Lecture Notes in Artificial Intelll

Subseries of Lecture Notes in Computer Science
Edited by J. G. Carbonell and J. Siekmann

Lecture Notes in Computer Science

Edited by G. Goos, J. Hartmanis and J. van Leeuwen

Springer
Berlin
Heidelberg
New York
Barcelona
Hong Kong
London
Milan
Paris
Singapore
Tokyo

Chengqi Zhang Dickson Lukose (Eds.)

Multi-Agent Systems

Theories, Languages, and Applications

4th Australian Workshop
on Distributed Artificial Intelligence
Brisbane, QLD, Australia, July 13, 1998
Selected Papers

 Springer

Series Editors

Jaime G. Carbonell, Carnegie Mellon University, Pittsburgh, PA, USA
Jörg Siekmann, University of Saarland, Saarbrücken, Germany

Volume Editors

Chengqi Zhang
Dickson Lukose
School of Mathematical and Computer Sciences
The Unviersity of New England
Armidale, N.S.W., 2351 Australia
E-mail: {chengqi,lukose}@cs.une.edu.au

Cataloging-in-Publication data applied for

Die Deutsche Bibliothek - CIP-Einheitsaufnahme

Multi-agent systems : theories, languages, and applications ; proceedings / 4th
Australian Workshop on Distributed Artificial Intelligence, Brisbane, QLD,
Australia, July 13, 1998. Chengqi Zhang ; Dickson Lukose (ed.). - Berlin ;
Heidelberg ; New York ; Barcelona ; Hong Kong ; London ; Milan ; Paris ;
Singapore ; Tokyo : Springer, 1998
  (Lecture notes in computer science ; Vol. 1544 : Lecture notes in artificial intelligence)
  ISBN 3-540-65477-1

CR Subject Classification (1998): I.2.11
ISBN 3-540-65477-1 Springer-Verlag Berlin Heidelberg New York

© Springer-Verlag Berlin Heidelberg 1998
Printed in Germany

Typesetting: Camera-ready by author
SPIN 10693067   06/3142 – 5 4 3 2 1 0   Printed on acid-free paper

Preface

This volume contains revised versions of selected papers presented at the Fourth Australian Workshop on Distributed Artificial Intelligence (DAI'98), together with a set of invited papers. Each paper has been reviewed by at least two program committee members. The workshop was held in Brisbane, Queensland, Australia on July 13, 1998. The goal of the workshop was to promote research in distributed artificial intelligence and multi-agent systems, both nationally and internationally. The papers cover a wide range of issues in the field of distributed artificial intelligence and multi-agent systems, such as theories, languages, and applications.

Many people contributed to the success of this workshop. We would like to thank all the authors who submitted papers to the workshop. Many thanks also to the members of the programme committee who diligently reviewed all the papers submitted. Finally, we thank the editorial staff of Springer-Verlag for publishing this contribution to the Lecture Notes in Artificial Intelligence series.

October 1998   Chengqi Zhang and Dickson Lukose

Programme Committee

Table of Contents

Team Formation by Self-Interested Mobile Agents*

Stanisław Ambroszkiewicz, Olaf Matyja, and Wojciech Penczek

Institute of Computer Science, al. Ordona 21, 01-237 Warsaw, Poland,
penczek, olaf, sambrosz@ipipan.waw.pl,
WWW home page: http://www.ipipan.waw.pl/mas/

Abstract. A process of team formation by autonomous agents in a distributed environment is presented. Since the environment is distributed, there are serious problems with communication and consistent decision making inside a team. To deal with these problems, the standard technique of token passing in a computer network is applied. The passing cycle of the token serves as the communication route. It assures consistent decision making inside the team maintaining its organizational integrity. On the other hand it constitutes a component of the plan of the cooperative work performed by a complete team. Two algorithms for team formation are given. The first one is based on simple self-interested agents that still can be viewed as reactive agents (see [14]) although augmented with knowledge, goal, and cooperation mechanisms. The second one is based on sophisticated self-interested agents. Moreover, the algorithm based on fully cooperative agents, which is an adaptation of the static routing algorithm in computer networks, is constructed in order to compare its performance with performances of the team formation algorithms.

Key words: team formation, cooperation mechanisms, autonomous agent, distributed computer networks.

1 Introduction

Cooperation is often considered as one of the key concepts of Multi-Agent Systems [4]. Among the cooperation mechanisms, the special interest is devoted to the notions of team [2, 7, 8, 23], teamwork [21, 11, 5], and team formation [3, 10]. Usually, it is assumed in applications (see [8, 21, 11]) that the members of a team are fixed and the research is focused on the teamwork. The research on team formation concerns mainly theoretical and fundamental aspects, so that there are very few realistic models of team formation processes. Our approach to team formation is quite practical, i.e., it is based on examples in the particular domain of distributed computer networks. Since the environment is distributed, it forces

* Partially supported by the State Committee for Scientific Research under the grant No. 8T11C 031 10 and ESPRIT project 20288 CRIT-2

all interactions inside a team, (i.e., information flow, decision making, goal real-izing) to be local. Thus, in order to maintain integrity of the team, a mechanism is needed for eliminating inconsistent decision making as well as contradictory information and goals inside the team. To manage with all these problems we adopt the standard technique of token passing in a computer network. The token is the sign of decision power, so that a member of the team who has currently the token has got the exclusive authority to decide on the status of the team. The passing cycle of the token serves for the following purposes: (1) It assures that the decision power is passed from one agent to another inside the team. (2) It determines the communication route. (3) It is a component of the plan of the cooperative work performed by a complete team. These three items correspond to organizational, information flow, and business structure of an enterprise [12]. Hence, our notion of team may be seen as a simple organizational form.

The crucial idea of our approach relies on the fact that the team is expanding locally, starting with a single agent. If the common goal of the expanding team becomes inconsistent according to the knowledge acquired from the dynamically changing environment, then the team starts shrinking by removing some of its members. As soon as the expanding team becomes complete, i.e., it has all the resources and capabilities needed to achieve the common goal, the members of the team perform the cooperative work. Another interesting feature of our approach is that the plan of the final cooperative work of the team is constructed and revised step by step during its formation. We introduce two algorithms that correspond to different types of self-interested agents participating in team formation. They are based on simple self-interested agents and 'electric' self-interested agents. Simple self-interested agents can be viewed as a reactive agents (see [14]) augmented with knowledge, goal, and cooperation mechanisms. The strategy of simple self-interested agents is very simple as it consists in making a fusion with any team that has got a consistent goal. This results in a situation, where the teams are expanding and shrinking very fast. The strategy of electric self-interested agents is more subtle. It is based on the idea of an electric circuit with resistors. Roughly speaking, the strategy determines a team to join by the agent, which assures maximal subjective probability (according to the agent's knowledge and calculations) for the agent to achieve his goal.

In order to have a basis for comparison of performances of our team forma-tion algorithms, we introduce the Ant-hill algorithm (based on fully cooperative agents called ants here) that is an adaptation of the static routing algorithm in computer networks, see [22]. As the working example we consider a network of servers and mobile agents that can move from one server to another in order to look for resources scattered randomly on the servers. To enhance cooperation between the agents, the entry to some servers is forbidden for some agents. Thus, if a resource, wanted by an agent, is on a forbidden server, then the agent needs help from other agents. If several agents need the same resource, then they have to compete for it. Agents can execute the following types of actions: take (drop) a resource from (to) a server, receive (give) a resource from (to) another agent, move from one server to another, or to end its activity.

Our team formation process may be seen as a cooperation mechanism [4] and as an instance of a cooperation structure [6]. However, the limit of space does not permit to discuss these issues in detail.

Since our notion of team is related to the classical notion of organization, our approach may be viewed as a first step towards understanding and construction of mechanisms for autonomous agents to form organizations.

The rest of the paper is organized as follows. In section 2 we formalize the distributed environment. In section 3 instances of the environment are presented. Section 4 is devoted to the concept of team and team formation. In section 5 the Ant-hill algorithm is presented. Section 6 contains two versions of our algorithm for the self-interested agents. Section 7 contains some details of the implementation, experimental results, and a comparison of performances of the three algorithms. Section 8 is devoted to the final conclusion.

2   Distributed environment

In order to present the example more formally, let us consider a graph $G = (V, E)$ representing a network of servers, where V is the set of vertices (servers), $E \subseteq V \times V$ is the set of edges (connections). Let $M = \{1, 2, \ldots, m\}$ be the set of mobile agents that can move from one server to another, $V_i \subseteq V$ be a subset of servers the agent i can enter, and R be the set of resources distributed randomly on the servers. There is one static gate-agent on each server v, denoted also by v, responsible for resource management on that server and for transportation of mobile agents. Here we assume that the gate-agents are obedient, that is, they fulfill the requirements of each mobile agent if this is only possible. Let $N = M \cup V$ denote the set of all the agents. Each mobile agent i is assigned an **original goal**, $G_i \subseteq R$, which consists in getting G_i with minimal effort and then to end its activity switching to an "off" state. The effort is related to agent's personal account, so that any action execution costs one unit, which is subtracted from the account. The gate-agents are always in "on" states, and have no goals. The following types of actions can be executed by agents:

- A mobile agent i can move from one server v to another v', provided $v, v' \in V_i$, i.e., the servers are available for him. This action is a joint action of agent i and the gate-agents v and v'.
- Agent i can give a resource r to another agent j. This is a joint action of the agents i and j, who are in a meeting state.
- A group of agents $N' \subseteq N$ can meet, provided they are at the same server. This is a joint action of the agents N'.
- A mobile agent can switch to the "off" state (terminal state).

Passing a resource between two agents is allowed only if the agents are in a meeting state at the same server. All the agents can 'gossip' at any opportunity by exchanging their knowledge concerning another agents (i.e., their resources and their sites) including themselves. Moreover, they calculate the most recent knowledge about other agents (for more details see [16]). The gossiping assures maximal spread of information in the system.

Let us note that the problem stated in the afore mentioned example and consisting in the proper cooperation while transporting resources can be solved using *coalition formation* methods, see [9, 13, 18, 19, 24]. However these methods are based on game theory, and in order to compute (sub)optimal coalitions (with possible utility transfer) each agent must know and consider the whole game and all the agents, which seems to be difficult for real applications. This results in a high computation cost not included in the agent's utility.

We are looking for a solution for an individual agent who knows initially almost nothing. He can get knowledge by wandering across the network and gossiping with other agents. The team formation method presented in the paper seems to be an appropriate solution.

3 Examples of cooperation mechanisms

The examples considered in this section are devoted for analyzing three different methods of agents' cooperation: bilateral exchange - Triangle example, signing a draft - Bridge example, and team formation - Lattice example.

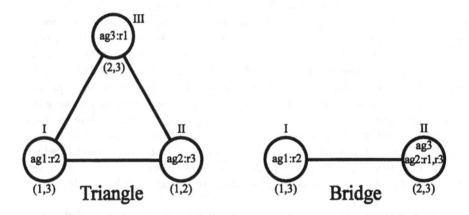

Fig. 1. Simple examples.

We start with defining two simpler methods of cooperation (bilateral exchange and signing a draft), and then we show that their application is quite limited in case of large distributed systems, calling for more sophisticated coordination mechanisms like team formation methods.

Triangle example. There are three servers: I,II,III, three agents: $1, 2, 3$, and three resources: r_1, r_2, r_3. Agent 1 can enter only server I and II and his goal is to get r_1, whereas agent 2 can enter only server II and III, and his goal is to get r_2. Agent 3 can enter only server III and I, and his goal is to get r_3. Initially, agent i resides at server i and has resource $r_{i+1(mod\ 3)}$, for $i \in \{1, 2, 3\}$.

The first cooperation mechanism, called **bilateral exchange**, is for implementing exchange of resources. The idea is that the involved agents first agree on exchanging resources and then follow their agreement by executing the appropriate actions. Let us notice that exchange of resources r, r' between two agents i, j is composed of two actions:
$a =$ (agent i gives r to agent j), and $a' =$ (agent j gives r' to agent i), which must be performed in a sequential order. The agents can achieve their goals by cruising between the servers and exchanging resources.

Bridge example. Another method of cooperation is called **signing a draft**. Agent j gets a resorce r from agent i and gives so called draft in reward. The draft is an equivalent of a written promise that agent j brings back either resource r' that agent i needs or resource r if r' is unreachable.

Consider the following example (see Figure 1). There are two servers: I,II, three agents: $1, 2, 3$, and three resources: $r1, r2, r3$. Agent 1 can enter only server I and his goal is to get $r1$, whereas agent 2 can enter only server II, and his goal is to get $r2$. Agent 3's goal is to get $r3$ and he can enter both servers, so that he can serve as *a bridge* between agents 1, and 2. Initially, agent 3 is on server II and has no resources, whereas agent 2 has $r1$, and agent 1 has $r2$, and $r3$. Notice that bilateral exchanges cannot be applied, because agent 3 has initially no resources.

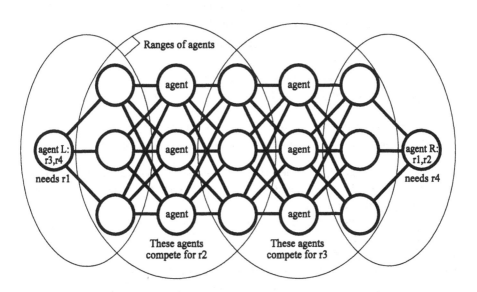

Fig. 2. Lattice $L(2, 3)$

Lattice example. Consider lattice $L(n, k)$ shown in Figure 2, where n is the number of sections (marked by ellipses) with agents, whereas k is the number of competing (for the same resource) agents in each section. Resources required by the agents from sections i with $i < \frac{n}{2}$ are possessed by the agent R, whereas the resources required by the agents from sections i with $i \geq \frac{n}{2}$ are possessed by agent L.

Notice that using simple cooperation mechanisms like *bilateral exchange* or *signing a draft* for construction of robust and generic protocols for lattices is a quite difficult job. Our experience shows that even if the information is perfectly distributed by gossiping, calculation of proper bilateral exchanges and signing a draft actions is too complicated. Therefore, in order to deal with such large and complex networks we introduce the notion of team.

4 Teams

The intuitive idea of our team formation method was presented in the introduction (see Section 1). In this section the concept of team is introduced formally.

Definition 1. Team *is defined as a 6-tuple* $\mathbf{T} = (T, JG, Res, pass, mode, token)$ *satisfying the following conditions :*

- $T \subseteq M$ *is the set of* team members, *consisting of at least two elements, such that the goals of the members are consistent, i.e.,* $G_i \cap G_j = \emptyset$ *for any* $i, j \in T$ *such that* $i \neq j$.
- $JG = \bigcup_{i \in T} G_i$ *is the* joint goal *of the team,*
- $Res \subseteq R$ *is the set of the resources owned by the team members,*
- $pass \overset{df}{:} [1, \ldots, p] \longrightarrow T$, *called the* token passing cycle, *is a sequence of agents' names of length* $p \geq |T|$,
- $mode \in \{expanding, shrinking, final\}$ *denotes the current mode of the team, which meaning is encoded into the name, and is also explained below.*
- $token \in T$ *is the pointer to a position in the passing cycle; this position distinguishes the agent, who is said to own the token at the moment.*

The passing cycle *pass* describes the order in which the token is passed, so that for any $k \in [1, \ldots, p]$, agent $i = pass(k)$ passes the token to the agent $j = pass(k + 1(mod\ p))$.

The intuitive meaning of the modes is as follows:
expanding: the team is trying to expand by getting new members,
shrinking: the team is getting rid of some of its members,
final: the team is realizing the goals of all its members.
A team is *completed* if it is able to realize its joint goal, i.e., the members of the team have all resources and capabilities to achieve all their goals. The capabilities mean here the possibility to enter some servers. In Bridge example, agent 3 has initially no resources, however his capabilities allow him to enter all servers in the network.

The joint goal of team $\mathbf{T}$, JG, is *impossible to achieve* if the resources or capabilities necessary for the team to achieve its goal are possessed by another team $\mathbf{T}$', that cannot be joined because the goal of $\mathbf{T}$', JG', is inconsistent with

JG, that is, $JG \cap JG' \neq \emptyset$, or **T'** has to join to **T"** that has goal inconsistent with the goal of **T**.

The agent who currently owns the token is called $representative_{\mathbf{T}}$ of the team, and he is supposed to have all the information about the team, i.e., to know **T**. This agent has the entire decision power of the team consisting in: changing the mode of the team and deciding on a fusion with another team. However, these decisions are subject to the following restrictions:

- switch to (or stay in) the expanding mode is permissible if, according to the current knowledge of the team representative, the joint goal is possible to achieve but the team does not have all resources and capabilities needed, so that some additional agents must joint the team,
- a fusion with another team **T'** is permissible, provided that team **T** is in the expanding mode, and the goal of team **T'** is consistent with the goal of team **T**, and both representatives of the teams do agree to join the teams,
- switch to (or stay in) the shrinking mode is obligatory if, according to the current knowledge of the representative, the team is not able to achieve its joint goal JG,
- switch to the final mode is obligatory, provided the team has all resources and capabilities needed for realizing the joint goal.

Obligations of a team member. No agent can be a member of two different teams at the same time. Any team member is obliged to comply with all the team rules. In particular, he cannot give away the resources he possesses, except the case where the team is in the final mode. Then, each of the members passes the resources, the other team members need, to the agent whose name is given by the passing cycle. Each agent is obliged to be as close as possible to the agent to whom he has given the token last time and from whom he will also get the token next time.

4.1 Recursive construction of teams

Joining two agents i, j into a new team

Suppose that two agents i, j, having resources Res_i, Res_j and goals G_i, G_j such that $G_i \cap G_j = \emptyset$, decide to make a team $\mathbf{T} = (T, JG, Res, pass, mode, token)$. Then $T \stackrel{df}{=} \{i, j\}$, $JG \stackrel{df}{=} G_i \cup G_j$, $Res \stackrel{df}{=} Res_i \cup Res_j$, $pass \stackrel{df}{=} (i, j)$, $token \stackrel{df}{=} i$, and $mode \stackrel{df}{=} expanding$, if $JG \not\subseteq Res$ or $final$ otherwise.

Joining agent j to team **T'**

If agent j and a representative of team **T'**, say agent i, decide to join agent j to team **T'**, making this way team $\mathbf{T} = (T, JG, Res, pass, mode, token)$,
then $T \stackrel{df}{=} T' \cup \{j\}$, $JG \stackrel{df}{=} JG' \cup G_j$, $Res \stackrel{df}{=} Res' \cup Res_j$, $token \stackrel{df}{=} i$, and $mode \stackrel{df}{=} expanding$ if $JG \not\subseteq Res$ or $final$ otherwise. If the passing cycle of **T'** is $pass = (k_1, k_2, \ldots, i, \ldots, k_{p_1})$, then the new passing cycle $pass_T \stackrel{df}{=} (k_1, k_2, \ldots, i, j, i, \ldots, k_{p_1})$.

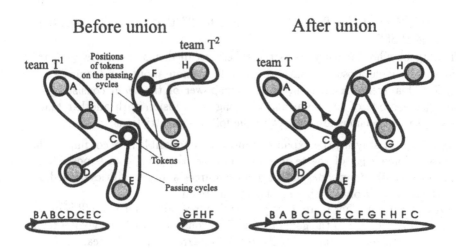

Fig. 3. Fusion of two teams.

Fusion of two teams

Consider two teams $\mathbf{T}^1, \mathbf{T}^2$, which are in the expanding mode. Their representatives: agent i of $\mathbf{T}^1$ and agent j of $\mathbf{T}^2$ agreed, during a meeting, to make a fusion of their teams into one team. Then, the resulting team, $\mathbf{T} = (T, JG, Res, pass, mode, token)$, is defined as follows:

- $T \stackrel{df}{=} T^1 \cup T^2$, $JG \stackrel{df}{=} JG^1 \cup JG^2$, and $Res \stackrel{df}{=} Res^1 \cup Res^2$,
- $mode \stackrel{df}{=} expanding$, if $JG \not\subseteq Res$ or $final$ otherwise.
- if the passing cycle of $\mathbf{T}^1$ is $pass_1 = (k_1, k_2, \ldots, i, \ldots, k_{p_1})$ and $pass_2 = (l_1, l_2, \ldots, l_{n-1}, j, l_{n+1}, \ldots, l_{p_2})$ is the passing cycle of $\mathbf{T}^2$, then the passing cycle of $\mathbf{T}$ is defined as $pass \stackrel{df}{=} (k_1, k_2, \ldots, i, j, l_{n+1}, \ldots, l_{p_2}, l_1, l_2, \ldots, l_{n-1}, j, i, \ldots, k_{p_1})$, see Figure 3, $token \stackrel{df}{=} i$.

Shrinking a team

Consider a team $\mathbf{T}$, which is in the shrinking mode. Let $representative_{\mathbf{T}} = k$ such that k appears in the passing cycle exactly once, i.e., $pass = (l_1, l_2, \ldots, l_{n-1}, k, l_{n+1}, \ldots, l_p)$ with $l_i \neq k$. Then the team is reduced to the team $\mathbf{T}'$ by removing from T the agent k, its goal from JG, its resources from Res, and constructing the new passing cycle as follows: $pass' \stackrel{df}{=} (l_1, l_2, \ldots, l_{n-1}, l_{n+2}, \ldots, l_p)$, $representative_{\mathbf{T}'} \stackrel{df}{=} l_{n-1}$. Notice that since $l_{n-1} = l_{n+1}$, the element l_{n+1} was removed from the passing cycle. Agent k becomes free from all the previous team obligations.

Final mode: the cooperative work is performed

As soon as a team is completed, its mode is changed to the final mode. Then, the passing cycle serves as a transportation route. Each member of the team gives all his unnecessary resources, which are transported along the token to the next agent in the passing cycle. Agent i is free to leave the team and go to 'off'-state if he has the resources he needs, and he is not needed in the further cooperative work of the team, that is, he has already given all the other resources, and his name occurs only once in the passing cycle. Then, after agent i has left, the team is reduced in the same way as in the shrinking mode.

4.2 Properties of the passing cycle

The passing cycle serves for the following purposes:
1. It assures that the decision power is passed from one agent to another inside the team.
2. It assures the communication flow inside the team, and in this way it maintains the organizational integrity of the team.
3. It assures that the cooperative work of the complete team is performed in the final mode.
These three items constitute together the organizational frame of team.

   The most important properties of the passing cycle, following from the construction, are formulated in the following Lemma.

Lemma 1. *Let* $\mathbf{T} = (T, JG, Res, pass, mode, token)$ *be a team. Then, the following conditions hold:*

  - *any member of the team occurs in the passing cycle at least once, i.e., for any* $t \in T$ *there is at least one* k *such that* $1 \leq k \leq p$ *and* $pass(k) = t$,
  - *for any* $k \leq p$, *there is a server where the agents* $i = pass(k)$ *and* $j = pass(k + 1 (mod\ p))$ *can meet,*
  - *no segment (of length at least 2) of the passing cycle can occur twice in the cycle, i.e., for any* k, k', l, l' *such that* $1 \leq k < l \leq p$ *and* $1 \leq k' < l' \leq p$, *if* $(pass(k), pass(k+1), \ldots, pass(l)) = (pass(k'), pass(k'+1), \ldots, pass(l'))$, *then* $k = k'$ *and* $l = l'$,
  - *if in the passing cycle agent* i *gives the token to agent* j, *then the agent* i *must receive the token from the same agent* j; *formally this condition is stated as: if* $(i, j, k_1, \ldots, k_n, i)$ *is a segment of the passing cycle and* $i \neq k_l$, *for* $l = 1, 2, \ldots, n$, *then* $k_n = j$.

The algorithms presented in the next two sections are based on the following assumptions:
1. The system and the initial configuration of the agents and the resources (see Section 2) are a common knowledge of all the agents. Locations of the agents and resources are changing dynamically in a distributive way, so that the initial knowledge becomes out-of-date very soon.
2. When two or more agents meet, then there is an opportunity to update their

knowledge about themselves as well as about the other agents and resources. The agents gossip at any meeting, exchanging and updating all their knowledge according to gossip automaton [16]. The gossiping concerns the agents (their positions and resources) as well as the current configuration of teams in the network. This assumption assures maximal spread of information in the system.

5 Ant–hill algorithm

In order to have a basis for comparing performances of the team formation algorithms we introduce the Ant-hill algorithm, which is an adaptation of the standard static routing algorithm in computer networks [22]. The agents modeled by the algorithm can be considered as fully cooperative, so that they are called *ants*.

Ant-hill algorithm implements the idea that the main and persisting goal of each ant is to reach a situation, where all resources are possessed by ants that need them. So that, the ants do their best in order to realize the common global goal of the system. This contrasts with the goal of a self-interested agent, who is interested only in getting the resources he needs.

Ants act according the knowledge-based protocol that may be sketched in the following way. Each ant tries to meet and gossip with as many ants as possible. Each ant tries to deliver any resource it finds to some ant, say B, that needs it. If no such ant B is reachable, the ant gives the resource to an ant that is either able to get to ant B or to get closer to B than A. More detailed description is given below.

- Let $dist_i(r)$ be the minimal number of passes of resource r, from one ant to another starting with i, necessary to deliver r to some ant that needs it.

  Before two ants i and j meet, they calculate how they should exchange their resources in order to achieve the common goal. For any resource r of ant i or j they calculate distances $dist_i(r)$ and $dist_j(r)$. The resource r is then given to j iff $dist_i(r) > dist_j(r)$, or it is given to agent i if $dist_i(r) < dist_j(r)$. Let $exchange(i,j)$ be the number of the resources that may be exchanged if the ants i and j meet.

- In order to find the best (according to the common goal) next server to enter, any ant i calculates the following $value_i(v)$ for each available server v in the neighborhood: $value_i(v) \stackrel{df}{=} \sum_{j \in N(v)} \frac{exchange(i,j)}{dist(v,i)+1}$, where $dist(v,i)$ is the distance from server v to the current position of the ant i, and $N(v)$ is the set of names of ants the ant i expects (according to its knowledge) to meet at server v. Having these calculations, the ant moves to the server v in the neighborhood with maximal $value_i(v)$, i.e., where it expects to be the most useful for the community.

- If ant i finds its resource, i takes it and then never gets rid of it. This and only this expresses its individual rationality towards achieving its own goal.

- If an ant waits *too long* in one place (*too long* is solved by setting a time-out), it is supposed to walk in a random direction.

Ant-hill algorithm serves as the basis for comparison to the team formation algorithms.

6 Two algorithms for team formation

In this section we present two algorithms for team formation. In order to present the algorithms formally, we should put them down as *knowledge&goal$_i$-based protocol* for any agent i. However, for the sake of the presentation, we give here only a sketch of the protocols. Let us note that the protocols for the ants are not goal-based because the ant goal is common and concerns the global states of the system.

In the algorithms presented below we make the following technical assumptions. If agent i gives the token to agent j, then the agent i is obliged to keep the distance to j as small as possible, because this is the agent j who will give him back the token next time. The problem of when the token is to be passed to the next team member is solved by setting a time-out. Even if according to the knowledge acquired and updated from gossiping, an agent has no chance to fulfill his goal, he is supposed to move around and gossip in hope to get new information making again his goal possible to achieve. The crucial point in the construction of the algorithms is the mechanism for deciding which team is needed (and how much) to realize the goal of the team. For this reason we consider two versions of the algorithm.

Let us note that a single agent is not considered as a team. The reason for that is that initially any agent is supposed to be free from all the team obligation introduced in Section 4. He can, for example, try to achieve his goal by using simple cooperation mechanisms like bilateral exchange or signing draft, see Section 3, or just wandering over the network in hope to find the resources he needs. To be bound to the team rules, the agent must first commit to them either by creating a new team with other agent or by joining an already existing team. However now for the simplicity of the presentation we consider a single agent as a team.

6.1 Simple algorithm

For this version the mechanism is quite simple and consists in making, by team **T**, a fusion with any team that has goal consistent with the goal of **T**. This results in a situation where the teams are expanding and shrinking very fast.

6.2 Electric algorithm

For this version of team formation, the mechanism is more subtle. It is based on the idea of electric circuit with resistors. We explain this using Figure 4. Since team A has a resource needed by team H, it is clear that team H has to make a fusion with team A. However, because of the movement ranges of its members, team H cannot get to team A, so that H needs intermediary teams to get there.

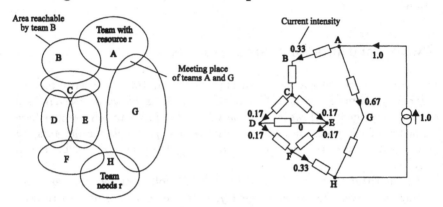

Fig. 4. Graph of movement ranges dependencies represented by an electric circuit

The graph of relations between the movement ranges of the teams, considered relatively to particular resources needed by a particular team, can be interpreted as an electric circuit with teams as nodes and resistors between the teams having the following resistance:

- 1 if the teams can meet via their representatives,
- $+\infty$ if the goals of the teams are mutually contradictory.

An option is to set resistance in a way that reflects the effort needed for resource transportation. Then, it is easy to calculate (see [20]) the value of the current intensity going by each node of the circuit. This value of node intensity can be interpreted as a measure of how much one is necessary by another team for getting a resource. For example, how much D is necessary by team H for getting resource r. However, this is not yet a good measure of necessity because although the value of team G is the biggest, it may happen that the union with G will cause the necessity to include all the other agents into the team. For example, G may need resources possessed by B, C, D, E, and F. On the other hand it may happen that teams H, F, E, C, B, and A together can form a complete team, which is able to realize all goals of these teams. Hence, to construct the appropriate measure of necessity, we must consider recursively the graph of movement ranges relatively to all resources needed by the teams that are candidates for fusion and theirs appropriate electric circuits. The detailed construction of the measure is given in [15].

7   Implementation of the algorithms

Our long distance target is to construct an architecture of self-interested agent that can be implemented in a real distributed environment like the Internet. The team formation mechanism can be viewed as a part of such architecture. In a computer network it is difficult to measure efficiency of a program, because many independent factors may change the timing, like other processes or changes in the speed of the network transmission. Thus, we decided to simulate the first version of the system at one computer in a fully controlled environment. All the algorithms described above have been implemented in C++. The concurrency among agents was simulated by random choice of agent activation and random order of agents' meetings at a server. In fact, the only difference between real and simulated concurrency consists in a possibility of passing by of two agents coming from one server to another in the opposite directions. However, such a situation can also be excluded in the real world if a transfer of a mobile agent requires synchronization of two gate-agents and the mobile agent. Simulation gives us an opportunity to observe precisely the behavior of each agent and to make statistics of the global performance.

The Lattice examples (see Figure 2) served as instances of distributed environment. They contained up to 50 agents (including gate-agents). For each algorithm and each size of these Lattice examples, 30 experiments were performed. General conclusions of the experiments are as follows. Self-interested agents are less efficient than ants, i.e., average performance of simple self-interested agent is about 4 times worse than the corresponding ant performance. This seems to be the price paid for selfishness of the self-interested agents and the submission to the team rules. Recall that a self-interested agent does not give away his resources unless he is a member of a complete team. When the world becomes larger, the performances of the simple agents are improving relatively to the ants, but they are still worse. However, the ants have a problem with switching to 'off'-state. Since the environment is distributed, ants may not be able to meet together at one server and get the common knowledge that the global goal is already realized. Without this knowledge, ants will be active forever gossiping and wandering along the network.

The most surprising observation is a very poor performance of the electric algorithm. Average performance of electric self-interested agent is about 17 times worse than the corresponding performance of simple self-interested agent. This seems to be caused by the fact that the electric self-interested agents want to join the best team among all consistent ones. Frequently, a team representative tries to unite his team to another large team, although the resulting joint team would be unable to achieve its goal, but the news about this fact has not yet reached the representatives of the teams. Thus, in the case of the electric algorithm, the teams are expanding much faster in size than in the simple algorithm, but the process of reduction is much more slower. So, the simple algorithm is much more flexible than the electric one.

8 Conclusion

For the tested examples the statistics show that the complexity of all the three algorithms is polynomial. We have observed that simple self-interested agents perform their job quite well relatively to reactive agents (ants). Although the performance of ants is better, they have a serious problem with finishing their activity in a distributed environment. The final conclusion of the experiments is that it is meaningful and useful to augment reactive agents with knowledge, goals, and knowledge&goal-based protocols according to the BDI–paradigm [1, 17]. On the other hand, in order to get efficient algorithms, agents' decision making should be reactive as much as possible. Self-interested agents of sophisticated decision making proved to be inefficient in, at least, the examples considered in the paper. The team formation method presented in the paper cannot be seen as a completely rational solution from the point of view of a single agent. However, this formation method is an example of a generic and robust cooperation mechanism. Intuitively, it is clear that the team formation process is an example of cooperation structure [6]. In order to prove so, a formal analysis of the team formation process is needed in terms of commitments, conventions, and joint actions [3, 7].

The organizational form of team is flat and extremely simple. There are only two roles the agents can take, namely "team representative" for an agent who has currently the token, and "passive role" for agents not having the token at the moment. It is clear that passing the token according to the order of the passing cycle can not be effective. The reason is that the token should be rather passed to the agent who needs it for expanding or shrinking the team. The same concerns the cooperative work in the final mode. The resources should be passed directly to the agents who need them instead of wandering a long way along the passing cycle. So that in order to improve the efficiency of team performance at least one additional role (say Mediator or Supervisor) is needed in the team to supervise the token passing and resource distribution. Since the environment is distributed and there are some problems with communication, one Mediator may not be able to perform the job. If however there are several Mediators in one team, then the Mediators must coordinate their decision to be consistent with each other and with the goal of the team. Hence, this impose a super structure of Mediators to be incorporated in the organizational form of team. Once the super structure is incorporated, the simple flat frame of team becomes a hierarchical one. This idea is closely related to more general framework of enterprise formation that is explored in our ongoing work.

References

1. M. E. Bratman. *Intentions, Plans, and Practical Reason.* Harvard University Press, 1987.
2. P.R. Cohen, and H.J. Levesque. Teamwork. *Nous, 35.*
3. P.R. Cohen, H.J. Levesque, and Ira Smith. On Team Formation. In G. H. Hintikka and R. Tuomela (eds.), *Contemporary Action Theory,* Volume 2: Social Action, Synthese Library, Kluwer Academic Publishers, Dordrecht, Netherlands, 1997, pp. 87-114.
4. J.E. Doran, S. Franklin, N. R. Jennings, and T.J. Norman. On cooperation in Multi-Agent-Systems. *The Knowledge Engineering Review,* 12(3), 1997.
5. B. Grosz, and S. Kraus. Collaborative plans for complex group actions. *Artificial Intelligence, 86,* 1996, pp. 269-358

6. M. d'Inverno, M. Luck, and M. Wooldridge. Cooperation Structures. In *Proc. IJCAI-97*, Nagoya, Japan, August 1997.
7. N. R. Jennings. Commitments and Conventions: The Foundations of Coordination in Multi-Agent Systems, *Knowledge Engineering Review* 8(3), 1993, pp. 223-250.
8. N. R. Jennings. Controlling cooperative problem solving in industrial multi-agent systems using joint intentions. *Artificial Intelligence* 75,1995.
9. S. Ketchpel. Coalitions formation among rational agents. In *Proc. MAAMAW-93*.
10. D. Kinny, M. Ljungberg, A. Rao, E. Sonenberg, G. Tidhar, and E. Werner. Planned team activity. In C. Castelfranchi and E. Werner (Eds.), *Artificial Social Systems, LNAI 830*, 1992.
11. H. Kitano, M. Tambe, M. Asada, Y. Kuniyoshi, I. Noda, and E. Osawa. The robocup synthetic agents' challenge. In *Proc. IJCAI'97*, 1997.
12. Ch. Klauck and H-J Mueller. Formal Business Process Engineering Based on Graph Grammars. To appear in *International Journal on Production Economics*, Special Issue on Business Process Reengineering 1997.
13. M. Klush and O. Shehory. Coalition formation among rational information agents. In *Proc. MAAMAW-96* Springer LNAI 1038, pp. 204-217, 1996.
14. P. Maes. Situated agents can have goals. In P. Maes, editor, *Designing Autonomous Agents: Theory and Practice from Biology to Engeneering and Back*. MIT and Elsevier, 1990, pp. 49-70.
15. O. Matyja. Team formation by autonomous agents. MS thesis, Warsaw Institute of Technology, Faculty of Electronics and Informatics, May 1998.
16. M. Mukund, and M. Sohoni. Keeping track of the latest gossip: Bounded time-stamps suffice, *FST&TCS'93*, LNCS 761, 1993, pp. 388-199.
17. A. S. Rao and M. P. Georgeff. Modelling rational agents within a BDI–architecture. In R. Fikes and E. Sandewall, editors, *Proc. of the 2rd International Conference on Principles of Knowledge Representation and Reasoning (KR'91)*, Morgan Kaufmann, 1991, pp. 473-484.
18. T.W. Sandholm and V.R. Lesser. Coalition among computationally bounded agents. *Artificial Intelligence* 94, 1997, pp. 99-137.
19. O. M. Shehory, K. Sycara and S. Jha. Multi-agent coordination trough coalition formation. In *Proc. ATAL-97*.
20. R.E. Scott. *Linear circuits.*, Addison-Wesley, Readings, Mass., 1960.
21. M. Tambe. Towards flexible teamwork. *Journal of Artificial Intelligence Research*, 7, 1997, pp. 83-124.
22. A. S. Tanenbaum. *Computer Networks.* Prentice-Hall Inc.Englewood Cliffs, New Jersey, 1981.
23. M. Wooldridge and N. R. Jennings. Towards a theory of cooperative problem solving. In *Distributed Software Agents and Applications (MAAMAW'94)*, LNAI 1069. Springer-Verlag, 1996, pp. 40-53.
24. G. Zlotkin and J.S. Rosenschein. Coalition, cryptography and stability: mechanisms for coalition formation in task oriented domains. In *Proc. AAAI-94*, Seattle, WA, 1994, pp. 432-437.

Conception, Behavioural Semantics and Formal Specification of Multi-agent Systems

Walid Chainbi

Mohamed Jmaiel   Ben Hamadou Abdelmajid

LARIS Laboratory
FSEG-SFAX, B.P. 1088
3018 SFAX, TUNISIA
Email: {wchainbi@yahoo.com}

Abstract. This paper has three purposes. First, it presents an approach to designing an agent based on communication and organization. We will show that this approach differs from most known in the DAI field. The underlying concepts of an agent have been identified from our study of cooperation in multi-agent systems. These concepts consist of communication concepts and organization concepts. The second objective of this paper is to show the application of labeled transition systems to deal with the behavioural semantics of a multi-agent system. An agent state is described by a triplet including beliefs, goals as communication concepts and roles as organization concepts. A transition consists of an execution step in the life-cycle of an agent. Third, we use the proposed semantics to define a formal specification language which is a first-order, multi-modal, linear-time logic. We illusrate our work with the well known prey/predator problem.

1   Introduction

The recent years have witnessed a large interest in agent-oriented approaches to developing systems. While an AI system represents a human being carrying out a task which needs knowledge, experience and a certain dose of reasoning, a DAI system is designed as a "society" of agents working together to achieve a global goal. The conception of multi-agent systems cover many meanings each referring to a peculiar trend in research. These trends can be grouped in two standpoints : The first point of view can be qualified by *individual* conception. It gathers all researchers who think that the solution goes only through the formal representation of an agent model [1] (agents as intentional systems). Accordingly, this consists in formalizing the mental state of an agent (its beliefs, its desires, its intentions ...). Most researchers work along those lines. For example, Shoham [2], Georgeff and Rao [3], Cohen and Levesque [4], Jennings and Wooldridge [5]. In our opinion, the proposed theories mask cooperation which is one of the main forces of multi-agent systems : we have the impression that their agents are isolated. The second point of view is qualified by *mass*[1] conception. It

---

[1] This term was used by Ferber in [1]

gathers people who consider that we should first think about *interaction*, then deduce the intentional structure of the agents and not the contrary. Our approach is in keeping with the latter standpoint. Indeed, starting from the study of cooperation in multi-agent systems [6], we identify the underlying concepts of an agent. These concepts consist of communication concepts and organization concepts. Communication in multi-agent systems as for human beings, is the basis of interaction and social organization. Communication consists of a set of psychological and physical processes relating the sender to the addressee(s) in order to reach some goals [12]. An organizational model defines how to dispatch the tasks between cooperative agents and their possible relations.

With respect to semantic models associated with multi-agent systems, two tendencies can be mentioned : a tendency toward Petri nets and a tendency toward logic. Previously, Chainbi [7] has used cooperative objects (a formalism which combines Petri nets and an object oriented approach) to model multi-agent systems. The combination between the two approaches has given a great deal of flexibility to the system structuring. This flexibility is basically due to the advantages of the object oriented approach. Unfortunately, cooperative objects have a weak analytic power. Purvis [8] try to use colored Petri nets to model multi-agent systems but the proposed model remains at a high abstraction level. The other models use formalisms associated with logical systems including Cohen & Levesque [4], Rao & Georgeff [3]. Their models are based on a possible world semantics where an agent's beliefs, knowledge, goals, and so on, are characterized as a set of so-called possible worlds, with an accessibility relation holding between them [5]. These models suffer from some drawbacks, notably the *omniscience* problem which implies that an agent has unlimited resources. In this paper, we exploit another formalism which doesn't belong to the afore mentioned tendencies to deal with the behavioural aspect of a multi-agent system : *labeled transition systems* which have been initially introduced to define the semantics of parallel systems. The proposed semantics is the basis for the definition of a formal specification language which is a first-order, multi-modal and linear-time logic.

This paper is organized as follows : Section 2 presents a preliminary in which we give some first-order notations. Section 3 describes the model : its static and dynamic parts. This section shows also the way we have used transition systems to model multi-agent systems. Section 4 presents a specification language $\mathcal{L}_w$ for the agent model.

2 Preliminary

In this section, we introduce some useful definitions for the formal specifications described below. These definitions deal with first-order logic.

Definition 2.1 [Signature]

Let N be the set of positive integers. A *signature* is a set Σ of function and constant symbols with a function $ar : \Sigma \longrightarrow N$. If $f \in \Sigma$ and

$ar(f) = n$ then f is n-ary and n is called the arity of f; if $n = 0$ then f is a constant symbol else it is a function symbol.

Definition 2.2 [Predicate calculus signature]

Predicate calculus *signature* is given by two different signatures Σ_f and Σ_r called functional and relational signature respectively. We define $\Sigma = \Sigma_f \cup \Sigma_r$. The elements of $\Sigma_f(\Sigma_r)$ are function (relation) symbols.

Definition 2.3 [Term]

Let X be an infinite countable set of variables We denote by $T_{\Sigma \cup X}$ the set of terms in first-order logic. $T_{\Sigma \cup X}$ is defined as follows :

(i) if $c \in \Sigma$ and $ar(c) = 0$ then $c \in T_{\Sigma \cup X}$

(ii) if $f \in \Sigma_f$ and $ar(f) = n \geq 1$ and if $t_1, ..., t_n \in T_{\Sigma \cup X}$ then $f(t_1, ..., t_n) \in T_{\Sigma \cup X}$

(iii) if $x \in X$ then $x \in T_{\Sigma \cup X}$

A term is obtained by the application of the rules (i), (ii) and (iii) a finite number of times.

The definition of a first-order logic formulae requires the definition of an atom.

Definition 2.4 [Atom]

Let $t_1, ..., t_n \in T_{\Sigma \cup X}$ be terms, and $R \in \Sigma_r$ be a relation symbol of arity n. An atom is the application of R on the terms $t_1, ..., t_n$, denoted by $R(t_1, ..., t_n)$. We denote by $At[X]$ the set of atoms and At the set of ground atoms (i.e., $X = \emptyset$).

First-order logic formulae over Σ are made up of atoms and quantifiers ($\exists$ and $\forall$) and connectors ($\Rightarrow, \wedge, \vee, \neg$).

Definition 2.5 [First-order logic formula]

Let $L_\Sigma[X]$ be the set of first-order logic formula over Σ. $L_\Sigma[X]$ is defined as follows:

(i) $At[X] \subseteq L_\Sigma[X]$

(ii) $True \in L_\Sigma[X]$; if $\varphi \in L_\Sigma[X]$ then $\neg\varphi \in L_\Sigma[X]$; and if $\varphi, \Psi \in L_\Sigma[X]$ then $\varphi \vee \Psi \in L_\Sigma[X]$.

(iii) If $x \in X$ and $\varphi \in L_\Sigma[X]$ then $\exists x\varphi \in L_\Sigma[X]$.

3 The model

The model describes three aspects :

- the *static aspect* deals with the agent state. It is made up of all the information an agent can handle,
- the *dynamic aspect* describes the operations which can modify the static aspect,
- the *behavioral aspect* deals with the relation between the underlying concepts of the intentional state of an agent, and with the modification of these concepts in time.

3.1 Static aspect

In our approach, the static aspect consists of the following concepts : beliefs, goals (local and global) and roles. This making up of the static aspect is justified by the following two points : On the one hand, no consensus has been reached in the DAI community regarding the components of the intentional state of an agent. Some studies adopt the concepts of beliefs, wants and intentions (example : Rao and Georgeff [3]). Some others contented themselves with beliefs, obligations and aptitudes (example : Shoham [2]). On the other hand, our approach is in keeping with *mass* conception which emphasizes the study of interaction as a preliminary to deduce the intentional structure of agents. Cooperation was our guiding line to deduce an agent model. Our study of cooperation had led us to deduce *roles* as organizational concepts, *beliefs* and *goals* as concepts related to communication.

Beliefs Beliefs are contingent knowledge about other agents' beliefs, their goals and their activities as well as the state of the environment. In more traditional AI terms, an agent's beliefs are its knowledge. Beliefs change due to the external environment of the agent, his communication with the others and his proper reasoning. Beliefs are a subset of the propositions that agents exchange. Generally, communication depends on the beliefs and the application domain. To represent beliefs, we adopt the idea of Wooldridge [9] who represented beliefs by ground atoms. We denote by *Bels* the set of all possible beliefs. $B \in Bels \implies B \in At$ We assume that the set of an agent beliefs should be finite since we deal with agents that have limited resources.

Example 1. The prey's position on the grid is a predator's belief. It can be represented by the atom $Position(prey, v_1, v_2)$: prey is an agent name and (v_1, v_2) are the coordinates of the prey on the grid.

Goals A goal is a potential state of the world to which the agent belongs. Goals and beliefs are the exchanged propositions between agents. The achievement of a goal is at the beginning of an agent behavior (e.g., his communicative actions). A goal may be *local* or *global* and can be expressed in terms of the agent beliefs. We represent an agent goal by a first-order formula. We denote by *Goals* the set of all possible goals. $G \in Goals \implies G \in L_\Sigma[X]$

Example 2. For a predator, getting closer to a prey from the western side is a local goal which helps reaching the global goal consisting in the capture of the prey. This local goal can be expressed in terms of the following beliefs : the prey's position and the predator's position on the grid. The formula used to represent this goal is :

$$\forall X \ \forall Y \ Position(prey, X, Y) \implies Position(\text{self}, X - 1, Y)$$
– self is the predator's identifier

Roles The role characterizes the responsibilities which would be attributed to an agent i.e., the tasks he is charged with. We adopt the definition of Salbert to the notion of task [10] : A task is an ordered set of actions which allows to reach a goal. Hence a role is represented by an ordered set of actions. An agent can perform at a point of time one of the following actions :

- *physical* actions are interactions between agents and the spatial environment,
- *communicative* actions are interactions between agents. They can be *emission* or *reception* actions,
- *private* actions are internal functions of an agent. They correspond to an agent exploiting its internal computational resources, and
- *decision* action can generate communicative, physical and private actions. A decision action can also update the agent's beliefs. We assume that the agent's goals are modified only after a negociation with the other agents (see the following section).

The actions to execute are determined by the resolution methods and communication protocols. We denote by APH the set of physical actions, APR the set of private actions, ACO the set of communicative actions such that $ACO = ACOE \cup ACOR$ where $ACOE$ is the set of emission actions and $ACOR$ is the set of reception actions, τ a decision action, which an agent can execute. In our description, we remain at a high level of abstraction i.e., we don't give the structure of actions and messages to be exchanged between agents. This is out of the scope of this paper, we are mainly interested in conceptual aspects rather than syntactic details. We use *Roles* to denote the set of all possible roles. $\forall role \in Roles, role \in Seq(APH \cup APR \cup ACO)$. Notice that the decision action doesn't belong to the action sequence representing the role.

Example 3.

Figure 1. The pursuit of a prey ($\otimes$) by a predator ($\Diamond$).

- The predator's role regarding the configuration given by figure 1, can be the sequence $< move\_right, move\_right, move\_up >$ denoting the execution of three physical actions.
- In the prey/predator problem, an agent may make a decision which allows him to know the current position of the prey. In this case, it generates a communicative action : the predator sends a request to his colleagues asking them for the prey's position.

3.2 Dynamic aspect

The dynamic aspect consists of the set of operations which can update the intentional state of the agent. The agent activity is made up of two sub-activities: interaction with the external environment (the other agents and the spatial environment), and an internal activity. The agent interacts with the other agents by executing communicative actions (emission actions and reception actions). Generally, an emission action does not modify the set of beliefs of an agent, whereas a reception action may have an impact on its beliefs. The agent can also execute physical actions on its spatial environment (e.g., moving on the grid in the prey/predator game). Each action from the spatial environment (a stimulus) on the agent will be interpreted. The results of the interpretation activity, agent beliefs and goals and resolution methods, form the parameters of the decision activity. The latter can update the agent beliefs. It can also modify the agent's role by generating any action (physical, private or communicative) which will be integrated into an interaction paradigm (for example an agenda). The interaction paradigm implicitly defines the metaphors used by the agents to interact and cooperate among each other [11]. The internal activity of an agent includes also its private actions which act on its beliefs.

3.3 Behavior

This section shows how transition systems can be used to model multi-agent systems. First we deal with the behavioural semantics of a single agent system. Then, we extend this model in order to represent the behavioural semantics of a multi-agent system.

An agent model The agent behavior describes the evolution of the agent state in time. It defines the relation between the static aspect and the dynamic aspect. The proposed model represents a multi-agent system by a triplet $< \mathcal{S}, \mathcal{A}, \Omega >$ consisting of a set $\mathcal{S}$ of states, a set $\mathcal{A}$ of actions, and a set Ω of state transitions. The behavior of an agent is described by the set of all possible executions which are finite or infinite sequences of the form

$$s_0 \xrightarrow{a_1} s_1 \xrightarrow{a_2} s_2 \ldots$$

where each s_i is a state and each a_i is an action. If the sequence is finite, then it ends with a state s_n. A state describes the complete instantaneous state of the system. An action is a system operation that is taken to be indivisible, and a sequence represents a possible execution in which each action a_i takes the system from state s_{i-1} to state s_i. The set Ω represents the set of all possible system executions. Before specifying the possible state transitions $s \xrightarrow{a} t$ caused by each action a of A, we define an agent state. An agent state consists of its beliefs, goals and roles.

Definition 3.1 [An agent state]

Let s_x be an agent state, s_x is a tuple $< K_x, B_x, R_x >$ defined as follows: K_x is the set of beliefs of the agent x, B_x are his goals, and R_x is his role.

Definition 3.2 [The state transition due to an action]

Let $< K, B, R >$ be a state of an agent and a an action. The state transition due to a physical, private or communicative action is described by :

$$< K, B, a.R > \stackrel{a}{\longrightarrow} < K', B, R > \text{ such that :}$$

(i) if $a \in APH \cup APR \cup ACOR$ then $K' = (K - Bels_a(s)) \cup Bels'_a(s)$ where :

$Bels_a(s)$ denotes the set of beliefs of the agent at a state s and on which the action a have an impact. This impact corresponds to the application of functions of Σ_f that is,

if $Bels_a(s) = \{R_1(\ldots), \ldots, R_k(\ldots)\}$ then there is $f_1, \ldots, f_k \in \Sigma_f$ such that $Bels'_a(s) = \{f_1(R_1(\ldots)), \ldots, f_k(R_k(\ldots))\}$.

(ii) if $a \in ACOE$ then $K' = K$

Example 4. Physical action

In the pursuit game, move_right is a physical action which a predator is able to do. The ground atom $Position(self, v_1, v_2)$ is an agent's belief which indicates its position on the grid. Let $Bels_{move\_right}(s) = \{Position(self, v_1, v_2)\}$ and B a predator's goal (e.g. getting closer to a prey from the southern side). Let the predator's role $= < move\_right, move\_right, move\_up >= R$. Then, we have

$$< K, B, R > \stackrel{move\_right}{\longrightarrow} < K', B', R' > \text{ where :}$$

$K' = (K - \{Position(self, v_1, v_2)\}) \cup \{Inc\_Abs(Position(self, v_1, v_2))\} = (K - \{Position(self, v_1, v_2)\}) \cup \{Position(self, v_1 + 1, v_2)\}$ such that Inc_Abs is a function which increments the first component of the agent coordinates on the grid ; $B' = B$; $R' = < move\_right, move\_up >$.

Private action

The distance which separates the predator from the prey can be calculated in terms of the number of boxes. It is a belief represented by the ground atom $Distance(self, prey, d)$. Calculating this distance is done by the private action distance_to_target. Let $Bels_{distance\_to\_target}(s) = \{Distance(self, prey, d)\}$. Let the agent's role $= < distance\_to\_target, move\_right, move\_up >$.

$$< K, B, R > \stackrel{distance\_to\_target}{\longrightarrow} < K', B', R' > \text{ where :}$$

$K' = (K - \{Distance(self, prey, d)\}) \cup \{f(Distance(self, prey, d))\}$ such that f is a function which updates the distance separating the prey and the predator; $B' = B$; $R' = < move\_right, move\_up >$.

Communicative action

send_message(m) is an emission action which a predator executes to ask its colleague for the prey's position. receive_message(m) is a reception action which a predator executes to know the new prey's position.

Definition 3.3 [The state transition due to a decision action]

Let $< K, B, R >$ be a state of an agent and τ a decision action. The state transition due to the execution of a decision action is described by $< K, B, R > \xrightarrow{\tau} < K', B, R' >$ such that :

(i) $K' = (K - Bels_\tau(s)) \cup Bels'_\tau(s)$

(ii) $R' = mod(R)$ where mod is an update function of the role resulting in the following operations :

- The generation of an action (physical, private or communicative). In this case the action will be integrated in the role and $mod(R) = Insert(R, a)$. – Insert is a function which integrates the action a in the role R
- The suppression of an action (physical, private or communicative). In this case $mod(R) = Delete(R, a)$. – Delete is a function which deprives the role of one of its actions
- The repetition of the two operations mentioned above.

Example 5. When the predator receives a message asking him for the prey's position, he decides to execute a communicative action to answer the sender of the request.

A multi-agent system model A multi-agent system represents a "society" of agents working together to achieve a global goal. In this section, we extend the behavioural semantics of an agent presented in the previous section to deal with the behavioural semantics of a multi-agent system.

Definition 3.4 [A multi-agent system state]

Let a multi-agent system made up of the agents $x_1, x_2, \ldots, x_i, \ldots, x_n$ a multi-agent system state SA is a tuple $<< K_{x_1}, B_{x_1}, R_{x_1} >, \ldots,$ $< K_{x_i}, B_{x_i}, R_{x_i} >, \ldots, < K_{x_n}, B_{x_n}, R_{x_n} >, BG >$ where: $< K_{x_i}, B_{x_i}, R_{x_i} >$ is the state of the agent x_i, and BG is the global goal of the system such that $\mathcal{R}$ $(B_{x_1}, B_{x_2}, \ldots, B_{x_n}) \implies BG$ where $\mathcal{R}$ is a relation which combines the local goals of the agents.

Note that $\mathcal{R}$ is closely related to the system to be modeled. For example, in the prey/predator problem, BG is the capture of the prey, B_{x_i} is getting closer to the prey from one side and $\mathcal{R}$ is the conjunction of all the local goals.

Definition 3.5 [The state transition due to an action]

Let $<< K_{x_1}, B_{x_1}, R_{x_1} >, \ldots, < K_{x_i}, B_{x_i}, R_{x_i} >, \ldots, < K_{x_n}, B_{x_n}, R_{x_n} >$ $, BG >$ be a state of our system, $A_i =< K_{x_i}, B_{x_i}, R_{x_i} >$ a state of an agent x_i $(i : 1..n)$. The state transition due to an action is described by the following inference rules :

(i) $a \in APH \cup APR$

$$\frac{< K_{x_i}, B_{x_i}, a.R_{x_i} > \xrightarrow{a} < K'_{x_i}, B_{x_i}, R_{x_i} >}{< A_1, \ldots, A_i, \ldots, A_n, BG > \xrightarrow{a} < A_1, \ldots, < K'_{x_i}, B_{x_i}, R_{x_i} >, \ldots, A_n, BG >}$$

If an agent is ready to execute a physical or private action, then the whole system is ready to execute the same action.

(ii) $a \in ACOE, \bar{a} \in ACOR$

$$\frac{< K_{x_i}, B_{x_i}, a.R_{x_i} > \overset{a}{\longrightarrow} < K_{x_i}, B_{x_i}, R_{x_i} >;}{< K_{x_j}, B_{x_j}, \bar{a}.R_{x_j} > \overset{\bar{a}}{\longrightarrow} < K'_{x_j}, B_{x_j}, R_{x_j} >}$$

$$< A_1, \ldots, A_i, \ldots, A_n, BG > \overset{a\bar{a}}{\longrightarrow}$$
$$< A_1, \ldots, < K_{x_i}, B_{x_i}, R_{x_i} >, \ldots, < K'_{x_j}, B_{x_j}, R_{x_j} >, \ldots, A_n, BG >$$

If an agent is ready to send a message a and another agent is ready to receive the same message, then the whole system is ready in this case to execute this interaction. We note it by $a\bar{a}$. One can see that in our approach, we model communication in a synchronous way.

(iii) τ a decision action

$$\frac{< K_{x_i}, B_{x_i}, R_{x_i} > \overset{\tau}{\longrightarrow} < K'_{x_i}, B_{x_i}, R'_{x_i} >}{< A_1, \ldots, A_i, \ldots, A_n, BG > \overset{\tau}{\longrightarrow} < A_1, \ldots, < K'_{x_i}, B_{x_i}, R'_{x_i} >, \ldots, A_n, BG >}$$

Each decision action executed by an agent changes the state of the system by changing the corresponding state of the decision-maker.

(iv) negotiation action : it is a finite sequence of communicative actions[2] initiated to update the goals of the agents. Indeed, under certain circumstances, it can be useful for an agent to modify his proper goal. We assume that the global goal can change if the agents perceive that it can't be achieved any longer. Let η be a negotiation action, we use the following axiom to describe its impact

$$< A_1, \ldots, A_i, \ldots, A_n, BG > \overset{\eta}{\longrightarrow} < A'_1, \ldots, A'_i, \ldots, A'_n, BG' >$$

where $A_i = < K_{x_i}, B_{x_i}, R_{x_i} >$; $A'_i = < K'_{x_i}, B'_{x_i}, R'_{x_i} >$
and $\mathcal{R} (B'_{x_1}, \ldots, B'_{x_i}, \ldots, B'_{x_n}) \Longrightarrow BG'$

The negotiation action is represented in the above definition (iv) at a high level of abstraction. That is, we have represented a negotiation action by a single (negotiation) action. Therefore, we do not discuss how a negotiation takes place in this paper.

4 Specification language

In this section, we define a specification language $\mathcal{L}_w$ which is a first-order, multi-modal and linear-time logic. The proposed semantics in the latter section is the basis for the evaluation of $\mathcal{L}_w$ formulae. In addition to the usual operators of first-order logic, $\mathcal{L}_w$ provides the temporal operators $\circ$(next time), $\square$(always), $\mathcal{U}$(until), $\bullet$(previous), $\blacksquare$(always in the past), $\mathcal{S}$ (since); and modal operators for belief, goal and role, and a number of other operators that will be informally

---

[2] Actually, the communicative actions used to negotiate are different from the usual communicative actions mentioned above. The latters cannot modify the goals whereas the formers are designed to update the agent goals.

described below. The formulae $(\mathcal{B}\ x\ \varphi)$, $(\mathcal{G}\ x\ \varphi)$ and $(Has\_Role\ x\ r\ \varphi)$ mean: agent x has a belief φ, has a goal φ, and has a role r that if executed would achieve φ respectively.

The syntax of $\mathcal{L}_w$ is provided in the sub-section that follows. The sub-section 2 describes the semantics of $\mathcal{L}_w$. For simplification, the semantics of $\mathcal{L}_w$ are given in three parts: the semantics of temporal formulae is given in the first part ; the semantics of formulae which apply to actions and roles are described in the second part ; the modelling of beliefs and goals is mentioned in the third part. The semantics of first-order fortmulae is defined as usual.

4.1 The syntax

The syntax of $\mathcal{L}_w$ is given by the following definition :

Definition 4.1 [$\mathcal{L}_w$ formulae]

Let $\mathcal{L}_w$ be the set of our specification language formulae. $\mathcal{L}_w$ is defined as follows:

(i) $L_\Sigma[X] \subseteq \mathcal{L}_w$;

(ii) if $\varphi \in \mathcal{L}_w$ then $\square\ \varphi \in \mathcal{L}_w$, $\circ\ \varphi \in \mathcal{L}_w$, $\varphi\ \mathcal{U}\ \psi \in \mathcal{L}_w$, $\blacksquare\ \varphi \in \mathcal{L}_w$, $\bullet\ \varphi \in \mathcal{L}_w$, $\varphi\ \mathcal{S}\ \psi \in \mathcal{L}_w$;

(iii) if $\varphi, \psi \in \mathcal{L}_w$ then $\varphi \vee \psi \in \mathcal{L}_w$, $\neg\varphi \in \mathcal{L}_w$;

(iv) if $x \in X$ (the set of variables) and $\varphi \in \mathcal{L}_w$ then $\exists x\varphi \in \mathcal{L}_w$;

(v) if $x \in Ag$ (the set of agents), and $\varphi \in \mathcal{L}_w$ then $\mathcal{B}\ x\ \varphi\ \in\ \mathcal{L}_w$, $\mathcal{G}\ x\ \varphi \in \mathcal{L}_w$;

(vi) if $x \in Ag$ (the set of agents), $a \in Ac$ (the set of actions), $\varphi \in \mathcal{L}_w$, and r a role then $OCCURRED\ a\ \in\ \mathcal{L}_w$, $Agent\ x\ a\ \in\ \mathcal{L}_w$, $Has\_Role\ x\ r \in \mathcal{L}_w$.

4.2 The semantics

This section describes the truth conditions of $\mathcal{L}_w$ formulae. Before, we give some definitions.

Definition 4.2 [precedence relation on state sequence]

Let $\mathcal{M}$ be a state transition sequence, and $ST(\mathcal{M})$ be the set of states including the transitions of $\mathcal{M}$. We define the immediate successor of a state $s \in ST(\mathcal{M})$ by the relation $\prec$ such that :

$\forall s, s' \in ST(\mathcal{M}) : s \prec s'$ iff s' is the immediate successor of s in $\mathcal{M}$.

We denote by $\prec^*$ the reflexive and transitive closure of $\prec$.

The set of accessible states from a given state is defined as follows :

Definition 4.3 [The set of accessible states]

Let $\mathcal{M}$ be a state sequence. The set of accessible states from a given state s is defined as follows : $\mathcal{A}(s) = \{e \in ST(\mathcal{M})|s \prec^* e\}$

Semantics of temporal formulae The semantics of temporal fromulae is given in a state sequence $\mathcal{M}$, with respect to a current time point s.

$< \mathcal{M}, s > \models \Box\, \varphi$	iff	forall $s' \in \mathcal{A}(s)$, $< \mathcal{M}, s' > \models \varphi$
$< \mathcal{M}, s > \models \circ\, \varphi$	iff	$< \mathcal{M}, s' > \models \varphi$ where $s \prec s'$
$< \mathcal{M}, s > \models \varphi\, \mathcal{U}\, \psi$	iff	there is $s' \in \mathcal{A}(s)$ such that $< \mathcal{M}, s' > \models \psi$
		and forall s'' $(s \prec^* s'' \prec^* s')$, $< \mathcal{M}, s'' > \models \varphi$
$< \mathcal{M}, s > \models \blacksquare\, \varphi$	iff	forall s' such that $s' \prec^* s$, $< \mathcal{M}, s' > \models \varphi$
$< \mathcal{M}, s > \models \bullet\, \varphi$	iff	$< \mathcal{M}, s' > \models \varphi$ where $s' \prec s$
$< \mathcal{M}, s > \models \varphi\, \mathcal{S}\, \psi$	iff	there is s' such that $s' \prec^* s$ and $< \mathcal{M}, s' > \models \psi$,
		and forall s'' $(s' \prec^* s'' \prec^* s)$, $< \mathcal{M}, s'' > \models \varphi$

Actions and roles In this section, we give the semantics of action and role formulae.

Semantics of action formulae With respect to an action, it may be interesting to reason about its occurrence. Hence, we use the following operators which could be applied on actions : *ENABLED* and *OCCURRED*. Let a be an action, (*ENABLED a*) means that the action a is ready to be executed. (*OCCURRED a*) means that the action a has just been executed. The semantics of the occurrence of an action are given in a sequence $\mathcal{M}$ and at a current time point s of $\mathcal{M}$:

$< \mathcal{M}, s > \models OCCURRED\ a$　　iff　　there is a state transition $s' \xrightarrow{a} s$ in $\mathcal{M}$

We can define (*OCCURRED a*) in terms of (*ENABLED a*) :

$(OCCURED\ a) \stackrel{\text{def}}{=} \bullet(ENABLED\ a)$.

The fact that an action a is of an agent x, is denoted by the formula (*Agent x a*) which semantics is given in a state sequence $\mathcal{M}$ as follows :

$< \mathcal{M}, s > \models Agent\ x\ a$　　iff　　there is $s' \xrightarrow{a} s$ in $\mathcal{M}$ and $a \in EL(R_x)$

– R_x is the role of the agent x.

– $EL(Se)$ denotes the set of elements composing the sequence Se.

To denote that an agent x is ready to execute an action a, we use the following abbreviation :

$(ENABLED\ x\ a) \stackrel{\text{def}}{=} (Agent\ x\ a) \wedge (ENABLED\ a)$.

Similarly, we use the abbreviation (OCCURRED x a) to denote that the agent x has just executed the action a.

$(OCCURRED\ x\ a) \stackrel{\text{def}}{=} (Agent\ x\ a) \wedge (OCCURRED\ a)$.

Semantics of role formulae Each agent has a role denoting its organizational component. A role is modelled as mentioned above by a sequence of actions. Next, we give the semantics of role formulae. The formula (*PERFORM x r*) means that an agent x fills its role r and its semantics is given by the following rule :

$< \mathcal{M}, s > \models PERFORM\ x\ r$　　iff　　exists s' such that $s \prec^* s'$, and forall $a \in EL(r)$, $< \mathcal{M}, s' > \models OCCURRED\ x\ a$

The past execution of a role r is denoted by the formula $\blacklozenge$ (*PERFORM x r*) which

means that an agent x has filled his role r. We use the following abbreviation :
$(PERFORMED \ x \ r) \overset{\text{def}}{=} \blacklozenge (PERFORM \ x \ r)$.
We use the formula $(Has\_Role \ x \ r \ \varphi)$ to denote that an agent x has a role r to achieve φ.
The semantics of this formula is given in $\mathcal{M}$ and a current time point s :
$< \mathcal{M}, s > \models Has\_Role \ x \ r \ \varphi$ iff $< \mathcal{M}, s > \models \Box \ ((PERFORMED \ x \ r) \Rightarrow \varphi)$
We're also interested in knowing whether an agent would succeed to achieve φ.
Let $(Succeeds \ x \ \varphi)$ be a formula denoting the success of an agent x to achieve φ. Formally : $(Succeeds \ x \ \varphi) \overset{\text{def}}{=} \exists r \in Roles \ (Has\_Role \ x \ r \ \varphi)$

Example 4.4 [The achievement of a goal]
Let $\varphi \equiv \forall X \ \forall Y \ Position(prey, X, Y) \Longrightarrow Position(\alpha, X - 1, Y)$ be the local goal of the predator α denoting getting closer to a prey from the western side. The achievement of φ is specified by the following formula: $\psi \equiv Succeeds \ \alpha \ \varphi$. Proving ψ requires that the agent has a role r to achieve φ $(Has\_Role \ \alpha \ r \ \varphi)$ and the agent succeeds to achieve φ.

Beliefs and goals In this section, we give the semantics of beliefs and goals of an agent. Beliefs are modelled by a finite set of ground atoms associated to each state. Similarly, goals are represented by a finite set of first-order logic formulae associated to each state. Syntactically, beliefs and goals have two parameters: an agent and a well-formed formula of $\mathcal{L}_w$. A belief formula is $(\mathcal{B} \ x \ \varphi)$ and means that agent x has φ as a belief. A goal formula is $(\mathcal{G} \ x \ \varphi)$ and means that agent x has φ as a goal. The formal semantics of beliefs and goals are given in a state transition sequence $\mathcal{M}$ with respect to a current time point s.
$< \mathcal{M}, s > \models (\mathcal{B} \ x \ \varphi)$ iff $\mathcal{NF}(\varphi) \in K_x$
$< \mathcal{M}, s > \models (\mathcal{G} \ x \ \varphi)$ iff $\mathcal{NF}(\varphi) \in B_x$
According to the semantics of beliefs, a formula is said to be believed at a point time s by an agent if and only if its normal form (denoted by $\mathcal{NF}$) belongs to the set of its beliefs at this time point. This setting enables to reduce the set of beliefs [3] . The set of beliefs is time-dependent. Indeed, K may be different at time point t_0 from the one at t_1. Thus, the agent can change his beliefs according to the semantics of the actions executed. Similarly, an agent is said having φ as a local goal (global respectively) if and only if its normal form belongs to the set of its goals at the time point s (all the time points respectively).

5   Conclusion

This paper proposes a study of multi-agent systems from conception to specification. Unlike most previous work where the authors adopt an individual conception, this paper emphasizes the study of interaction as a preliminary to deduce the intentional structure of an agent. We have talked about beliefs and goals as communication concepts, and roles as organization concepts. In future, we hope

---

[3] In fact, we augment the set of beliefs without augmenting its reserved space.

to extend the work presented in this paper in a number of ways. First, the underlying axiomatic system to $\mathcal{L}_w$ need to be developed -we are currently working at this level. Second, the negotiation is given at a high abstraction level, specially the underlying protocols and the common language enabling information exchange need to be studied. Third, the agent model as described in this paper need to be implemented. Stated another way, the following question should be addressed : given a specification φ, expressed in $\mathcal{L}_w$, how do we construct a system S such that S satisfies φ ? In this regard, we know that there are two general approaches in the literature : to directly execute φ (for example the programming language called Concurrent Metatem[4] [13]), or compile φ into a directly executable form. Both approaches involve generating a model that satisfies the specification.

References

1. J. Ferber, *Les systémes multi-agents : un aperçu général*, [T.S.I, Volume 16, 1997].
2. Y. Shoham, *Agent Oriented Programming*, [Artificial intelligence, 60 (1), 1993].
3. A.S. Rao & M.P. Georgeff, *An abstract architecture for rational agents*, [In R. Fikes and E. Sandewall editors, Proceedings of knowledge representation and Reasoning (KR & R-91), page 473-484. Morgan Kaufmann Publishers : San Mateo, CA, April 1991].
4. P.R. Cohen & H.J. Levesque, *Intention is choice with commitment*, [Artificial Intelligence, 42, pp. 213-261, 1990].
5. M. Wooldridge & N.R. Jennings, *Agent Theories, Architectures, and Languages : A Survey*, [LNAI 890, Springer-Verlag 1994].
6. W. Chainbi, *Cooperation in Multi-agent Systems*, [Internal report, LARIS, F.S.E.G, Sfax, April 1997].
7. W. Chainbi & C. Hannachi & C. Sibertin-Blanc, *The multi-agent Prey/Predator problem : A Petri net solution*, [In Proc. of the symposium on Discrete Events and Manufacturing Systems, CESA'96 IMACS Multiconference, IEEE-SMC, Lille-France, July 9-12, 1996].
8. M. Purvis & S. Cranefield, *Agent modelling with Petri Nets*, [In Proc. of the symposium on Discrete Events and Manufacturing Systems, CESA'96 IMACS Multiconference, IEEE-SMC, Lille-France, July 9-12, 1996].
9. M. Wooldridge, *This is MYWORLD : The Logic of An Agent-Oriented DAI Testbed*, [LNAI 890, Springer-Verlag 1994].
10. D. Salbert, *De l'interaction homme-machine individuelle aux systèmes multi-utilisateurs : L'exemple de la communication homme-homme médiatisée*, [Phd thesis, IMAG, Joseph Fourier University, Grenoble, France 1995].
11. S. Bandinelli & E. Di Nitto & A. Fuggetta, *Supporting cooperation in the SPADE-1 environment*, [IEEE Transactions on Software Engineering, Vol.22, No 12, December 1996].
12. T. Bouron, *Structures de communication et d'organisation pour la coopération dans un univers multi-agents*, [Phd. thesis, Paris 6 University, November 1992].
13. M. Fisher, *A survey of Concurrent Metatem-the language and its applications*, [In D. Gabbay and H.J. Ohlbach, editors, Proc. of the first Int.Conf. on Temporal Logic(ICTL-94). Springer Verlag, 1994].

---

[4] This language is based on the direct execution of temporal logic

Learning Message-Related Coordination Control in Multiagent Systems

Toshiharu Sugawara
sugawara@brl.ntt.co.jp

Satoshi Kurihara
kurihara@square.brl.ntt.co.jp

NTT Optical Network Systems Laboratories

3 − 1 Wakamiya Morinosato, Atsugi

Kanagawa 243-0198, Japan

Abstract

This paper introduces the learning mechanism by which agents can identify, through experience, important messages in the context of inference in a specific situation. At first, agents may not be able to immediately read and process important messages because of inappropriate ratings, incomplete non-local information, or insufficient knowledge for coordinated actions. By analyzing the history of past inferences with other agents, however, they can identify which messages were really used. Agents then generate situation-specific rules for understanding important messages when a similar problem-solving context appears. This paper also gives an example for explaining how agents can generate the control rule.

Keyword: Multi-agent Learning, Reasoning about coordinated interactions, Multi-agent Planning

1 Introduction

How agents can select globally coherent actions is one of the main issues in multi-agent systems. However, to describe what the appropriate coordinated activities are is quite difficult because agents have to take into account not only locally available information, but also non-local information such as a system's environment, domain data that other agents have, and inference states of other agent. It is almost impossible for systems designers to completely describe all problem-solving situations (especially in an open system). If the situations are completely described, it is still difficult to achieve coherent activities because necessary information is not appropriately sent/received, and thus, is not correctly inferred [3, 7].

Agents have to decide what information should be sent, to whom, and when. Sending all information to other agents can build a global view of the situation in all agents, but it is not efficient because of the costs of communication, processing the received messages, and creating the global view. Furthermore, all information is not worthwhile to send/receive; only a part of the information is used in agents' decisions in each problem-solving situation.

To partly overcome these issues, the purpose of this paper is to introduce a learning mechanism by which agents can identify important messages in a specific situation through experience. At first, agents may not be able to identify the important message because of the inappropriate rating, incomplete non-local information, or insufficient knowledge for coordinated actions. By analyzing the history of past inferences with other agents, they can identify which messages were really used. Agents then generate situation-specific rules for understanding the important messages. We already proposed a learning method for coordinated activities (not only messages but also local actions) in [10], where there is a strong assumption that all agents are homogeneous. In this paper, the application of the learning method is extended to other types of systems that have the same inference architecture, but may have different knowledge. Instead, it focuses on only messages among agents for the first step. Another difference from the previous work is that functional organization is introduced to identify where an agent sends messages to.

The learning discussed here is applicable to the domains where the problem-solving contexts do not change frequently. We assume that the learned message control rules can be applied to future identical situations. If the context changes, the problem detection mechanism will find the message control problem and this learning will be reapplied.

This paper is organized as follows. In the next section, some assumptions and definitions are made; then an overview of learning is given. Next, the detailed learning steps are described. Following that, an example problem from LODES, which is the multiagent system that manages and troubleshoots problems in internetworking [8, 9], is illustrated. Finally, the results in this paper are compared with those in our previous work [10].

2 Preliminaries

2.1 System Assumptions

A plan is a partially-ordered set of tasks to achieve the current goal or to verify the current hypothesis of solutions. A task may be a subplan, which may further be divided into smaller tasks and the associated partial order. An individual task that cannot be divided into smaller tasks is called an operation, which must correspond to an executable form such as a program, a test tool, or a command. (This is called a monitoring unit in [1].) The execution of a plan means that all the subplans are executed in a manner consistent with the specified partial order.

The agent discussed here is assumed to have a planner component, which can generate a plan and pass[1] each operation in the plan to the executor component according to the specified partial order. The planning (and the scheduling) is based on the task-relations that are described in the TÆMS framework (see the next section). It is also assumed, for simplicity, that all models of the problem, the inference states, and local and non-local agents are expressed by a set of variables. Thus, all results of executed plans and control information (such as the current plan, the messages from other agents, and the current goal) as well as application domain data are bound to the corresponding variables. When an agent receives a message from a coordinating agent, it can detect the arrival of the message, interleave the execution of the current plan, and then read

---

[1]The component for deciding the order of all operations is sometimes called a scheduler

the message. According to the importance rating[2] and the content of the message, the planner/scheduler decides to resume the current plan execution, or to analyze the message in detail because important tasks may be associated with it. Another assumption of the agent is to keep a history of decisions and events. This history, which is called the *inference trace*, is utilized to reproduce the model in the past diagnostic process.

2.2 TÆMS framework

It is assumed, for generality, that agent's activities are described in TÆMS framework, a task-centered coordination model proposed by Decker and Lesser [2] based on generic coordination relationships. In this model, each agent makes planning and scheduling decisions based on a subjective view of its own and other agents' task structures, which consist of the relationships among these tasks such as *enable-*, *facilitate-*, and *support-*relations[3] and resource usage patterns (such as *use*-relation).

2.3 Types of messages

Agents exchange messages with other agents for coordination. There are the following four types of messages for this purpose.

(1) A meta-level control message (such as 'stop' 'start' and 'interrupt')
(2) A message for requesting the verification of a goal and execution of a plan or an operation (and its reply)
(3) A message for requesting the value of a variable (and its reply)
(4) A message for sending the value of a variable

A message contains the sender, the receiver, and the content describing the requested task. Note that it is not necessary for agents to always use all types of messages.

2.4 Inference Traces

An inference trace is a sequence of nodes that express decisions, executions of operations, and events (such as a message from another agent). Each node is a unit of agent's action (this is called an *action unit* or *AU* hereafter) that cannot be divided. A message during a unit of action is recognized as it arrives after the the action. A node has the following information:

(a) (Decision) Why a goal was selected as a hypothesis, why a plan was selected, why a plan was suspended, why a plan was abandoned, and why a message was sent (a decision generates one node).
(b) (Execution) Variable values bound in each operation, and the execution time (this is optional) of each operation (one operation generates one node).

---

[2]This rating is referred to as a *message rating* below.

[3]The support-relation is a new relationship that was not in the original formulation discussed in [2]. This relates to how a task in an agent can affect the subjective view of its own and other agents' task structures by changing the importance rating of other tasks. When a task is requested of other agents that may have different goals, for example, the agent must decide which goal is more appropriate for the current problem. Even in a local agent, the problem situation is gradually understood by executing tasks; thus, the agent may have to decide that the current goal is not appropriate, but another goal is. Support-relations, therefore, express the semantics of inference in the domain, although enable- and facilitate-relations are relatively syntactical. It is possible that support-relation may be qualitative or quantitative depending on the systems design. This rating change can, in turn, cause the agent to choose one task over another for execution.

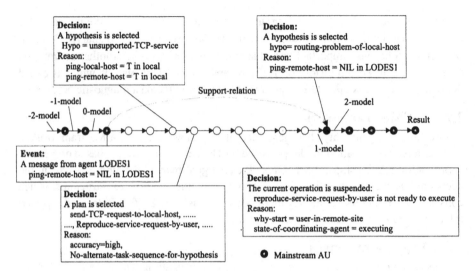

Figure 1: An Example of Inference Trace

(c) (External event) When and what type of event occurred (one event generates one node).

The variables and their data that are bound during the AU execution are also attached to the corresponding node. The model in an agent, which can be expressed as the collection of bound variables (and the semantics), can be generated from the inference trace. Fig. 1 shows the inference trace created in a LODES agent.

2.5 Functional Organization of Agents

When an agent decides the content, the time, the order, and the importance of communications with others, it has to take into account the roles that the target agents play in the agent organization as well as in the human organization, where people often change the content of what they are communicating depending on who they are talking to. The functional organization of agents is introduced to provide the framework for identifying when and with whom each agent should communicate.

Because the way to which the agents are organized highly depends on the system architecture, problem structure, and application structure, the functional organization is defined in abstract form in this paper. We assume the organization's structure is hierarchical, as shown in Fig. 2. Let A be the set of all agents. Given a problem P, the functional organization is a family of the set $\{O_{x_1,\ldots,x_n}(P)\}$ such that $O_0(P) = A$, $O_{x_1,\ldots,x_n}(P) = \cup_{m=1}^{N} O_{x_1,\ldots,x_n,m}(P)$, and $O_{x_1,\ldots,x_n,m}(P) \neq O_{x_1,\ldots,x_n,m'}(P)$ if $m \neq m'$.

The functional organization may be independent of or dependent on the problem structures. For example, in office scheduling where agents work as secretaries, the functional organization probably reflects the titles or positions in the company organization. In a heterogeneous multi-agent system, the functional organization must reflect the specialty/domain of each agent. In LODES, agents are given knowledge about the classification of problems; datalink-(Ethernet, token ring etc.), network- (IP-related) and transport-level (TCP, UDP etc.) problems. Its functional organization dynamically changes depending on which class the current hypothesis shared by the group of agents

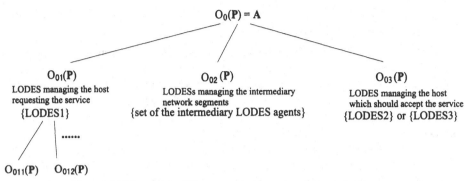

Figure 2: Hierarchical Structure in Functional Organization

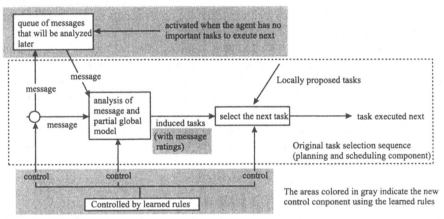

Figure 3: Scheduling Flow with Learned Rules

belongs to. Fig. 2 describes the functional organization when LODES agents diagnose a network-level problem.

2.6 How the learned rules affect reasoning activities

A coordination problem relating to communications may occur when the importance of tasks associated with a message of type (2) (3) or (4) in section 2.3 is not appropriately rated. In general the ratings of the associated tasks will be calculated by reasoning how the tasks contribute to global problem solving, based on the agent's partial global model.[4] Thus, further analysis and calculation occur in the receiver. Moreover, if the partial global model does not contain some important information or is not inferred correctly, the rating may not be appropriate: As a result, important requested tasks will be omitted or postponed, and unnecessary tasks will be executed.

To cope with this problem, two approaches come to mind. Agents:

- create a more informative partial global model so that necessary data are included, or

---

[4]In this paper a partial global model is a world model in an agent, including local and non-local information such as control, planning, other agents and domain data. The word "partial" expresses "incomplete."

- adding rules for calculating the ratings of messages, schedule the further analysis of the message according to the ratings.

[10] took the former approach for homogeneous agents. This approach is definitely general and enables an agent to make informed choices if there is enough reasoning time. Although the primary interest of this paper is to extend the learning method in [10] to non-homogeneous cases, we adopt the second the second approach as the initial means to understanding the performance of the simple approach. A rating attached to a message is called a *message rating*, hereafter.

The rules are generated in sender and receiver agents. A sender agent calculates the rating of message being sent. The rating, which may be expressed in numbers or characters, is attached to each message. In a receiver agent, the rating of the received message is also calculated using the learned rules. Ratings of messages may be identified only in one of the sender and receiver. If the ratings are calculated in both sender and receiver agents and their ratings are in conflict, the agent adopts the receiver's (futher discussion in Section 5).

The learned control rules affect the agent's reasoning in two ways (Figure 3). First, an agent can identify the rating of a being sent/received message in a situation-specific manner by just looking at the contents (without the partial global model). This identification can postpone the analysis of non-important messages; [5] thus, unnecessary tasks do not block other tasks. Second, the message ratings identified by learned rules can adjust the local task scheduling; the agent can reflect the message ratings to calculate the ratings of the induced tasks, although how much the rules should raise/lower the rating depends on application domains.

3 Steps of the Learning Process

The learning process is invoked after each problem is solved. Each domain problem is called the *instance* in this paper. The learning component in the agents follow these steps based on recorded inference traces of activity locally stored in the agents:

1) Mainstream Determination identifies the tasks and messages that contributed to achieving the final result.
2) Problem Detection locates a message control problem in the trace where the agent selected incoherent behaviors about the messages.
3) Multiple-Point Model Reproduction generates a number of models at and after the point the message control problem is detected. These models are used for identifying the situation where the learned rule is applied and for identifying the same instances of diagnosis.
4) Message Control Modification adds context-sensitive rules to raise/lower the detected message so as to avoid recurrence of the problem in this situation
5) Situation Identification and Refinement determines how to best characterize the context-sensitive situation where the generated rules should be applied.

Our basic paradigm has strong similarities to case-based reasoning and case-based planning [4]. Case-based reasoning is usually applied to a system whose domain has a

---

[5]Postponed messages will be analyzed when the agent has no further tasks to do.

weak domain theory. Our learning will, however, be applied to the domain that has a strong theory, because it is hard for agents in distributed environments to appropriately decide actions with a lack of non-local information.

3.1 Mainstream Determination

The first step in the learning process is to identify the mainstream AUs and messages of the instance (remember that an AU is an unit of actions of agents which cannot be divided). These can be obtained by tracing backwards through enable- and support-relations from the final result in the inference trace as follows. The AU that directly led to the final result is a mainstream AU. An AU that enabled (required precondition of) a mainstream AU is a mainstream AU. A goal or hypothesis that induced a mainstream AU is a mainstream goal. An AU whose results supported a mainstream AU is a mainstream AU. A message that induced or enabled a mainstream AU is a mainstream message. Thus, this process is also activated in the sender agent. An AU that produced a mainstream message is a mainstream AU. An AU that produced the content of a mainstream message is a mainstream AU. A variable bound in a mainstream AU is called a mainstream variable. Note that an AU corresponds to a decision, event or task execution; therefore, these words are sometimes used instead of AU (for example, "mainstream task").

3.2 Problem Detection

This step isolates situations in which any of the following inappropriate actions occurs:

(Pa) A mainstream message and the associated task were not appropriately rated; thus, the message was not sent soon enough in the sender agent or was not analyzed quickly in the receiver agent. In this case, either the corresponding mainstream AU did not executed in a timely manner or other non-mainstream AUs had higher priority.

(Pb) A non-mainstream message was sent with a high rating or the associated tasks have the higher ratings; this message may produce unnecessary tasks for the receiver agent and thus delay the inference.

These cases are detected by applying, in turn, a number of problem detection rules which are previously defined. An example problem detection rule is shown in Fig. 4, where a mainstream AU (task) is not executed soon enough because the mainstream message, which associates the task corresponding to the AU, is not appropriately rated. The detected problem is called a *Message-related Coordination Problem* or a *Message Control Problem* (MCP), and the detected message is called an *ill-controlled message* (ICM). An agent thinks that a message caused the problem (Pa), but another may think that it caused the problem (Pb). Such a case is called a *mixture MCP* and is considered in the situation identification step below.

3.3 Multi-level Model Reproduction

The aim of this step is to create a number of models in the sender and receivers when an ICM occurs (if this message is multicast, more-than-one agents receive it). The models created here will be used to identify situations where the learned rule should be applied. Even in the completely identical instances, the partial global model in the receiver agent may be slightly different because of the timing of the message arrival and the local task

```
Condition:
   execution-order(T1 T2 T3)      ;; Order of selections
   mainstream(T1),mainstream(T3);; T1 and T3 were the Mainstream AUs (Tasks).
   no-mainstream-between(T1 T3)  ;; No executed mainstreams in between T1 and T3,
                                 ;; thus T2 is not a mainstream task.
   task-enabled-by(T3 (T1 M1))   ;; T3 was enabled by the task T1 and the message M1.
   before(M1,T2)                 ;; M1 arrived before T2 was selected.
   Message-rating (M1) = low
   Decision-at(M1, at(M1)) = analysis-Postponed
   ;; The rating of the message was so low that its analysis was postponed.
Then: message-has-the-low-rating(M1)
```

Figure 4: An Example of Rules for Detecting a Message Control Problem (Pa).
This rule states that the execution of a mainstream task (T3) is delayed (task T2, which does not contribute to the final result, is executed before T3) because an important message (M1) has been rated lowly. Such a situation will appear in the network diagnosis example below.

execution. Here we also assume that, if instances are really identical, the models in the receiver agent will have few differences. Further discussion on the difference of orders of task executions and message arrivals will be done in Section 3.6.

First, agents create the models they had just before the ICM was sent/received. This model can be generated from the inference trace because it contains all of the data and the results of decision-making. Then the non-mainstream variables, AUs, and messages are eliminated from the model. The resulting model is called the *0-step-ahead model of the MCP* or *0-model* for simplicity in this paper. Note that the sent or received message that causes the coordination problem is not included in the 0-model. The 1-model (-1-model) is the model that are generated when the next (previous) mainstream AU is selected after (before) the MCP. The n-model ($n < 0$ and $n > 0$) is also defined in the same manner. Note that if we consider a model as the set of the bound variables a n-model is the subset of the model the agent actually has.

An n-model ($n > 0$) means the look-ahead model obtained after the mainstream executions of n AUs, and a $-n$-models ($n > 0$) means the n-step previous model of the agent. The n-models ($n < 0$, in this paper) are used to decide whether or not the last and past instances are identical. We assume that in the completely identical instances (see Section 3.5.1), the timing of arrival does not differ very much, one or two action units, at most. Thus the agent stores 0-, -1-, or -2-models. However, how many models are stored is a design issue.

3.4   Message Control Modification

This step involves adding (or modifying if the message control rules were already generated) the control rules for determining the rating of being sent/received messages. The learned rules are expressed in an "if-then" form. The first aim of this step is to create/modify the "then" part.

The then-part is easy to create; that is, the message rating of the ICM is set to the appropriate value in which the (non-) mainstream message will (not) be read and soon analyzed in the receiver agents. This rule is generated in both sender and receiver agents, thus the receiver agents have to report the appropriate message rating to the sender to put it into the rule. For the mixture MCP, the sender creates two rules for the current MCP; one for raising the ratings and the other for lowering them.

The if-part is divided into two portions for identifying the situation where the generated rule is applied and for identifying the type of message that should be controlled.

The second aim of this step is to create the latter portion. This portion is also easily generated by describing the type and the contents of the ICM in sender/receiver agents (as described in Section 2.3).

3.5 Situation Identification and Refinement

The conditions for identifying the situation where the learned rule should be applied are generated by the following steps.

3.5.1 Instance Identification

This refinement method uses a number of inference traces of identical instances. We can say that two instances are identical if the finally generated mainstream high-level models described in their inference traces are identical. Namely, the following sets are identical (note that these are compared after the inference process although the if-part in the learned rule should identify the situation during the inference process); (1) the set of agents and their functional organization when the MCP occurred; (2) the 0-model; (3) the content of the ICM; (4) the type of the MCP (namely, (Pa) or (Pb)); and (5) the final result. The 0-model may slightly be different because of the timing of the MCP arrival, thus the condition (2) will be extended as follows; (2') the agent has to be able to choose the pairs the n-model of the past instance and the current instance such that the sets of variables in their n-models are identical and one of the selected model is 0-model, at least (further discussion on this topics will appear in Section 3.6). It is possible that an agent may decide that the last inference is identical to a past instance but another agent may decide otherwise. Such a case is detected in the next step.

When the same inference appears after the (initial) rule is generated by learning, this learning is invoked again only if the learned rule does not affect the inference. This situation occurs when the message rating is not sufficiently raised/lowered in the previous learned rule.

3.5.2 Instance-type ID

The group of agents which were the sender of the ICM or which were the receiver claiming the MCP ((Pa) or (Pb)) have to identify the type of current instance.

(ID1) The agent in this group locally retrieves the past instances identical to the current instance and gets their instance IDs. If it cannot find any identical past instance, it selects "new" instead of the ID.

(ID2) All agents in this group exchange the set of IDs or "new."

(ID3) They carry out the intersection of all sets of IDs. If they find one ID, it is the ID of the current instance. If one of the agents sends "new" or the intersection is an empty set, all agents decide the new ID for the current instance.

The new ID must be generated by encoding all agents' IDs (such as the IP addresses or the MAC numbers) so that the same ID is never generated by the other set of agents.

3.5.3 If-Part and Its Generalization

This step generates the conditions to identify the situation where the learned rule is applied. It is important that the local data at the arrival of the ICM can only be used. If the current instance has a new ID, the if-part is generated based on the 0-model. The conjunction of all mainstream variable-and-value pairs in the 0-model is put into the if-part of the learned rule (see Section 4) in the sender and receiver agents. This if-part may not appropriately characterize the situation. It is often over-specific because the rule is applied only when the problem-solving situation is completely identical; for example, the situation is recognized as the different one because of the delay of messages. The if-part is improved in the following steps using a number of instances.

Suppose that the ID is not new. The agent locally retrieves the past instances with the ID. First, the agent calculate the n-models of the past instances and the current instance which are satisfied with the condition (2') in Section 3.5.1. The set of variables in these n-models is called the *base-variable set* of this ID.

Next, the if-part is refined using the current and past instances using comparative analysis [5, 6][6]. We assume that the base-variable whose value is not identical is not important for distinguishing the situation from others; thus, it is eliminated. The conjunction of the remaining variables and their values (and the message type and content condition generated in Section 3.4) are set as the if-part of the new rule.

The generated rules may be in conflict; for example, when an agent claimed both (Pa) and (Pb) in the same situation such rules may be generated. These conflict rules should be discarded; this phenomenon often appears in the early stage of inference because the agent does not have sufficient information to determine the message rating thus it cannot solely distinguish when the message is important.

3.5.4 Use of Functional Organization

It must be noted that, like a mixture MCP, a (non-)mainstream in a message found in the step for problem detection may (not) be important for not all, but only one of the receiver agents. The message was not important in the last instance, but will be important for for the same or similar instance in the future. We think that the message rating will depend on the functional role of the agent in the organization.

Let us denote the functional organization for the current instance by $\{O_{x_1,...,x_n}(P)\}$. First consider the sender agent. Before learning, the agent probably sent the message to all agents (i.e. O_0) with the same rating. However, it will vary the rating of messages depending on the receivers' roles in the organization according to the following steps with the past instances.

(F1) Select the smallest set $O_{X_1,...,X_n}$ such that all agents which said that the detected ICM causes the MCP (Pa) (or (Pb)) are contained.

(F2) Then add, into the if-part, the new condition so that it restricts applying the rule to only the message to the agents in $O_{X_1,...,X_n}$.

(F3) If the MCP is a mixture and the agents cannot be distinguished by the functional organization, the sender gives up creating the rule (the decision may be taken by the receivers).

F1 and F2 show that some agents that never claimed (Pa) (or (Pb)) may also receive the message with a higher (lower) rating. When this new rating causes another MCP for these agents, the sender agent gives up to create a rule (and thus the receiver decides its rating), since it cannot distinguish which agent really need the message being sent.

---

[6]This may not be powerful, especially for or-conditions, but has so far been adequate for our needs. We can use another powerful refinement methods instead of the comparative analysis.

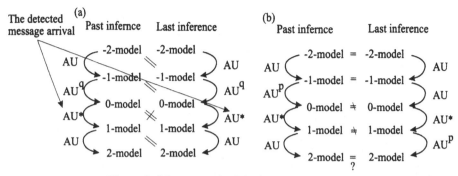

Figure 5: Message arrival timing and n-models

Next consider each receiver agent. If the receiver agent always claims only one of (Pa) or (Pb) in the instances, the agent keeps the learned rule and applies it to future identical instances. If it always claims no problem (in this case another agent claimed (Pa) or (Pb)), the learned rule is not applied[7].

3.6 Comment on Instance Identification

We have to discuss the instance identification because this is a central issue in experience-based learning. We want to emphasize that all agent's decisions are made based on its partial global (0-)model, even if that the sequences/orders of AUs in the inference before the generated (0-)models, (especially non-mainstream AUs,) are different. In Figure5 (a), the 0-model (−1-model) of the last inference and the −1-model (−2-model) of the past inference are identical.[8] In this example, although the sequences of the executed AUs may be different (that is, their execution orders are different) before −2-model, the results of executed tasks and received messages do not cause any difference in reasoning around the 0-model, where we must remember that our purpose is to understand the rating of a being sent/received message from the agent's partial global model. Therefore, if the 0-model of the last inference is identical to one of the n-model (n <= 0) of a past inference (or vice versa), the inferences (at least when the message arrives) can be said to be identical.

However, we must analyze the effect of a message near the 0-model. Suppose that −2-models of the past and last inferences are equal. These models includes all information about the agent's control and planning as well as the application domain. Thus, the agent usually selects the same AU after the −2-models. The only event that could affect the next AU selection is a message arriving at a different time. For example, when another message (the event AU^p in Figure 5 (b)) arrives just before or after the 0-model, the resulting agent's 0-models are different. A similar situation also occurs when the AU^q in Figure 5 (a) is another message. In both cases, the agent cannot find an n-model equal to the 0-model; thus, the instance identification decides that these inferences are different.

---

[7]Strictly speaking, the rule is not generated because no MCP are detected

[8]Precisely, the −1-model of the last inference is identical to the −2-model of the past one; thus, both of them induce the same AU activity. The resulting models are also identical.

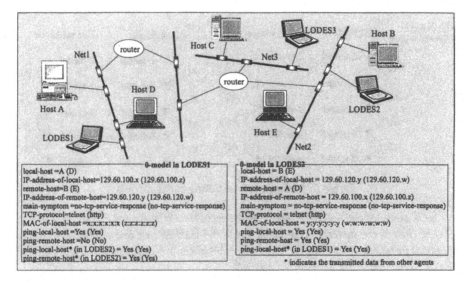

Figure 6: The Example Environment where the troubles are reported

4 An Example in Computer Network Troubleshooting

This learning method is implemented in our LODES system. We will show a LODES example that arises when the priority for processing a received mainstream message is incorrectly set in a particular situation.

4.1 Example Description

Consider the following two causes of trouble in the environment shown in Fig. 6.

(C1) Host B has no routing data for sending packets to the network, Net1.

(C2) B is off-line or the power is off.

The symptoms for these troubles reported by a host A user are identical; that is, the user tried to telnet to host B, but there was no response from B.

After the symptom is reported to LODES1, LODES1 decides that this is not a local problem; thus, it invokes LODES2 for coordinated diagnosis. (LODES agents between Net1 and Net2 are also invoked, but they do not play important roles in this diagnosis.) Note that because any observational result in LODES1 for these two troubles is identical (i.e., there is no B's response to any test or request packet) LODES1 cannot distinguish the causes of these two troubles by itself.

Before learning, the LODES agents can diagnose the problem but not efficiently because unnecessary tasks are induced by non-mainstream messages. For example, the cause of C1 cannot be isolated solely by LODES2 because LODES2's observations imply that B works correctly. Only the message indicating that the communication it expected from B has not occurred (e.g. the ICMP echo reply from B cannot be observed by LODES1. This result is stored into the variable "ping-remote-host" in LODES1) can change LODES2's decision. LODES2 can, however, diagnose the problem by itself if it is C2, and no information from LODES1 is necessary. A message from LODES1 may lead to executions of unnecessary tasks. However, since LODES1 cannot distinguish the causes of this problem either, it cannot decide the rating of the result "ping-remote-host" locally. It is also true that LODES2 cannot identify whether or not the received message is important because it has not isolated the cause of the trouble yet.

4.2 First Diagnosis

Suppose that initially the rating of the message "ping-remote-host" is low (this rating is appropriate for C2). Consider the cause of the trouble, C1. LODES2 cannot isolate the cause without coordination with LODES1. In this case, a message about the result of "ping-remote-host" from LODES1 is a mainstream message (See Fig. 1 which is the trace of LODES2). At first, LODES2 strongly believed that host B had no problems because all tests by LODES2 expressed B's correct behaviors. This message, furthermore, had a low rating. Thus LODES2 postponed analyzing it and performed a number of unnecessary AUs, as shown in Fig. 1. This figure shows that LODES2 decided that the trouble was not IP-related, but TCP- or upper-level-related. It then selected the hypothesis "unsupported-TCP-service." LODES2 then created the plan for verifying it. However, one of its operations, which required collaboration with LODES1, intermediary LODES agents between Net1 and Net2, and the manager in LODES1's site was not ready to execute. As a result, the current plan was suspended and the next hypothesis, which has the support relation with the message "ping-remote-host," was selected. This decision enabled LODES2 to eventually isolate cause C1.

4.3 Learning Steps

Let us now look at, by learning, how LODES1 and LODES2 identify the rating of LODES1's message on the variable "ping-remote-host."

The mainstream determination step is simple; thus, details of its process are omitted here. The marked mainstream AUs are shown in Fig. 1. It is also obvious that, by applying the rule shown in Fig. 4 in LODES2's problem detection step, LODES1's message on "ping-remote-host" belongs to the problem (Pa). This result is transmitted to LODES1 and other intermediary LODES agents.

In the multi-level model reproduction step, the LODES agents create 0-, −1-, and −2-models from the inference trace. These models are expressed by a set of variable-value pairs. An important part of the 0-models in LODES1 and LODES2 is shown in Fig. 6. Because the instance ID of this example is "new," the rule is created in a simple manner. For example, the created rule in LODES1 is shown in Fig. 7 (a). Furthermore, by using the functional organization for this example, the word "LODES2" in this rule is replaced by $O_{03}(P)$ for more general uses (This is not shown in Fig. 7 (a)). Of course, this rule is too specific to be applied to similar cases such as when the same trouble is reported between hosts A and C.

If the same problem occurs between the hosts in network segments Net1 and Net2 (e.g. hosts D and E), this rule is more generalized by comparative analysis. In this new instance of trouble, LODES1 and LODES2 execute the same inference (but the rule by the last instance cannot be applied because its if-part is too specific). Before the situation identification step, all learning actions are identical so we omit the details. All mainstream AUs, the MCP type, the message type, and the variable set in the 0-models are identical, so this new instance has the ID identical to the previous example.

```
IF local-host = A, remote-host = B, ...., ping-remote-host in LODES2 = Yes,
   the-message-type = (sending-value-of-variable ping-remote-host LODES2)
THEN the message (sending-value-of-variable ping-remote-host LODES2)
   has the high rating.
```

(a) The rule created from the first instance
The if-part is the conjunction of the variable and value pairs appeared in Fig. 6.

```
IF  ;; Rule in LODES1
   main-symptom = no-tcp-service-response, ping-local-host = Yes,
   ping-remote-host = No, ping-local-host in LODES2 = Yes,
   ping-remote-host in LODES2 = Yes,
   the-message-type = (sending-value-of-variable ping-remote-host LODES2)
THEN
   the message (sending-value-of-variable ping-remote-host LODES2) has
   the high rating.
```

(b) The rule created after the first and second instances

Figure 7: Rules created from the example diagnoses

The 0-models in LODES1 and LODES2 are also described in Fig. 6 (the values in parentheses). By comparative analysis, the variables that have different values can be eliminated from the if-part of the previous rule. The obtained rule is described in Fig. 7 (b).

Furthermore, the word LODES2 in this rule is also replaced by $O_{03}(P)$ for general uses. This rule is useful for other cases such as the same trouble between hosts A and C. Although LODES3 has no experience in diagnosing this instance, the sender (LODES1) can set the high rating of the message.

4.4 How LODESs distinguish cases C1 and C2

Let us compare causes C1 and C2. Initially LODES1's message on the variable ping-remote-host has a low rating; thus, it does not lead to an MCP in the case of C2. The generated rule is not selected in the case of C2 because LODES1 has the 0-model, where the value of the ping-local-host in LODES2 is "no" or this value has not yet arrived.[9] This phenomenon also happens in LODES2.

5 Implementation and Discussion

This learning method is implemented in our newest version of the LODES system, which runs on a KCL/FreeBSD/Pentium (II). We artificially produced troubles, C1 and C2, and LODESs can actually generate the rule in the environment. The rule in the case of C1 can eliminate nine non-mainstream AUs (as shown in Fig. 1). Some eliminated AUs are operations following message exchanges; thus, the diagnostic time (not CPU-time) can be reduced by about 10%.

Our approach is symbolic, fully distributed, and agent-centered. It is quite different from other learning research in DAI, whose approaches are based on statistics or reinforcement learning [11, 12].

Compared to [10], CPU time for this learning is shorter. In [10], it is assumed that all agents are homogeneous. All models (0-models) are fully exchanged and the comprehensive global model is generated in agents; however, these communications and

---

[9]The AU for deciding that the value of ping-local-host is "no" takes more time because LODES2 has to wait for a few seconds and retry again in order to make sure that there is truly no response.

model creation processes are CPU expensive. The generated rule in [10], however, describes well the situation where the generated rule should be applied. We can consider two reasons for this. First, it is clear that the global view is very powerful for generating rules. Agents can take into account control problems on the rating of local goals, local plans, and local operations as well as messages. Another reason is the ability of identifying the same instances. For example, if all agents are homogeneous, LODES1 understands that the C1 troubles between hosts A and B, and between hosts A and C are the same instances, because LODES1 agents can recognize the models of LODES2 and LODES3. However, if all agents are not homogeneous, LODES1 cannot understand that these two are the same instances. The local models of LODES1 are identical, but the models in LODES2 and in LODES3 cannot be compared.

The generated rule is iteratively improved in this learning. However, the rule may change the situation of inference. As a result, the inference will be recognized as a new instance. In our framework, if this new instance has another MCP, it will be rectified by the learning method. We must discuss the case in which the inference trace has two MCPs. The rule for the first MCP may change the situation where the second MCP appears, so that the latter rule cannot be generated well. To prevent such a phenomenon, the agent can restrict the learning of the rule only for the first MCP.

As shown in Section 2.6, if the ratings of a message in the sender and receiver agents are in conflict, the agent adopts the receiver's. However, this is not generally true; the rule generation also has to iteratively be applied. Our idea is that if the reciever's choice is not appropriate thus cuases the same or another message related problem, this problem is also detected and the learned rule will be modified.

This paper only discusses changing the rating of messages, which is possible by changing the rating of the local plan and/or operation to remedy the coordination problem. For example, the MCP detected by the detection rule in Fig. 4 can be eliminated by lowering the rating of the local task T2. In other situations, an important plan whose outcome supports sending a mainstream message was not selected; thus, the mainstream message was sent with low rating. To change the control of local tasks, the agent must generate a more global model. This is one issue to be investigated in the future.

6 Conclusion

A method for learning the appropriate rating of messages for coordinated actions has been proposed. If at first, agents cannot decide whether or not the arrived message is really used because of inappropriate ratings and a lack of knowledge for coordinations, by analyzing past inference traces, they can identify which messages were really used. Agents then generate situation-specific rules for understanding important messages. An example for explaining how agents can generate the control rule has also been described. Our current work is to extend this framework to identify what are really important local tasks and important messages.

References

[1] Cockburn, D and Jennings, N. R. "ARCHON: A Distributed Artificial Intelligence System for Industrial Applications," in Foundations of Distributed Artificial Intel-

ligence," eds. by O'Hare, G. M. P. and Jennings, N. R., pp. 319 - 344.

[2] Decker, K. and Lesser, V. R. "Quantitative Modeling of Complex Environments," International Journal of Intelligent Systems in Accounting, Finance and Management, special issue on Mathematical and Computational Models of Organizations: Models and Characteristics of Agent Behavior, 1993.

[3] Decker, K.S. and Lesser, V.R. "Designing a Family of Coordination Algorithms," Proceedings of the First International Conference on Multiagent Systems, San Francisco, June 1995. AAAI Press.

[4] Hammond, K. J., "Case-Based Planning: Viewing Planning as a Memory Task," Academic Press, 1989.

[5] Hudlická, E. and Lesser, V. R., "Meta-Level Control Through Fault Detection and Diagnosis," Proceedings of the 1984 National Conference on AI, 1984, pp. 153-161.

[6] Hudlická, E. and Lesser, V. R., "Modeling and Diagnosing Problem-Solving System Behavior," IEEE Transactions on Systems, Man, and Cybernetics, Vol. 17, Number 3, May/June 1987, pp. 407-419. (Also published in Readings in Distributed Artificial Intelligence, A. Bond and L. Gasser (eds.), Morgan Kaufmann Publishers, California, 1988, pp. 490-502.)

[7] Lesser, V. R., "A Retrospective View of FA/C Distributed Problem Solving," IEEE Transactions on Systems, Man, and Cybernetics, 21(6):1347-1362, Nov./Dec. 1991.

[8] Sugawara, T. "A Cooperative LAN Diagnostic and Observation Expert System," Proc. of IEEE Phoenix Conf. on Comp. and Comm., pp. 667-674, 1990.

[9] Sugawara, T. and Murakami, K. "A Multiagent Diagnostic System for Internetwork Problems," Proc. of INET'92, Kobe, Japan, 1992.

[10] Sugawara, T. and Lesser, V. R. "On-Line Learning of Coordination Plans," COINS Technical Report, 93-27, Univ. of Massachusetts, 1993. (The shorter version of this paper is also published in Proc. of the 12th Int. Workshop on Distributed AI, 1993.)

[11] Tan, M. "Multi-agent reinforcement learning: Independent vs. cooperative agents," In Proceedings of the Tenth International Conference on Machine Learning, pages 330-337, 1993.

[12] Weiss, G. "Some studies in distributed machine learning and organizational design," Technical Report FKI-189-94, Institut fur Informatik, TU Munchen, 1994.

Multi-agent Reinforcement Learning System Integrating Exploitation- and Exploration-Oriented Learning

Satoshi Kurihara and Toshiharu Sugawara
NTT Optical Network Systems Labs
3-1 Morinosato-wakamiya, Atsugi, Kanagawa, 243-01 JAPAN
Tel:+81 462 40 3611, Fax:+81 462 40 4730
Email:{kurihara, sugawara}@square.brl.ntt.co.jp
Rikio Onai
Real-World Computing Partnership
Tsukuba Mitsui Bld. 13F, 1-6-1 Takezono, Tsukuba, Ibaraki, 305 JAPAN
Tel:+81 298 53 1672, Fax:+81 298 53 1640
E-mail:onai@trc.rwcp.or.jp

Abstract

This paper proposes and evaluates MarLee, a multi-agent reinforcement learning system that integrates both exploitation- and exploration-oriented learning. Compared with conventional reinforcement learnings, MarLee is more robust in the face of a dynamically changing environment and is able to perform exploration-oriented learning efficiently even in a large-scale environment. Thus, MarLee is well suited for autonomous systems, for example, software agents and mobile robots, that operate in dynamic, large-scale environments, like the real-world and the Internet. Spreading activation, based on the behavior-based approach, is used to explore the environment, so by manipulating the parameters of the spreading activation, it is easy to tune the learning characteristics. The fundamental effectiveness of MarLee was demonstrated by simulation.
Keywords: Multi-agent reinforcement learning; Exploitation-oriented; Exploration-oriented; Spreading activation; Dynamic environment.

1 Introduction

The use of artificial intelligence for building autonomous systems in complex, dynamic environments like the Internet is attracting much interest. We have been studying behavior-selection mechanisms (planning, search algorithms, etc.) for possible application to autonomous mobile robots, software agents, and so on.

Several behavior-selection mechanisms that enable an autonomous system to effectively respond to changes in the dynamic environment have been proposed. These include: a subsumption architecture [9], real-time reactive planning [10], an agent network architecture (ANA) [7], and our previously proposed multi-agent real-time reactive planning [11]. Although these systems react efficiently to their environments, they are still incapable of efficient adaptation to changes. Therefore, autonomous systems need to be capable of "reinforcement learning" so that they can independently adapt to different situations they encounter.

To learn, it is necessary to gather information about the environment; however, in the real-world, it is impossible to obtain comprehensive information in advance. Therefore, autonomous systems operating in a real-world environment must be provided with sensors and be able to model the environment as they go along gathering information locally. In addition, because a real-world environment is volatile and changes dynamically, the learning ability of the autonomous systems must also be quite robust. Effective exploration of a large environment must therefore take the state of the environment into account. In regard to reinforcement learning, there are two basic methods: exploitation-oriented learning and exploration-oriented learning.

Profit-sharing [3] is a typical exploitation-oriented learning method: when a reward is given, the entire behavioral series up to that point is immediately reinforced. Profit-sharing is considered to be a robust learning method for two reasons. First, it requires only a few training iterations. Second, unlike Q-learning [2] (which is a typical exploration-oriented learning method), when the environment changes, the reinforcement values corresponding to the portions that were not affected by the changes are maintained. Unfortunately, the portions that are affected must be re-learned.

Q-learning [2] has attracted a great deal of interest in the nineties. C. J. C. Watkins et al. demonstrated that if the exploration of an environment can be completed without incident, then optimal learning results can be obtained [2]. However, this approach has several weaknesses. For example, in order to determine suitable "Q values", the state of the environment must be accurately identified. Q-learning thus takes much more time than profit-sharing to complete the required number of training iterations. Furthermore, if the environment changes while learning is underway, all of the previously learned results (the Q-table) are adversely affected which reduces the overall learning efficiency.

The environment in this study is assumed to be dynamic and large, so even if exploitation-oriented learning can perform adaptively, highly accurate learning results are difficult to obtain. Although exploration-oriented learning is affected by changes in the environment and requires considerably more learning steps, it nevertheless enables highly accurate learning. Therefore, the ideal approach would be to integrate the two learning methods in a way that harnesses the unique strengths of each approach.

It would clearly not be very efficient to explore the entire space of a dynamically changing, large-scale environment in which points where rewards can be obtained are scattered throughout. For example, it would be more efficient to begin exploring in the vicinity of a reward point rather than to begin exploring from a place without any reward points in the immediate vicinity.

We have proposed an integrated learning system called MarLee (Multi-Agent Reinforcement Learning System integrating Exploitation/Exploration). It uses one agent to perform exploitation-oriented learning (the exploitation agent) and multiple agents to perform exploration-oriented learning (exploration agents). The overall learning flow starts with the learning of the exploitation agent. When the exploitation agent encounters a reward point, the exploitation agent generates an exploration agent that then pursues exploration-oriented learning of the area around the reward point. Meanwhile, the exploitation agent resumes its learning, and when it encounters another reward point it generates another exploration agent, and so on.

The area to be explored by each exploration agent initially depends on the value of the reward obtained by the exploitation agent. The area is gradually increased according to the exploration rate. Although exploration-oriented learning, such as Q-learning, cannot be effectively applied to a dynamically changing environment, a robust exploration capability can be achieved by implementing an exploration method that uses a spreading activation model [7] based on a behavior-based approach [8].

In Sec. 2 we describe MarLee in detail, and in Sec. 3 we present the results of our simulation. In Sec. 4 we discuss the overall results of our research, and in Sec. 5 we conclude with a summary and take a look at our future work.

2 MarLee

2.1 Simulation environment

Before describing MarLee, we will outline the simulation environment we used to evaluate its performance. Consider an autonomous system **A** moving within grid-structured space S (a grid world). **A** can move one block in each step

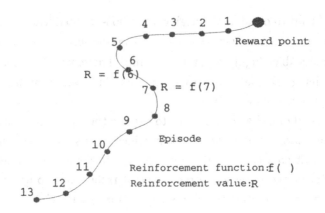

Figure 1: Reinforcement function.

within S, either up, down, left, or right. Several reward points B are positioned at various locations within S, and the amount of each reward is different. There are also obstacles within S, which **A** cannot cross. Neither the number nor position of the Bs vary, but those of the obstacles do.

In the initial state, **A** has only the following knowledge: S is a grid world, and **A** can move within S in the four compass directions. **A** has no information regarding the locations of the rewards or the obstacles and is only able to retain or learn information about the path it takes through the environment. Multiple **A**s can be present in the environment at the same time, and these **A**s can communicate with each other.

A's purpose is to determine the location of and best routes to the reward point B. Also, **A** should learn that even if B_1's reward is low, it is more efficient to go to it than to go to B_2 if B_1 is closer. Finally, and most importantly, **A** should react flexibly to obstacles coming into or going out of existence and maintain its learning performance.

2.2 Overview of MarLee

MarLee consists of one exploitation agent and multiple exploration agents.

2.2.1 Exploitation agent

The exploitation agent performs the same kind of learning as in profit-sharing. In profit-sharing, a state-transition series (an episode) is the unit of learning, and the episodes and the reinforcement value assigned to each episode are retained.

The reinforcement values are allocated in the same way as in profit-sharing:

one is assigned for each point of an episode based on a reinforcement function $R = f(h)$, where R is the reinforcement value, and h is the distance between the reward point and the point of the episode [1](see Fig. 1). In profit-sharing, the performance of the reinforcement function greatly affects the learning performance. Several specialized methods of calculating the reinforcement value exist [3] [6] but we will use a standard method instead.

There are several differences between using an exploitation agent and using profit-sharing. When the exploitation agent obtains a reward, it generates an exploration agent, which performs exploration-oriented learning centered around the point where the reward was obtained and covers an area proportional to the amount of the reward. The exploration agent performs its learning independently of the exploitation agent. The exploitation agent meanwhile resumes its learning; when it encounters another reward point, it generates another exploration agent, and so on [2].

Optimal learning is obtained by the exploration agent when it completes its learning of the area. So, the exploitation agent only performs its learning on the path segments up to the peripheries of the areas that are explored by the exploration agents.

2.2.2 Exploration agents

The exploration agents perform their learning in a manner similar to Q-learning. The only difference is that they perform a spreading activation, which is similar to an ANA [7], of the learned Q-values in order that their learning becomes more robust. Behavior-selection networks such as ANA consist of many simple agents (similar to Minsky's agent [5]) that use spreading activation for mutual coordination, which enables them to achieve their overall purpose. Because each agent acts autonomously, which makes centralized control unnecessary, the system is both robust and expandable. There are two types of spreading activations: forward spreading and backward spreading. The former type gives rise to environment-oriented behavior selection, while the latter type gives rise to goal-oriented behavior selection. In MarLee, only backward-spreading activation is used.

An exploration agent begins by exploring its assigned area in a random manner. It generates and allocates a "memory agent" to each point that it encounters. These memory agents are similar to the simple autonomous entities of an

---

[1]For example, $R = \frac{Reward}{h}$.

[2]In the simulation environment described in Sec. 2.1, the exploitation agent is implemented in one A and the exploration agents are implemented in other As.

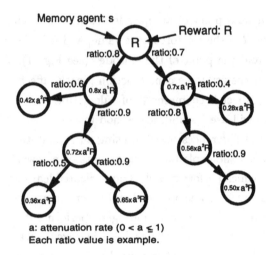

a: attenuation rate (0 < a ≤ 1)
Each ratio value is example.

Figure 2: Spreading activation.

ANA, and spreading activation is achieved through their cooperative actions.

Each memory agent does not move, but instead stores the various kinds of information including the activation energy (which is the Q-value) spread to it, a list of the other memory agents it is connected to[3], and the ratios of its Q-values to the connected neighbors's Q-values.

When the number of memory agents allocated to a certain area reaches a certain threshold value and the total number of connections between memory agents exceeds a certain "calculated exploration ratio" (to be explained later), the exploration agent stops exploring. The spreading activation process begins by taking the reward point as the starting point.

Each memory agent shares the Q-values it receives from its neighbors with the other neighboring memory agents. As shown in Fig. 2, when memory agent s receives reward R, it attenuates R by the ratio 0.8, and so on. Once this process is completed, the area being explored is expanded, new memory agents are allocated, and the sequence of steps is repeated.

We mentioned earlier that the area explored by an exploration agent centers around a reward point. The reward-dependent heuristic distance is the radius of the circle. In our simulation, the manhattan distance was used. When the "exploration ratio" [4], which indicates how carefully an area is to be explored,

---

[3] Even though two memory agents are next to each other, their relationship cannot be regarded as connected unless an exploration agent moves between them. A memory agent can be connected to up to four other memory agents (located above, below, to the right, or to the left of the agent).

[4] If n equals the total number of memory agents allocated by the exploration agent and r_i

exceeds a threshold value, the heuristic distance is increased so that the area to be explored gradually expands. As the area explored by each exploration agent expands, the areas eventually overlap, until finally the entire environment has been completely explored. This means that in situations where sufficient learning time is made available, MarLee achieves the same exploration-oriented learning results as if the entire environment was explored by a single exploration-agent (learning by exploration-oriented learning alone).

However, for mobile robots and software agents and so on, there are many situations in which it is difficult to allocate sufficient learning time. In other words, because exploration requires much more time than exploitation, situations will arise in which it is necessary to use learning results even though the explorations are not completed. MarLee overcomes this problem somewhat because it uses the exploitation agent to compensate for the areas that have not yet been explored. Therefore, MarLee is more adaptive than exploration-oriented learning alone when the results have to be used before the explorations are completed.

3 Simulation

3.1 Comparative Evaluation of MarLee

A snap-shot of MarLee learning is shown in Fig. 3. The black indicate areas that the exploration agents explored, and the gray areas are groups of episodes learned by the exploitation agent. The existence of two black areas shows that two exploration agents were generated.

We compared the learning performance of MarLee against that of exploitation-oriented learning (profit-sharing) and exploration-oriented learning (Q-learning) alone. In the simulations described in Secs. 3.1 and 3.2, evaluation was done after the learning was finished. Here, we evaluated the performance while the learning was still underway.

The environment used for this simulation was a 200×200 square grid with 16 reward points. In each assessment trial, 12 million learning steps were performed. For example, when MarLee consisted of the exploitation agent and four generated exploration agents and each one took one learning step, MarLee performed five learning steps.

---

be the number of memory agents for memory agent m_i, then the exploration ratio is equal to $\frac{\sum_{i=1}^{n} r_i}{4n} \times 100$.

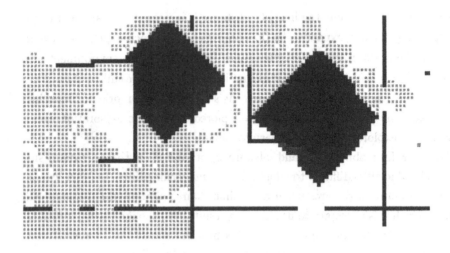

Figure 3: Snapshot of MarLee learning.

Average learning rates vs. number of learning steps The average learning rates for each learning method plotted against the number of learning steps is shown in Fig. 4. The average learning rate is the average value for learning all the points (mentioned in Sec. 3.1). If a point has not been learned as an episode or the memory agent has not been allocated to the point, A moves in a random direction until it encounters an episode or an memory agent.

As shown in Figure 4, MarLee had the lowest average learning rate in all stages. When learning was performed based on exploitation-oriented learning alone, the average learning rate remained high and was variable.

As mentioned above, ultimately, both MarLee and exploration-oriented learning alone can perform optimal learning. However, MarLee has a lower average learning rate than exploration-oriented learning alone in the early stages. This is because when learning is performed based on exploration-oriented learning alone, the learning results cannot be applied to points that have not yet been explored. The exploitation agent in MarLee compensates for areas that have not yet been explored. MarLee thus learns efficiently by integrating exploitation- and exploration-oriented learning.

Average learning rates vs. learning time The average learning rates for each learning method plotted against the learning time is shown in Fig. 5. The learning time for one learning step is different for each method. The shorter the time for each step, the better.

In MarLee, many exploration agents perform learning in parallel, so each

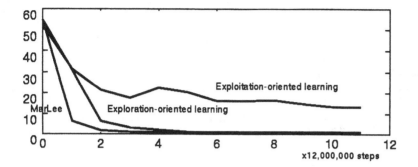

Figure 4: Average learning rate vs. the number of learning steps

area explored by an exploration agent is not so big, and these explored areas are excluded from the target area of the exploitation agent. Therefore, the learning time for each step is no longer than that for exploitation-oriented learning alone.

For example, ten exploration agents performing one learning step is equivalent to an exploration-oriented learning alone performing ten learning steps. Therefore, the area explored by exploration-oriented learning alone is bigger. However, when the area expands, the efficiency of the spreading activation process declines by a factor of two. Therefore, exploration-oriented learning alone takes longer than MarLee. In our simulation, in the final stage, learning by exploration-oriented learning alone took about 50 times longer than learning by MarLee. This shows that MarLee maintains learning efficiency even when the environment is big.

4 Discussion

4.1 Robustness

If an exploration agent's memory agent is damaged, the exploration agent can still perform the spreading activation process by excluding the damaged memory agent and automatically selecting a new route. This improved robustness of MarLee makes it an effective learning method for autonomous systems in dynamic environments.

4.2 Learning time

When the spreading activation process is performed the starting point is always a reward point as a result of the calculation cost. Therefore, by modifying the current spreading method into a procedure in which a new spreading activation

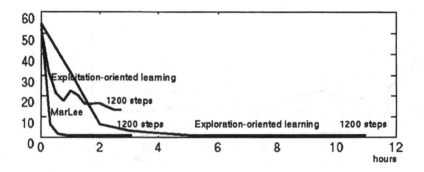

Figure 5: Average learning rate against learning time.

process is only done for the area between the current and last state of the exploration area, it should be possible to reduce the calculation cost to some extent (current research is addressing this point).

4.3 Effective movement of exploitation agent

In addition to exploitation-oriented learning by the exploitation agent, another important purpose of MarLee is to find as many reward points as possible. This suggests that it would be preferable to have several exploration agents learning in several areas, rather than having a single exploration agent learn many episodes. Because the exploitation agent cannot recognize the routes over which it travels, it cannot know how many areas have yet to be explored. This problem can be resolved to some extent by using information from the exploration agents. Each exploration agent allocates memory agents to the areas it has explored, and these agents know the directions in which they are connected. There are three kinds of connections: those with the other memory agents, those with episodes by way of the exploitation agent, and those that are null. In directions that have no connections, it is likely that there are areas that have not been explored by the exploitation agent. The exploitation agent may somehow be able to obtain the connection information from the memory agents and then move in the direction of the exploration agent with the most number of unconnected links.

4.4 Applying MarLee

The use of multiple exploration agents would support a number of useful applications, for example, software agents that have the ability to autonomously acquire information matching users' preferences from the Internet. These software agents would have the ability to send mobile agents to any particular resource point in the network at will. The pervasive use of single autonomous mobile robots in the real-world clearly prevents the use of this multi-agent framework as it is. However, MarLee could be applied to these kinds of situations by having the robot perform exploitation- and exploration-oriented learning in turn. We are now in the process of evaluating this approach.

4.5 Negative reinforcement learning

Up to now, we have only discussed positive reinforcement learning. However, with MarLee, it is also quite simple to use reverse the spreading activation (in which activation values are "absorbed" instead of spread) so as to implement negative reinforcement learning. **A** uses the results of its learning always to move towards states with higher reinforcement values, but consider what happens when we add a "pitfall" to the grid world S. To prevent **A** from approaching this pitfall and falling in, we simply need to perform "activation absorption" spreadeings centered at the bottom of the pitfall. Then, by overlapping this "negative spreading activation " with the result of the positive spreading activation done for the purpose of getting a reward, it is quite easy to integrate the two learned knowledge bases. **A** will thus take the optimal approach to a reward point that avoids the pitfall.

4.6 Other research

Learning that integrates exploitation- and exploration-oriented learning has attracted a great deal of interest [1] [4]. MarcoPolo learning [4] uses three kinds of modules: one that performs exploitation-oriented learning, one that performs exploration-oriented learning, and one that monitors the other two types of modules. The monitoring module decides which learning process to use based on the progress currently being made by the learning modules; the overall learning consists of the "learning phase of both modules" and "the decision-making phase of the monitoring module", so MarcoPolo maintains high learning performance. Main difference between MarLee and MarcoPolo exists in the use of exploration-oriented learning. In MarcoPolo, exploration-oriented learning is performed only by one module. The extention of MarcoPolo to a multi-agent model will be described as a future work. We will also compare both learning systems.

5 Conclusion

We have proposed a multi-agent reinforcement learning system that integrates exploitation- and exploration-oriented learning (MarLee). It is more robust in dealing with dynamic changes in the environment and it is capable of highly efficient exploration-oriented learning even in large-scale environments, such as the real-world or the Internet. By applying a spreading activation model based on the agent network architecture for environmental exploration, learning characteristics can be easily tuned by manipulating the spreading parameters. The fundamental effectiveness of MarLee was demonstrated through simulation. In future works, we intend to perform a more detailed assessment of MarLee through simulation and actual application.

References

[1] A. G. Barto, S. J. Bradtke, and S. P. Singh: Learning to act using real-time dynamic programing, *Artificial Intelligence*, Vol. 72, No. 1 – 2, pp. 81 – 138 (1995).

[2] C. J. C. Watkins and P. Dayan: Technical Note: Q-Learning, *Machine Learning*, Vol. 8, pp. 55 – 68 (1992).

[3] J. J. Grefenstette: Credit Assignment in Rule Discovery Systems Based on Generic Algorithms, *Machine Learning*, Vol. 3, pp. 225 – 245 (1988).

[4] K. Miyazaki, M. Yamamura, and S. Kobayashi: MarcoPolo: A Reinforcement Learning System Considering TradeOff Exploitation and Exploration under Markovian Environments, *Journal of Japanese Society for Artificial Intelligence*, Vol. 12, No. 1, pp. 78 – 89 (1997) (in Japanese).

[5] M. Minsky: The Society of Mind, Simon & Schuster, 1986.

[6] J. H. Holland and J. S. Reightman: Cognitive Systems Based on Adaptive Algorithms, *Pattern-Directed Inference System*, D. A. Waterman and F. Hayes-Roth (eds.), Academic Press, 1978.

[7] P. Maes: The Agent Network Architecture (ANA), *SIGART Bulletin*, Vol. 2, No. 4, pp. 115 – 120, 1991.

[8] P. Maes: Behavior-Based Artificial Intelligence, *Proceedings of the Second International Conference on Simulation of Adaptive Behavior (From Animals to Animals 2)*, The MIT Press/Elsevier, pp. 2–10, 1993.

[9] R. A. Brooks: A Robust Layered Control System for a Mobile Robot, *IEEE Robotics and Automation*, vol. 2, No. 1, pp. 14 – 23 (1986).

[10] R. J. Firby: An Investigation into Reactive Planning in Complex Domains, *AAAI'87*, pp. 189 – 208 (1987).

[11] S. Kurihara and R. Onai: Adaptive Selection of Reactive/Deliberate Planning for the Dynamic Environment, *Lecture Notes in Artificial Intelligence 1237, Proceedings of the MAAMAW'97*, 1997.

Motivated Behaviour for Goal Adoption

Michael Luck*   Mark d'Inverno[†]

* Department of Computer Science, University of Warwick, CV4 7AL, UK
  mikeluck@dcs.warwick.ac.uk

[†] Cavendish School of Computer Science, Westminster University, London W1M 8JS, UK
  dinverm@westminster.ac.uk

Abstract. Social behaviour arises as a result of individual agents cooperating with each other so as to exploit the resources available in a rich and dynamic multi-agent domain. If agents are to make use of others to help them in their tasks, such social behaviour is critical. Underlying this cooperation is the transfer or adoption of goals from one agent to another, a subtle and complex process that depends on the nature of the agents involved. In this paper we analyse this process by building upon a hierarchy previously constructed to define objects, agents and autonomous agents. We describe the motivated *self-generation* of goals that defines agent autonomy and the adoption of goals between agents that enables social behaviour. Then we consider three classes of goal adoption by objects, agents and autonomous agents. The first of these is merely a question of instantiation, the second requires an understanding of the relationship of the agent to others that are engaging it, and the third amounts to a question of negotiation or persuasion.

1 Introduction

The notion of *autonomy* has associated with it many variations of meaning. According to Steels, autonomous systems must be automatic systems and, in addition, they must have the capacity to form and adapt their behaviour while operating in the environment. Thus traditional AI systems and most robots are automatic but not autonomous — they are not independent of the control of their designers [29]. Autonomous systems are independent and exercise *self-control*. To do this, it is argued, they must be *motivated*.

Autonomous agents possess goals which are *generated* within rather than *adopted* from other agents. These goals are generated from *motivations* which are higher-level non-derivative components characterizing the nature of the agent. For example, consider the motivation *greed*. This is not a goal in the classical artificial intelligence sense since it does not specify a state of affairs to be achieved, nor is it describable in terms of the environment. However, it may, if other motivations permit, give rise to the generation of a goal to rob a bank. The distinction between the motivation of greed and the goal of robbing a bank is clear, with the former providing a reason to do the latter, and the latter specifying what must be done.

This view of autonomous agents is based on the generation and transfer of goals between entities. Specifically, an entity is an agent if it can be viewed as satisfying a goal. This goal must first be created and then, if necessary and appropriate, transferred to another entity. It is this adoption of goals that changes an entity from an object to an agent, and it is the *self-generation* of goals that is responsible for its autonomy.

Key to understanding the nature and behaviour both of individual agents, and of any interactions between them, is this notion of autonomy. In a series of papers, we have described and formally specified an extended theory of agent interaction, based on *goals* and *motivations*, which takes exactly this standpoint. The theory describes a framework for categorising different agents [14], which has been used as a basis for investigating aspects of the relationships between agents [16], providing an operational account of their invocation and destruction [6] and analysing their complexity [8], as well as for reformulating existing systems and theories [3,4,7]. In all this, however, one aspect has either been omitted or only briefly alluded to, namely a detailed account of the generation of goals from motivations, and goal adoption between agents. This paper addresses that omission, by showing how the formal framework may be used to provide a detailed operational account of the processes of goal generation and adoption.

First, we provide some context for the concept of motivation and its use in directing reasoning and behaviour with a short review of related work, and then consider the role of motivation in autonomous behaviour in more detail. Section 4 provides a brief outline of the formal agent framework, giving a selection of Z schemas that describe salient aspects, so that a reasonable context is available within which to situate this work. Then we analyse how motivations are used in goal generation and subsequently goal adoption. At each point we describe the processes involved both informally and formally using the Z notation. Finally, we summarise and and present concluding remarks.

2   What and Why Motivation?

According to Halliday, the word *motivation* does not refer to a specific set of readily identified processes [9]. It is frequently discussed in terms of *drive* and *incentive*. Drives are related to physiological states such as the deprivation of food, hormones, etc, while incentives refer to external stimuli that affect motivation such as the presence of food, as an incentive to eat. Research on motivation is currently being pursued from a variety of perspectives including psychology and ethology. Our focus, however, is on providing an effective control mechanism for governing the behaviour and reasoning of autonomous agents through the use of motivations. Though we focus on a computational approach, in this section we will discuss related work.

Some psychological research has recognised the role of motivations in reasoning in a similar way to that suggested here. Kunda [12] informally defines motivation to be, "any wish, desire, or preference that concerns the outcome of a given reasoning task" and suggests that motivation affects reasoning in a variety of ways including the accessing, constructing and evaluating of beliefs and evidence, and decision making. Such arguments are supported by a large body of experimental research, but no attempt is made to address the issue of how motivations may be represented or applied in a computational context.

Computational work has also recognised the role of motivations. Simon [25] takes motivation to be "that which controls attention at any given time," and explores the relation of motivation to information-processing behaviour, but from a cognitive perspective. Sloman [27,26] has elaborated on Simon's work, showing how motivations are relevant to emotions and the development of a computational theory of mind.

Problem solving can be considered to be the task of finding actions that achieve the current goals. Typically, goals are presented to systems without regard to the problem-solving agent so that the reasoning process is divorced from the reality of an agent in the world. Clearly, this is inadequate for research concentrating on modelling autonomous agents and creatures, which requires an understanding of how such goals are generated and selected. Additionally, it is inadequate for research that aims to provide flexibility of reasoning in a variety of contexts, regardless of concerns with modelling artificial agents. Such flexibility can be achieved through the use of motivations which can lead to different results even when goals remain the same [13].

In proposing to develop a 'computational architecture of a mind', Sloman makes explicit mention of the need for a "store of 'springs of action' (motives)" [27]. In the same paper, he tries to explicate his notion of a *motive* as being a representation used in deciding what to do, including desires, wishes, tastes, preferences and ideals. The key feature of a motive, according to Sloman, is not in the representation itself, but its role in processing. Importantly, Sloman distinguishes between motives on the one hand, and 'mere subgoals' on the other. "Sometimes," he claims, "a mere subgoal comes to be valued as an end," because of a loss of 'reason' information. First-order motives directly specify goals, while second-order motives generate new motives or resolve conflicts between competing motives — they are termed *motive generators* and *motive comparators*. "A motive produced by a motive generator may have the status of a desire." This relatively early work presents a broad picture of a two-tiered control of behaviour: motives occupy the top level, providing the *drive* or *urge* to produce the lower level goals that specify the behaviour itself. In subsequent work, the terminology changes to distinguish between *nonderivative* motivators or goals and *derivative* motivators or goals, rather than between motivators and goals themselves. Nevertheless, the notion of derivative and nonderivative mental attitudes makes one point clear: that there are two levels of attitude, one which is in some sense innate, and which gives rise to the other which is produced as a result of the first.

In a different context, the second of Waltz's 'Eight Principles for Building an Intelligent Robot' requires the inclusion of "innate *drive* and evaluation systems to provide the robot with moment-to-moment guidance for its actions."[30] In elaborating this principle, Waltz explains that the action of a robot at a particular time should not just be determined by the current sensory inputs, but also the "desires" of the robot, such as minimizing energy expenditure (laziness), and maintaining battery power levels (hunger). This research into robotics, artificial life, and autonomous agents and creatures has provided the impetus for a growth of interest in modelling motivations computationally, and a number of different representations for motivations and mechanisms for manipulating them have been developed at both subsymbolic and symbolic levels (eg. [1,10]).

3 Motivated Behaviour in Autonomous Agents

A given stimulus does not always evoke the same response. If the external situation is constant, differences in response must be ascribed to changes in the internal state of the responding agent. These differences are due to the motivations of the agent.

An agent possesses a fixed range of identifiable motivations of varying strength. These motivations can be regarded as being innate, and certain behaviours may be associated with one or more motivations. For example, the behaviour of feeding is associated with the motivation of obtaining food, or hunger. In most cases, the execution of such a behaviour reduces the strength of the associated motivations, so that in the case of feeding, the motivation to obtain food is reduced. These behaviours are known as *consumatory behaviours*; other behaviours which are not associated with any particular motivation, but which make the conditions of a consumatory behaviour come true are known as *appetitive behaviours*. For example, a go-to-food behaviour might make the conditions (that there is food within reach) of the feeding behaviour become true.

This view of motivation is somewhat simplified, and although much behaviour occurs in functional sequences with appetitive behaviours leading to consumatory ones, complex interactions between motivations and behaviours are possible [11]. For example, a single factor could directly cause many activities, or cause an action which in turn leads to other behaviours, or even cause some motivations to decrease so that others would increase in turn. In addition there are inhibitory relationships between behaviours in animals and also relationships that increase the strength of other behaviours. Moreover, the combination of motivations may lead to different or variable behaviours. These are all difficult issues which must be addressed in attempting to construct accurate behavioural models of real and artificial agents. Our concern, however, is not with providing such accuracy, but in constructing *simple* yet *adequate* models which will allow effective control of behaviour.

We can define autonomous agents to be agents with a higher-level control provided internally by motivations. Thus we can specify motivations of *curiosity*, *safety*, *fear*, *hunger*, and so on. In a simple agent design, we might then associate the motivation of *curiosity* with the goal of *avoiding obstacles* which, in turn, is associated with the actions required to achieve such results. Motivations will also vary over time according to the internal state of the agent. For example, if the agent spends a long time without food, then the hunger motivation will increase. When the agent feeds, the hunger motivation will decrease.

Each motivation thus has a strength associated with it, either variable depending on external and internal factors, or fixed at some constant value. A motivation can thus be represented by a triple, $< m, v, b >$ known as an *m-triple* where m is the kind of motivation, v is a real number, the strength (or intensity [26]) value associated with that motivation, and b is a boolean variable taking the value *True* when the strength value, v, is fixed, and *False* when it is variable. An autonomous agent can be regarded as embodying a set of n motivations, M, which comprises the *m-triples*, $< m_1, v, b >$ ... $< m_n, v, b >$. Thus the set of motivations, M, is a function of the kind of agent being considered, while each motivation in this set at a particular point in time is a function of an instance of a particular kind of agent and its environment together. In order to act on motivations, a threshold value for strength may be necessary, which must be exceeded to force action. Alternatively, the highest strength value may be used to determine the motivation currently in control.

More sophisticated mechanisms are possible such as those described by Norman and Long [22,23], Sloman [2,26] and Moffat and Frijda [21,20]. In addition, other representations for motivations and mechanisms for manipulating them have been developed at both subsymbolic and symbolic levels (eg. by Schnepf [24], Maes [17–19] and Halperin [10]). All are possible instantiations of the model described in the remainder of this paper, but the details are unimportant at present. It is enough to note that the abstract model provides the framework within which such mechanisms can be incorporated according to the particular need.

4 The Agent Framework

As has been described elsewhere in more detail [14], we propose a four-tiered hierarchy comprising *entities*, *objects*, *agents* and *autonomous agents*. The basic idea underlying this hierarchy is that all components of the world are entities. Of these entities, some are objects, of which some, in turn, are agents and of these, some are autonomous agents. In this section, we briefly outline the agent hierarchy. Many details are omitted — a more complete treatment can be found in [14].

Entities can be used to group together attributes for any useful purpose without adding a layer of *functionality* on top. They serve as a useful abstraction mechanism by which they are regarded as distinct from the remainder of the environment, and which can organise perception. An object is just something with abilities and attributes and has no further defining characteristics. An agent is just an object that is useful, typically to another agent, where this usefulness is defined in terms of satisfying that agent's goals. In other words, an agent is an object with an associated set of goals. One object may give rise to different instantiations of agents which are created in response to another agent. This definition of agency relies upon the existence of these other agents which provide goals that are adopted in order to instantiate an agent. In order to escape an infinite regress of goal adoption, we can define autonomous agents which are just agents that can generate their own goals from motivations.

For example, a table can be an object. It has attributes specifying that it is stable, made of wood, is brown in colour and has a flat surface. Its capabilities specify that it can support things. If I support my computer on a table, however, then the table is my agent for supporting the computer. The table may not actually possess the goal, but it is certainly satisfying, or can be *ascribed*, my goal to support the computer. A robot which rivets a panel onto a hull is also an agent, and if it has motivations such as hunger and achievement, then it is an autonomous agent.

Mathematically, we can describe this view of agents and provide a complete formal specification of it using the Z specification language. Below, we present the basic components of the framework. Our use of the notation should be self-explanatory and we will not, therefore, give excessive detail here, though details can be found in [28].

Before we can move to a definition of any of these entities, we must first define some primitives. First, *attributes* are simply features of the world, and are the only characteristics which are manifest. They need not be perceived by any particular entity, but must be potentially perceivable in an omniscient sense. Second, *actions* are discrete events which change the state of the environment. Third, *goals* are describable states of affairs to be achieved in the environment. Finally, *motivations* are any desires or preferences that can lead to the generation and adoption of goals and which affect the outcome of the reasoning or behavioural task intended to satisfy those goals.

We define an entity to have a non-empty set of attributes, as just something identifiable. An object is then an entity with a non-empty set of actions or capabilities.

$$Entity == [attributes : \mathbb{P}\, Attribute;\ capableof : \mathbb{P}\, Action;\ goals : \mathbb{P}\, Goal;$$
$$motivations : \mathbb{P}\, Motivation;\ |\ attributes \neq \{\ \}]$$

Similarly, an agent is an object with a non-empty set of goals, and an autonomous agent is an agent with non-empty motivations. Note the use of schema inclusion for incremental definition, by which earlier schemas are included and used subsequently.

$$Object == [Entity\ |\ capableof \neq \{\ \}]$$
$$Agent == [Object\ |\ goals \neq \{\ \}]$$
$$AutonomousAgent == [Agent\ |\ motivations \neq \{\ \}]$$

In summary, if there are attributes and capabilities, but no goals, then the entity is an *object*. If there are goals but no motivations, then the entity is an *agent*. Finally, if neither the motivation nor goal sets are empty, then the entity is an *autonomous agent*. Thus, we have constructed a formal specification which identifies and characterises agents and autonomous agents. Most usefully, perhaps, the specification is constructed in such a way as to allow further levels of specification to be added to describe particular agent designs and architectures.

5 Goal Generation

The framework described above involves the generation of *goals* from *motivations* in an autonomous agent, and the adoption of goals by, and in order to create, other agents. In this section, we build on earlier initial work in outlining goal generation and adoption [5]. We give a complete description and specification of how an autonomous agent, *defined* in terms of its high-level and somewhat abstract *motivations*, can construct goals. Earlier work, while describing the introduction of goals, did not consider the later stages of releasing entities from agency obligations, an omission corrected here.

An autonomous agent will try to find a way to mitigate motivations, either by selecting an action to achieve an existing goal as above for simple agents, or by retrieving a goal from a repository of known goals. Thus, our model requires a repository of known *goals* which capture knowledge of limited and well-defined aspects of the world. These goals describe particular *states* or *sub-states* of the world with each autonomous agent having its own such repository.

As stated elsewhere [16], in order to retrieve goals to mitigate motivations, an autonomous agent must have some way of assessing the effects of competing or alternative goals. Clearly, the goals which make the greatest positive contribution to the motivations of the agent should be selected unless a greater motivational effect can be achieved by *destroying* some subset of its goals. The motivational effect of generating or destroying goals not only depends on the motivations but also on the goals of the agent. For example, an autonomous agent should not generate a goal that it already possesses or that is incompatible with the achievement or satisfaction of its existing goals.

Formally, the ability of autonomous agents to assess goals is given in the next schema, *AssessGoals*. The schema describes how an autonomous agent monitors its motivations for goal generation. First, the *AutonomousAgent* schema is included and the new variable representing the repository of available known goals, *goalbase* is declared. Then, the motivational effect on an autonomous agent of satisfying a set of new goals is given. The *motiveffectgenerate* function returns a numeric value representing the motivational effect of satisfying a set of goals with a particular configuration of motivations and a set of existing goals. Similarly, the *motiveffectdestroy* function returns a numeric value representing the motivational effect of removing some subset of its existing goals with the same configuration. The predicate part specifies that the goal base is non-empty, and that all the current goals must be goals that exist in the goalbase. For ease of expression, we also define a *satisfygenerate* function, related to *motiveffectgenerate*, which returns the motivational effect of an autonomous agent satisfying an additional set of goals. The *satisfydestroy* function is defined analogously.

$$
\begin{array}{|l}
\_\ AssessGoals _____ \\
AutonomousAgent \\
goalbase : \mathbb{P}\ Goal \\
motiveffectgenerate : \mathbb{P}\ Motivation \rightarrow \mathbb{P}\ Goal \rightarrow \mathbb{P}\ Goal \rightarrow \mathbb{Z} \\
motiveffectdestroy : \mathbb{P}\ Motivation \rightarrow \mathbb{P}\ Goal \rightarrow \mathbb{P}\ Goal \rightarrow \mathbb{Z} \\
satisfygenerate : \mathbb{P}\ Goal \rightarrow \mathbb{Z} \\
satisfydestroy : \mathbb{P}\ Goal \rightarrow \mathbb{Z} \\
\hline
goalbase \neq \{\} \\
goals \subseteq goalbase \\
\forall\ gs : \mathbb{P}\ goalbase \bullet \\
\quad (satisfygenerate\ gs = motiveffectgenerate\ motivations\ goals\ gs) \wedge \\
\quad (satisfydestroy\ gs = motiveffectdestroy\ motivations\ goals\ gs)
\end{array}
$$

Now we can describe the generation of a new set of goals in the *GenerateGoals* operation schema. First, the agent changes, indicated by $\Delta AutonomousAgent$, and the previous schema is included. The predicate part simply states that there is a set of goals in the goalbase that has a greater motivational effect than any other set of goals, and the current goals of the agent are updated to include the new goals.

$$
\begin{array}{|l}
\_\ GenerateGoals _____ \\
\Delta AutonomousAgent \\
AssessGoals \\
\hline
goalbase \neq \{\ \} \\
\exists\ gs : \mathbb{P}\ Goal \mid gs \subseteq goalbase \bullet \\
\quad (\forall\ os : \mathbb{P}\ Goal \mid os \in (\mathbb{P}\ goalbase) \bullet \\
\quad\quad (satisfygenerate\ gs \geq satisfygenerate\ os) \wedge \\
\quad\quad goals' = goals \cup gs)
\end{array}
$$

Once generated by an autonomous agent, goals exist in multi-agent system until, for whatever reason, they are explicitly destroyed by that autonomous agent. This represents the end of the life of a goal. The destruction of goals is defined in a similar way to the generation of goals, and formally in *DestroyGoals*. This schema states that an agent destroys the subset of its goals, the destruction of which provide the greatest motivational benefit.

$$
\begin{array}{|l}
\underline{\quad DestroyGoals \quad\quad\quad\quad\quad\quad\quad\quad\quad\quad\quad\quad\quad\quad\quad} \\
\Delta AutonomousAgent \\
AssessGoals \\
\hline
goalbase \neq \{\,\} \\
\exists\, gs : \mathbb{P}\ Goal \mid gs \subseteq goalbase \bullet \\
\quad\quad (\forall\, os : \mathbb{P}\ Goal \mid os \in (\mathbb{P}\ goalbase) \bullet \\
\quad\quad\quad\quad (satisfydestroy\ gs \geq satisfydestroy\ os) \wedge \\
\quad\quad\quad\quad\quad\quad goals' = goals \setminus gs)
\end{array}
$$

6 Goal Adoption

Since we are interested in multi-agent worlds, we must consider the world as a whole rather than just individual agents. In this world, all autonomous agents are agents and all agents are objects. We also identify further sub-categories of entity. Before proceeding, therefore, we distinguish those objects which are not agents, and those agents which are not autonomous and refer to them as *neutral-objects* and *server-agents* respectively.

An agent is then either a server-agent or an autonomous agent, and an object is either a neutral-object or an agent.

$$
NeutralObject == [Object \mid goals = \{\}]
$$
$$
ServerAgent == [Agent \mid motivations = \{\}]
$$

We can then describe the world as a collection of neutral objects, server agents and autonomous agents.

$$
\begin{array}{|l}
\underline{\quad World \quad\quad\quad\quad\quad\quad\quad\quad\quad\quad\quad\quad\quad\quad\quad\quad\quad} \\
entities : \mathbb{P}\ Entity \\
objects : \mathbb{P}\ Object \\
agents : \mathbb{P}\ Agent \\
autonomousagents : \mathbb{P}\ AutonomousAgent \\
neutralobjects : \mathbb{P}\ NeutralObject \\
serveragents : \mathbb{P}\ ServerAgent \\
\hline
autonomousagents \subseteq agents \subseteq objects \\
agents = autonomousagents \cup serveragents \\
objects = neutralobjects \cup agents
\end{array}
$$

In multi-agent systems agents may wish, or need, to use the capabilities of other entities. They can make use of the capabilities of these others by *adopting* their goals. For example, if Anne needs to move a table which cannot be lifted alone, she must get someone else to adopt her goal before it can be moved. Similarly, if she wants

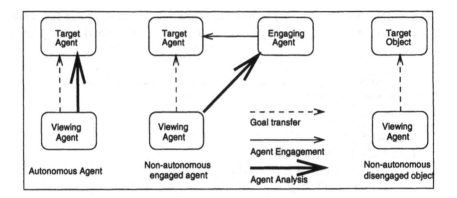

Fig. 1. Goal Adoption in Non-Autonomous and Autonomous Agents

tea, then she must make use of a kettle to boil water, a teapot to make the tea and subsequently a cup from which to drink it. Each of these objects can be ascribed, or viewed, as adopting Anne's goals in order that her thirst can be relieved. This notion of goal adoption underlies social behaviour, and an understanding of the ways in which in can be achieved is fundamental for effective modelling and simulation. In general, entities may serve the purposes of others by adopting their goals. However, the ways in which they adopt goals depends on the kind of object. They may be either neutral-objects, server-agents or autonomous agents, and each requires a separate analysis by the agent with a goal to be adopted, which we call the *viewing* agent.

In the description given in the previous section, goals may be generated only by autonomous agents. Both non-autonomous (server) and autonomous agents, however, can adopt goals. With autonomous agents, goal adoption amounts to a problem of *negotiation* or *persuasion*, requiring an analysis of the *target* autonomous agent. With non-autonomous agents, goal adoption requires an analysis of both the agent intended to adopt the goal, and any other agent *engaging* that agent. With objects, no analysis is required, since agents are *created* from objects with the relevant associated goals.

Figure 1 shows three fundamental cases of goal adoption which we consider in detail below. In the figure, there are three kinds of agent. A *target* agent or object is one that is intended to adopt goals. An *engaging* agent is one whose goals are currently (already) adopted by the target agent. A *viewing* agent is an agent that seeks to engage a target agent or object by having it adopt goals. It is a viewing agent because the way in which goal adoption is attempted is determined by its view of the situation. We consider the three cases of goal adoption below.

6.1 Goal Adoption by Neutral Objects

In the simplest case, goal adoption by non-autonomous agents occurs by instantiating an agent from a neutral object with the goals to be adopted. In this case, no *agent* exists before the goals are adopted, but the act of goal transfer causes an agent to be created from a neutral object using those particular goals. Thus, for example, a cup in Anne and Bill's office, which is just an neutral-object, becomes an agent when it is used for storing Anne's tea. In this case it *adopts* or *is ascribed* her goal of storing liquid. It is possible to create the agent from the object because the cup is not being used by anyone else; it is not *engaged* by another agent. An entity can only be a neutral object if it is not *engaged*.

Below, we specify a function that creates a new entity by ascribing a set of goals to an existing entity. It is *total*, valid for any entity and any set of goals, and is just a formal way of associating goals with an entity, and will be used subsequently.

$$EntityAdoptGoals : (Entity \times \mathbb{P}\ Goal) \rightarrow Entity$$

$$\forall gs : \mathbb{P}\ Goal;\ old, new : Entity \bullet$$
$$EntityAdoptGoals(old, gs) = new \Leftrightarrow new.goals = old.goals \cup gs$$
$$\wedge\ new.capableof = old.capableof \wedge new.attributes = old.attributes$$

We now specify how a non-autonomous disengaged object, or neutral-object is instantiated as a server-agent. In Z, a variable with a '?' indicates an input. Thus, a neutral-object and a set of goals are input, the entities in the world change, indicated by $\Delta World$, and the sets of objects and agents are updated accordingly. First, the set of neutral objects no longer includes the originally disengaged object. Second, the set of server agents now includes the newly created server-agent. Finally, the schema states that there is no change to the set of autonomous agents. In addition, the variables, *entities*, *objects* and *agents*, are updated by removing the neutral-object and adding the newly instantiated server-agent. The final three predicates are redundant since they necessarily follow from the previous predicates, but are included to detail how all the state variables are affected. In subsequent schemas, such redundancy is not included.

$\_NeutralObjectAdoptGoals$ _____

$o? : NeutralObject$
$gs? : \mathbb{P}\ Goal$
$\Delta World$

$o? \in neutralobjects$
$neutralobjects' = neutralobjects \setminus \{o?\}$
$serveragents' = serveragents \cup \{EntityAdoptGoals\ (o?, gs?)\}$
$autonomousagents' = autonomousagents$

$entities' = entities \setminus \{o?\} \cup \{EntityAdoptGoals\ (o?, gs?)\}$
$objects' = objects \setminus \{o?\} \cup \{EntityAdoptGoals\ (o?, gs?)\}$
$agents' = agents \setminus \{o?\} \cup \{EntityAdoptGoals\ (o?, gs?)\}$

For completeness, we specify the related operation where an entity is released from all of its agency obligations. Here, a server-agent reverts from a server-agent to a neutral-object. It is possible that a cup can be engaged for two separate goals. For example, it may be engaged as a vase for flowers and as a paper-weight for loose papers if there is a breeze coming from a nearby open window. If the window is closed and the flowers are removed, the cup is released from all its agency obligations and reverts to being a neutral-object.

Formally, this operation is defined by the *RevertToNeutralObject* schema. It uses the axiomatic function, *EntityRemoveGoals*, defined similarly to *EntityAdoptGoals*, which removes a set of goals from an entity.

$$EntityRemoveGoals : (Entity \times \mathbb{P}\ Goal) \rightarrow Entity$$

$\forall gs : \mathbb{P}\ Goal;\ old, new : Entity \bullet$
$\quad EntityRemoveGoals(old, gs) = new \Leftrightarrow new.goals = old.goals \setminus gs$
$\quad \wedge\ new.capabilities = old.capabilities \wedge new.attributes = old.attributes$

The predicates in the following schema check that the input goals are the same as the set of current goals of the server-agent. This ensures that the server-agent is released from *all* of its agency obligations. The variables, *neutralobjects, serveragents* and *autonomousagents*, are updated accordingly.

___RevertToNeutralObject_____
$sa? : ServerAgent$
$gs? : \mathbb{P}\ Goal$
$\Delta MultiAgentSystem$
_____
$sa? \in serveragents$
$gs? = sa?.goals$
$neutralobjects' = neutralobjects \cup \{EntityRemoveGoals\ (sa?, sa?.goals)\}$
$serveragents' = serveragents \setminus \{sa?\}$
$autonomousagents' = autonomousagents$

6.2 Goal Adoption by Server Agents

If the target object is *engaged* by other agents then it is itself an agent, so the protocol for goal adoption changes. In this case, there are several ways to *engage* the target object.

The first involves supplying the target object with more goals that does not affect the existing agency obligations. In this case the agent is *shared* between the viewing agent and the existing engaging agents. The second involves trying to persuade any engaging agents to *release* the engaged object so that it becomes a *neutral*-object and can therefore subsequently be engaged by the viewing agent as required. (This may relate to the issue of goal adoption for autonomous agents, which is considered later). The third possibility involves *displacing* the engaging agent so that the engaged object becomes a neutral-object and can then subsequently be ascribed other goals. This possibility is dangerous since it may cause conflict with the previous engaging agents.

As an example, suppose that a cup is currently in use as a paper-weight for Anne, so that the cup is *Anne's* agent with her goal of securing loose papers. Suppose also, that Bill wishes to use the cup to have some tea. The first way for Bill to engage the cup is for him to attempt to use the cup without destroying the existing agency relationship between Anne and the cup. Since this would involve an awkward attempt at making tea in, and subsequently drinking from, a stationary cup, he may decide instead to try other alternatives. The second alternative is to negotiate with Anne to release the cup so that it can be used for storing tea while the third alternative is for Bill to displace the goal ascribed to the cup by removing the cup from the desk and pouring tea into it. The cup is no longer an agent for Anne and is now ascribed the goal of storing tea for Bill. It has switched from being engaged by Anne to being engaged by Bill, and this is equivalent to the agent reverting to an object and then being re-instantiated as a new agent. This method may not be an appropriate strategy, however, because in destroying the agency obligation of the cup as a paper-weight, there is a risk of conflict between Anne and Bill.

The adoption of goals by server-agents is formalised in the next schema, in which a server-agent is ascribed an additional set of goals. It describes the alternative where the cup is serving as a paper weight and is then subsequently given the goal of storing flowers. The schema checks that the adopting agent is a server-agent in the system and that the new goals are distinct from the existing goals.

$$
\begin{array}{l}
\rule{0pt}{0pt}\\
\hline
\textit{ServerAgentAdoptGoals} \\
\hline
a? : ServerAgent \\
gs? : \mathbb{P}\, Goal \\
\Delta World \\
\hline
a? \in serveragents \\
gs? \cap a?.goals = \{\} \\
neutralobjects' = neutralobjects \\
serveragents' = serveragents \setminus \{a?\} \cup \{EntityAdoptGoals\,(a?, gs?)\} \\
autonomousagents' = autonomousagents \\
\hline
\end{array}
$$

In some situations, a server-agent is released from some but not all of its agency obligations. Suppose, for example, that a window is open in A's office and that a cup is being used as a paperweight by A and a vase by B. If the window is subsequently closed, then the cup may be released from its agency obligations as a paperweight but still remain an agent because it is holding flowers. Formally, the operation schema representing this change of agency obligation is specified in the next schema. Notice that the goals that are removed from an agent in this operation must be a *proper* subset of its goals. The server-agent, sa?, is removed from the set of server-agents and replaced with the agent that results from removing the goals, gs?, from a?.

$$
\begin{array}{l}
\rule{0pt}{0pt}\\
\hline
\textit{ServerAgentReleaseGoals} \\
\hline
sa? : ServerAgent \\
gs? : \mathbb{P}\, Goal \\
\Delta MultiAgentSystem \\
\hline
sa? \in serveragents \\
gs? \subset sa?.goals \\
neutralobjects' = neutralobjects \\
serveragents' = serveragents \setminus \{sa?\} \cup \{EntityRemoveGoals\,(sa?, gs?)\} \\
autonomousagents' = autonomousagents \\
\hline
\end{array}
$$

6.3 Goal Adoption by Autonomous Agents

In the example above, the second possibility for goal adoption by server-agents involves Bill persuading Anne to first release the cup from its existing agency. The cup would then become a neutral-object and could be instantiated as required by Bill. In general, such persuasion or negotiation may be more difficult than the direct physical action required for goal adoption in non-autonomous entities. Autonomous agents are motivated and as such, only participate in an activity and assist others if it is to their motivational advantage to do so (that is, if there is some motivational benefit). They create their own agendas and for them, goal adoption is a *voluntary* process as opposed to an *obligatory* one for non-autonomous agents. In a similar example, Anne might ask Bill to assist in moving a table, but Bill may refuse.

Formally, the operation of an autonomous agent adopting the goals of another is specified in the following schema where the set of autonomous agents is updated to include the newly instantiated target autonomous agent. Note that this does not detail the persuasion involved, but simply the state change resulting from the goal adoption.

$$
\begin{array}{l}
\rule{3cm}{0.4pt}\ AutonomousAgentAdoptGoals \rule{5cm}{0.4pt} \\
AssessGoals \\
aa? : AutonomousAgent \\
gs? : \mathbb{P}\ Goal \\
\Delta World \\
\rule{8cm}{0.4pt} \\
aa? \in autonomousagents \\
autonomousagents' = autonomousagents \setminus \{aa?\}\cup \\
\qquad\qquad\qquad\qquad\qquad \{EntityAdoptGoals\ (aa?, gs?)\} \\
agents' = agents \\
objects' = objects \\
\neg\ (\exists\ hs : \mathbb{P}\ Goal\ |\ hs \subseteq goalbase \wedge hs \neq gs?\ \bullet \\
\qquad satisfygenerate\ hs > satisfygenerate\ gs?)
\end{array}
$$

In general, goals must be adopted through explicit autonomous agent initiative, as opposed to an ascription of goals for non-autonomous agents. However, in some contexts the ascription of goals to autonomous agents may be meaningful. Suppose, as a dramatic yet unlikely example, that Anne incapacitates Bill in some way and places him by the door to function as a draft excluder. In this situation, the autonomous agent, Bill could be *ascribed* the goal of keeping out the draft even though he has not explicitly adopted this goal. Such cases can be described by considering the autonomous agent as an agent in an obligatory relationship. In this thesis, however, we restrict *autonomous goal adoption* to the explicit and voluntary generation of goals that have been recognised in others. In our view, this is the only case in which *cooperation* takes place as opposed to mere *engagement* [16].

6.4 Autonomous Goal Destruction

For a number of reasons an autonomous agent may destroy adopted goals. For example, suppose Anne wishes to move a table and has persuaded Bill to help. If Anne subsequently destroys some important agency relationship of Bill's, it is possible that Bill may then destroy the goal he has adopted from Anne of moving the table. As with goal adoption, for an autonomous agent to destroy goals, this must be considered the most motivationally beneficial course of action. This scenario is formalised below and is similar to the previous schema.

$$
\begin{array}{l}
\underline{\quad AutonomousAgentDestroysGoals \quad\quad\quad\quad\quad\quad\quad\quad\quad\quad} \\
aa? : AutonomousAgent \\
gs? : \mathbb{P}\ Goal \\
\Delta MultiAgentSystem \\
AssessGoals \\
\underline{\quad\quad\quad\quad\quad\quad\quad\quad\quad\quad\quad\quad\quad\quad\quad\quad\quad\quad\quad\quad\quad\quad\quad\quad} \\
aa? \in autonomousagents \\
gs? \subseteq aa?.goals \\
autonomousagents' = (autonomousagents \setminus \{aa?\}) \cup \\
\quad\quad\quad\quad\quad\quad\quad\quad\quad\quad\quad\quad \{EntityRemoveGoals\ (aa?, gs?)\} \\
agents' = agents \wedge objects' = objects
\end{array}
$$

7 Discussion

Social behaviour by which individual agents interact and cooperate is an intricate and complex process which both structures and depends on the distribution of goals in a global system. If target agents are already involved in significant social interactions with others, it may not be possible to initiate new interactions with them. If such new interaction is possible, however, this will change the distribution of goals among agents in the system, potentially impacting on existing relationships, and certainly imposing structure to constrain new ones. In any of these situations, such social behaviour can only arise through the generation of goals by one agent, and the adoption of goals by another. The preceding sections have provided an operational specification of these processes so that the roles of goals and motivations are clarified and explicated.

Using the Z notation provides a way to formalise these mechanisms which first removes ambiguity from the analysis, and second enables an easy transition to be made to practical systems. Moreover, the specification of goal generation and adoption is one part of a much larger yet integrated theory of agent interaction which covers agent taxonomy [14], formal systems specification [15,4], agent relationships [16], and the construction of implemented agent systems [16].

Research on motivation is currently being pursued from a variety of perspectives including psychology and ethology, while computational research into motivation is also significant. The notion of motivation is not new. Simon, for example, takes motivation to be "that which controls attention at any given time," [25]. Sloman [26] has elaborated on Simon's work, showing how motivations are relevant to emotions and the development of a computational theory of mind. Others have used motivation and related notions in developing computational architectures for autonomous agents such as the *motives* of Norman and Long [22], and the *concerns* of Moffat and Frijda [20]. What is new about the current work is the role of motivation in defining autonomy and in enabling goal generation and adoption.

The agent hierarchy distinguishes clearly between objects, agents and autonomous agents in terms of goals and motivations. Such an analysis of the entities in the world not only provides appropriate structures so that different levels of functionality may be established, but also information as to how multiple entities or agents can cooperate to solve problems which could not be solved alone. By basing the distinctions on function and purpose, we do not arbitrarily differentiate between cups and robots, for example, especially when it is not useful to do so. Instead, our motivation and goal based analysis allows us to concentrate precisely on important aspects of multi-agent interaction and problem-solving. In that context, we have considered the roles of goal generation and adoption. We have specified how and why goals must be generated in some autonomous agents in response to motivations, grounding chains of goal adoption, and further, how goals are adopted by objects, agents and autonomous agents in this agent model.

References

1. C. Balkenius. The roots of motivation. In J. Meyer, H. L. Roitblat, and S. W. Wilson, editors, *From animals to animats 2, Proceedings of the Second International Conference on Simulation of Adaptive Behavior*. MIT Press/Bradford Books, 1993.
2. L. P. Beaudoin and A. Sloman. A study of motive processing and attention. In *Prospects for Artificial Intelligence: Proceedings of AISB93*, pages 229–238, Birmingham, 1993.
3. M. d'Inverno and M. Luck. A formal view of social dependence networks. In C. Zhang and D. Lukose, editors, *Distributed Artificial Intelligence Architecture and Modelling: Proceedings of the First Australian Workshop on Distributed AI, LNAI 1087*, pages 115–129. Springer, 1996.
4. M. d'Inverno and M. Luck. Formalising the contract net as a goal directed system. In W. Van de Velde and J. W. Perram, editors, *Agents Breaking Away: Proceedings of the Seventh European Workshop on Modelling Autonomous Agents in a Multi-Agent World, LNAI 1038*, pages 72–85. Springer, 1996.
5. M. d'Inverno and M. Luck. Development and application of a formal agent framework. In M. G. Hinchey and L. Shaoying, editors, *Proceedings of the First IEEE International Conference on Formal Engineering Methods*, pages 222–231. IEEE Press, 1997.
6. M. d'Inverno and M. Luck. Making and breaking engagements: An operational analysis of agent relationships. In C. Zhang and D. Lukose, editors, *Multi-Agent Systems Methodologies and Applications: Proceedings of the Second Australian Workshop on Distributed AI, LNAI 1286*, pages 48–62. Springer, 1997.
7. M. d'Inverno and M. Luck. Engineering AgentSpeak(L): A formal computational model. *Journal of Logic and Computation*, 8(3):233–260, 1998.
8. M. d'Inverno, M. Luck, and M. Wooldridge. Cooperation structures. In *Proceedings of the Fifteenth International Joint Conference on Artificial Intelligence*, pages 600–605, Nagoya, Japan, 1997.
9. T. Halliday. Motivation. In T. R. Halliday and P. J. B. Slater, editors, *Causes and Effects*. Blackwell Scientific, 1983.
10. J. R. P. Halperin. Machine motivation. In J. A. Meyer and S.W. Wilson, editors, *Proceedings of the First International Conference on Simulation of Adaptive Behaviour: From Animals to Animats*, pages 238–246. MIT Press/Bradford Books, 1991.
11. R. A. Hinde. *Ethology: Its nature and relations with other sciences*. Fontana Press, 1982.
12. Z. Kunda. The case for motivated reasoning. *Psychological Bulletin*, 108(3):480–498, 1990.
13. M. Luck. *Motivated Inductive Discovery*. PhD thesis, University of London, 1993.

14. M. Luck and M. d'Inverno. A formal framework for agency and autonomy. In *Proceedings of the First International Conference on Multi-Agent Systems*, pages 254–260. AAAI Press / MIT Press, 1995.

15. M. Luck and M. d'Inverno. Structuring a Z specification to provide a formal framework for autonomous agent systems. In J. P. Bowen and M. G. Hinchey, editors, *The Z Formal Specification Notation, 9th International Conference of Z Users, LNCS 967*, pages 48–62. Springer, 1995.

16. M. Luck and M. d'Inverno. Engagement and cooperation in motivated agent modelling. In *Distributed Artificial Intelligence Architecture and Modelling: Proceedings of the First Australian Workshop on Distributed AI, LNAI 1087*, pages 70–84. Springer, 1996.

17. P. Maes. The dynamics of action selection. In *Proceedings of the Eleventh International Joint Conference on Artificial Intelligence*, pages 991–997, Detroit, 1989.

18. P. Maes. How to do the right thing. *Connection Science*, 1(3):291–323, 1989.

19. P. Maes. A bottom-up mechanism for behaviour selection in an artificial creature. In J. A. Meyer and S.W. Wilson, editors, *Proceedings of the First International Conference on Simulation of Adaptive Behaviour: From Animals to Animats*, pages 238–246. MIT Press/Bradford Books, 1991.

20. D. Moffat and N. H. Frijda. Where there's a will there's an agent. In M. Wooldridge and N. R. Jennings, editors, *Intelligent Agents: Theories, Architectures, and Languages, LNAI 890*, pages 245–260. Springer, 1995.

21. D. Moffat, N. H. Frijda, and R. H. Phaf. Analysis of a model of emotions. In *Prospects for Artificial Intelligence: Proceedings of AISB93*, pages 219–228, Birmingham, 1993.

22. T. J. Norman and D. Long. Goal creation in motivated agents. In M. Wooldridge and N. R. Jennings, editors, *Intelligent Agents: Theories, Architectures, and Languages, LNAI 890*, pages 277–290. Springer, 1995.

23. T. J. Norman and D. Long. Alarms: An implementation of motivated agency. In M. Wooldridge, J.P. Muller, and M. Tambe, editors, *Intelligent Agents: Theories, Architectures, and Languages, LNAI 1037*, pages 219–234. Springer, 1996.

24. U. Schnepf. Robot ethology: A proposal for the research into intelligent autonomous systems. In J. A. Meyer and S.W. Wilson, editors, *Proceedings of the First International Conference on Simulation of Adaptive Behaviour: From Animals to Animats*, pages 465–474. MIT Press/Bradford Books, 1991.

25. H. A. Simon. Motivational and emotional controls of cognition. In *Models of Thought*, pages 29–38. Yale University Press, 1979.

26. A. Sloman. Motives, mechanisms, and emotions. *Cognition and Emotion*, 1(3):217–233, 1987.

27. A. Sloman and M. Croucher. Why robots will have emotions. In *Proceedings of the Seventh International Joint Conference on Artificial Intelligence*, pages 197–202, Vancouver, B.C., 1981.

28. J. M. Spivey. *The Z Notation: A Reference Manual*. Prentice Hall, 2nd edition, 1992.

29. L. Steels. When are robots intelligent autonomous agents? *Journal of Robotics and Autonomous Systems*, 15:3–9, 1995.

30. D. L. Waltz. Eight principles for building an intelligent robot. In J. A. Meyer and S.W. Wilson, editors, *Proceedings of the First International Conference on Simulation of Adaptive Behaviour: From Animals to Animats*. MIT Press/Bradford Books, 1991.

Physically Based,
Self-Organizing Cellular Automata

Alan Dorin

School of Computer Science and Software Engineering,
Monash University, Clayton, Australia 3168
ph. +61-3-9905-5524, fx. +61-3-9905-5146
aland@csse.monash.edu.au

Abstract. A physically based system of interacting polyhedral objects is used to model self-assembly and spontaneous organization of complex structures. The surfaces of the polyhedra in the simulation are covered with bonding sites in states akin to those of cellular automata. The bonding sites interact with sites on neighbouring polyhedra to apply forces of attraction and repulsion between bodies and to trigger transitions in their states. Using only these mechanisms, the elements exhibit chaining, membrane and cluster formation, and differentiation / segregation. Examples of each of these phenomena are given along with explanations as to how they are formed. Assembly without the guidance of an external agent or central control is infrequently used in the construction of complex artificial structures, but is the norm for biological construction. This paper presents a model by which the construction of complex structures may be simulated using multiple reactive, artificial agents, acting independently under artificial physical and chemical laws.

Keywords: Artificial Life, Cellular Automata, Physical Modelling, Self - Organization / Assembly, Molecular Dynamics

1 Introduction

Living organisms are problem solvers. Not only at the level at which they seek food, evade predators, construct shelter or play chess, but also at the microscopic level. At this level the components of an organism are continually and co-operatively acting to maintain the organism's physical identity. Organisms are self-assembling, parallel machines whose many and varied components maintain a stable organization under perturbation. This is achieved through the local physical and chemical interactions of the individual elements themselves. There is no external agent or co-ordinating body which acts to place the correct materials, operate the appropriate reactions and so forth within the body of the organism. The parts of the living system independently move into position at the time required for life's processes to proceed.

This paper draws on work in a number of disparate fields to simulate aspects of the defining processes of living things. By simulating the parallel behaviour of usually microscopic components, it is hoped that an understanding of the assembly and maintenance of life may be reached. It is clearly beyond current technology and understanding to fully simulate such processes with anything but extremely remote semblance to the behaviour of actual life. Nevertheless, it *is* becoming feasible to examine at least some of the possibilities, identifying problems of comprehension and computation along the way. With this proviso, the following sections of the introduction outline a few fields which have bearing on the present effort. Section 2 introduces physically-based, Self-Organizing Cellular Automata (SOCA). This is a simulation framework for experiments with collections of rigid, polyhedral elements acting under simulated physical and chemical laws. Section 3 further details the SOCA system and describes a set of experiments with self-assembling structures. In section 4 further research using SOCA is described, then conclusions for this paper are presented. Acknowledgments and a bibliography appear in the final sections.

1.1 Physical Simulation

The non-interpenetration and collision of solids, and their movement under internally and externally generated forces is modelled in the SOCA system. The techniques employed have found wide application in computer graphics and animation, for example [20,27]. Real world, internally generated forces particularly relevant to SOCA include those produced by electro-magnetic attraction and repulsion. Externally generated forces of interest in this study include forces acting between solids, fluids, and the action of gravity or other global forces where applicable.

1.2 Cellular Automata

Cellular Automata (CA) have been widely studied as examples of complex dynamical systems [12,31], under the banner of artificial life [17], and originally as examples of components in a self-reproducing machine [4,11]. The global behaviour usually said to be *emergent* [5] from the local interactions is a source of fascination for researchers struggling to understand complex behaviour in the real world. To some extent, this complexity appears to stem from simple agents or automata operating in complex environments [26].

The cells in a CA grid act in parallel to collectively solve problems. Not necessarily problems in the sense that a chess player or robot controller solves problems, but problems akin to those solved by biological organisms and their components in maintaining their organization [6].

1.3 Philosophy of Biology

Autopoiesis has been coined by Maturana and Varela [19] to describe the organization of living things. The view may be summarized thus: a living thing is the matter contained within a space defined by a set of chemical processes which produce the components of which they themselves are constructed. An organism is a network of self-sustaining, self-bounding chemical processes. Such a view of life places it as a subset of auto-catalytic reactions as described by Kauffman [16] and within the scope described by Prigogine [23]. The extension of this to the virtual space as discussed in [6], includes representational physics and chemistry of relevance to the current study.

1.4 Self-Organization / Self-Assembly

Self-organization and assembly occur under what may loosely be described as a *physics* without which there are no principles guiding the interaction of components. The SOCA system simulates real world physics and may be used to explore self-assembly and self-organization[1] within the limits imposed by the simulated rules of interaction.

Although they are physical objects, Penrose's wooden machines [22] are similar in spirit to the constructions presented in this paper. The presence of a seed structure in a set of Penrose's machines allows the assembly of more complex machines from the components provided. Once a particular form of machine has been constructed, a mechanical trigger severs it into two or more compound structures with features identical to the seed which began the process.

Ingber has built simple machines to model the mechanical properties of cells [15]. His drinking straw and elastic constructions behave in ways not unlike the elements of the SOCA system, although they are unlike the machines of Penrose. Ingber's units form geometric shapes as they find their stable, minimum energy state.

Other authors have explored systems with some similarities to these. A mechanical system of blocks and magnets [14] has been used to study the formation of intermediate products during self-assembly. The simulation of cellular development by Fleischer [10] and the self assembly of the T4 bacteriophage [13] have also been modelled. The physical simulation in the latter model is unsophisticated. Of course there are also many studies of self-organization with no reference to physical simulation in the sense that it is modelled in SOCA, rather a *physics* (although it may not be called such) is modelled according to the researcher's particular needs. Steels [29] investigates the development of language as if it were a self-organizing system. Banzhaf uses binary strings to explore auto-catalysis and metabolic formation [1]. Saitou and Jakiela [24,25] have examined the process of sub-assembly (that is, the ordering of assembly processes within larger scale assembly processes) in detail.

1.5 Reactive, Distributed Artificial Intelligence

Components in many self-assembling systems may be viewed as purely reactive agents. They are unable to plan but respond directly to their surroundings. The stimuli to which a component is capable of responding are dictated by that component's physical composition and properties. This paper shows how simple reactive elements may self-assemble into larger structures without an explicit global plan or complex inter-element communication. The elements rely purely on (simulated) mechanical and chemical properties to realize a plan implicit in their structure and the virtual physics / chemistry of the environment. The resulting structure is not organized by an external agent in the way that, for example, a clock or bridge is built by robots or people. Instead, the structure appears as a result of many local interactions between agents 'responsible' for their *own* behaviour (position / orientation and movement). The systems of interest consist of many reactive artificial agents that interact to spontaneously form at least one complex structure.

1The terms self assembly / organization are used so loosely as to have become interchangeable. A suitable working definition requires only that the terms indicate construction of a unity from components acting under forces / motives internal or local to the components themselves, and arising through their interaction with the environment. That is, assembly or arrangement according to a distributed plan or goal implicit in the structure and behaviour of the parts, not explicitly stated or held by a central controlling entity.

Attempts have been made to utilize the emergent properties of interacting reactive agents. Drogoul and Dubreuil [8] demonstrate Eco-Problem-Solving (EPS) after Ferber and Jacopin [9]. The agents in these works aim to satisfy their own goals. The result of their local interactions is a global stable state in which all agents are satisfied and a correct solution to the problem at hand is found. In this respect EPS is similar to the SOCA system presented here. Where EPS differs from SOCA is in the explicit nature of the goals of each agent. The SOCA agents do *not* have explicit goals to satisfy although the system as a whole does have one or many stable states. Perhaps the differences between SOCA and EPS are better understood by making the analogy between SOCA elements and virtual chemicals reacting in various ways to form molecules, an analogy explored in the next subsection.

1.6 Molecular Dynamics & Supramolecular Inorganic Chemistry

Recent papers in supramolecular chemistry grapple with self-assembly [18]. One way of understanding the interactions of groups of molecules is to visualize them according to the shapes they form and the bonding sites the shapes present to their surroundings. Molecules of different types have differently arranged bonding sites which fit together to form large collections of molecules (supramolecules). By some reports [21] it is helpful to visualize molecules as polyhedra whose vertices are bonding sites. The resulting supramolecules are visualized as organized collections of polyhedra[2].

The system described in this paper is ideal for the simulation of such behaviour. To date, self-assembly in chemistry has been examined by mixing real chemicals. Efforts have been made to utilize simulated Newtonian physics to allow models of molecules constructed from empirical data to fall into natural minimum energy states, a practice called *molecular dynamics*. The system presented in this paper allows for the full simulation of the movement of rigid polyhedra acting under the influence of forces centered on bonding sites across their geometry. It should be of interest to those exploring the chemistry of self-assembly.

2 The SOCA System

The elements in the SOCA system are simulated, rigid, convex polyhedra suspended in a fluid. The densities and geometric properties of the elements may be specified. Collisions are detected, analytically derived impulses prevent bodies from interpenetrating. The implementation details of this are in many respects similar to those of Baraff [2].

The fluid model incorporates viscosity acting on the bodies as fluid drag. A vector field specifying the direction of fluid flow at any location in space is also modelled. For the purposes of this paper the fluid is stationary at large scales. Small scale Brownian motion helps 'jiggle' the elements in the fluid into stable states. Effects of solids on the fluid medium are ignored, only effects of the fluid on solids within it are considered. This is in keeping with the fluid models found in [7, 30].

2The models described in the supramolecular chemistry lierature visualize bonding sites at the verteces of the polyhedra. This scheme was not adopted for the experiments described here although modification of the SOCA software to emulate the chemist's approach is trivial.

In addition to the above properties, the faces of each element have a state visualized as their colour. This is analogous to the state of a CA cell. Lookup tables stored with each element dictate the behaviour of a face depending on its current state and the state of the faces on *other* elements within its vicinity.

Faces may apply forces to the bodies on which they lie in response to the presence or absence of faces on other elements in particular states. The forces act at the center of the face in question and therefore provide linear and angular acceleration to the element on which they lie. The scale of the force generated is determined using a lookup table particular to the element on which the face resides. This value may be scaled according to the surface area of the face and the range over which the neighbouring face is detected.

There exists a special 'inert' state similar to the quiescent or background state of CA's. An inert face does not interact with any faces around it.

Besides generating a force, a face may undergo a change of state. This is triggered, like the application of forces, by the presence or absence of faces on other elements in particular states and at particular distances. It is not possible for a face on one polyhedron to control the behaviour of a face on another. The face may however *trigger* a response dictated by the transition table of the neighbouring body.

In sections 3.1 and 3.2, the properties of SOCA elements utilizing empty transition tables are explored. Section 3.3 on the formation of clusters of SOCA elements, utilizes the transition table to alter the state of the elements according to their environment. The properties of dynamic SOCA elements, elements with faces which change in such a way as to produce mobile or active structures, are not discussed in this paper.

3 Self-Assembling Structures

For the following experiments, the face of an element may be in one of the states 'blue', 'green', 'grey' or 'red' (after the colours in which they are drawn) or in the 'inert' state[3].

The dimensions of the elements used in the following examples were arrived at after some experimentation but are not mandatory. The system is sensitive to changes in dimensions of its elements for various reasons. Most notably, short or small elements are less stable than long elements under forces tending to align them in specific directions. This is due to the reduced lever arm available on a short element for the application of torque. [Fig 1]

Additionally, the difference between forces experienced by a pair of opposite faces, say on a cube is less than the difference between opposite end caps on a long rectangular prism because in the SOCA system, as in real life, forces attenuate across space. In these experiments all forces between element faces obey the standard inverse square law of force propagation. The strength of each force is independent of the surface area of the face on which it acts. The density of all elements is identical unless otherwise stated.

3Figures are rendered as clearly as possible within the limits imposed by black and white reproduction. The figure captions are written to clarify the orientation of the bodies. Colour figures are available from the author should they be required.

3.1 Chaining

A tube or cord is a geometric structure along which energy or matter may pass. It is a continuous structure able to span distances with a minimum expenditure of energy and material. Long, narrow, flexible, structures play vital roles throughout the natural and artificial worlds. Elephants marching around a ring, ropes, chains, wires, threads, tendons, muscle fibres, arteries, veins, capillaries, nerve cords, sinuses, hairs, all these things loosely fit into this category.

A common behaviour in chemistry and a useful property of many artefacts is referred to here as 'chaining'. For example, polymerization is chemical chaining in which many identical molecules or repeated sets of molecules link up end to end to form a molecular tube, cord or similar. A chain of metal rings is an artificial example of this structure, rope a variation on the theme. Chaining is a simple way to create tubes and cords from many identical elements.

To model chaining in the SOCA system, elements of length eight times the width of their square cross section were set up to act like ferrous magnets, one end cap in the green state, the other blue. The mid-sections of the elements were inert for this experiment. As with magnets it was arranged that opposite poles attract and like poles repel. Under these conditions all elements have the same transition table (since all magnets behave alike). Table 1 shows the forces between faces for this experiment.

	Inert	Blue	Green
Inert	0.0	0.0	0.0
Blue	0.0	-1.0	+1.0
Green	0.0	+1.0	-1.0

Table 1. Force table for ferrous magnet simulation

A positive force indicates a direction *towards* the neighbouring face (attraction), a negative force a direction *away* from the neighbouring face (repulsion). Interactions between inert faces and any other face always result in a force of 0.

When a blue face on a SOCA element encounters a green face on a neighbouring element, a force acting at the center of the blue face is generated in a direction towards the center of the green face (and vice versa because each element has the same transition table) [Fig 1]. As indicated above, the strength of the force is scaled to decay according to an inverse square law.

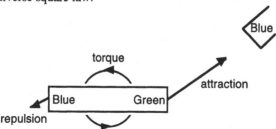

Fig. 1. Diagram illustrating resultant torque on a body undergoing attraction at one end, repulsion at the other

An environment homogeneously populated with elements of this type organizes itself into element pairs. Sometimes a short chain of three elements arises, but this is unstable and is hardly the desired behaviour [Fig 2a]. The stable state for the elements is a pair aligned head to tail (ie. blue to green and green to blue). From a distance, the net attraction or repulsion to the end point of one of these pairs is zero since the forces generated by blue and green ends cancel out.

To encourage chaining, the inert sides of the elements were replaced with grey sides. Table 2 shows the forces acting between elements in the new system.

	Inert	Grey	Blue	Green
Inert	0.0	0.0	0.0	0.0
Grey	0.0	-0.25	0.0	0.0
Blue	0.0	0.0	-1.0	+1.0
Green	0.0	0.0	+1.0	-1.0

Table 2. Force table for ferrous magnet simulation with repulsion along the length of the bodies

Table 2 is the same as table 1 but for the addition of a small repulsive force between the grey lengths of the SOCA elements. The small repulsion prevents pairs of elements from mating at both ends and encourages chaining [Fig 2a,b&c]. The stable form for a system of these elements, like those above, is a circle. In this case it is a circle of circumference greater than the degenerate two-link 'circle' (pair) in the earlier experiment and requires the chaining of more than two elements to be complete. The circumference of the minimum stable circle is proportional to the force applied between pairs of grey faces.

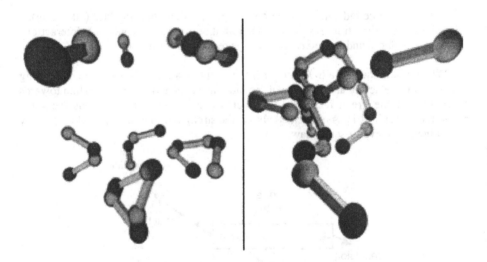

Fig. 2a & b. Chaining blue ends to green ends, elements form:
(a) small clumps (No repulsion along element lengths as in Table 1.),
(b) compact chains (Slight repulsion along element lengths).

Fig. 2c. Chaining blue ends to green ends - long extended chains of elements
(Repulsion along element lengths as in Table 2)

As has been shown, without any repulsion between grey faces the minimum stable 'circle' has a 'circumference' of two elements. Circles containing nine elements have been observed. In theory larger structures could be formed but in practice these are not easily assembled. This seems to be due to the inevitable presence of twists and turns in the chain which keep the two free ends from meeting. The grey faces of all elements in the chain repel one another and keep the structure from attempting to self-intersect. They resist the pull of the free ends to form a clean circle and tend to meander. The resulting structure has more in common with a helix than a circle.

Under conditions where the minimum circle size has been established, circles larger than the minimum stable circle have nevertheless been seen to form. Should an element of one of these large circles be dislodged by a collision with an element from outside, the circle may close out the dislodged element and form a structure closer in circumference to the minimum stable circle.

3.2 Boundary Formation

In many circumstances in the natural and artificial worlds, it is useful to separate something from its surroundings by means of a material barrier. The cell membrane is such a barrier, as are the skin and the walls of the stomach. A bottle and a balloon are artificial barriers.

Table 3 illustrates one way in which SOCA elements can be made to self-assemble into a boundary. All green faces attract one another, all blue faces repel one another. The effect is to have the elements' green faces forming the inside surface of a spherical boundary. The blue faces settle into a minimum energy outer surface. [Fig 3]

	Inert	Blue	Green
Inert	0.0	0.0	0.0
Blue	0.0	-1.0	0.0
Green	0.0	0.0	+1.0

Table 3. Force table for boundary formation

The boundaries formed using table 3 are unstable and slow to form. The instability manifests itself as oscillations in the arrangements of the elements and an insecure hold on components within the structure. A more stable configuration can be achieved using the behaviour specified by table 4.

	Inert	Grey	Blue	Green
Inert	0.0	0.0	0.0	0.0
Grey	0.0	-1.0	0.0	0.0
Blue	0.0	0.0	-4.0	-1.0
Green	0.0	0.0	-1.0	+4.0

Table 4. Force table for boundary formation with repulsion along the length of the bodies

Repulsion between faces along the length of the elements in the grey state (as opposed to the inert state) proves to be a useful stabilizer. Additionally, a small amount of repulsion between blue and green faces accelerates assembly by forcing 'un-linkable' ends apart. By altering the ratio of repulsion between the grey / grey and green / green faces to the attraction between blue / blue faces, boundaries of different diameter may be assembled. The repulsive forces must not be so great as to force the elements too far apart or the attractive forces will be insufficient to orient the elements over the greater diameter of the structure.

In this example, the number of elements in the boundary also effects its diameter. In each case the system settles into its state of minimum energy. The more elements there are, the more tightly packed they must be to form a sphere of some diameter, the higher the attraction on the inner surface needed to counter the repulsion between grey faces tending to expand the structure.

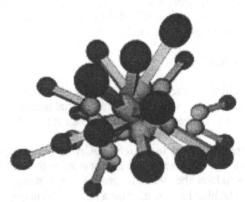

Fig. 3. Boundary formation, green end caps inward, blue outward

The boundary presented mimics to some degree the formation of liposomes [3]. Fatty acids in water orient their hydrophilic heads outward to form a hollow sphere which isolates the acid's hydrophobic tails from the water [Fig 4]. Single surface spheres like those created by the SOCA elements are formed by fatty acids surrounding droplets of oil placed in water.

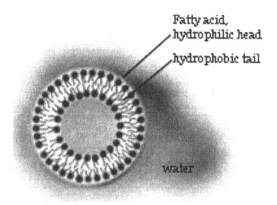

Fatty acid,
hydrophilic head
hydrophobic tail

water

Fig. 4. Liposome formation

3.3 Cluster Formation

It is not always desirable to have all SOCA elements participating in the formation of one structure like the membrane above. It may be necessary to assemble a complex structure hierarchically. To illustrate, a simple bridge constructed of steel girders is not assembled one girder at a time. A few girders are first bolted to one another and to a floor to form a sub-unit of the bridge. Several of these sub-units are then joined to form the complete bridge. How may hierarchical subassembly be achieved in SOCA?

A means of ensuring that SOCA elements self-assemble in stages triggered by their environmental conditions is required. This mechanism is implemented in the manner of Cellular Automata. The SOCA elements have, in addition to the table of forces generated between faces, a lookup table storing the transitions a face of a particular state may undergo when it encounters faces on neighbouring elements. This table contains, for each face state and each state it may encounter on a neighbouring face, a threshold which triggers the application of the transition. The transition itself, and its priority are also stored. The neighbourhood region falls within a constant range of a face's center.

A transition table may, for example, tell a green face that if it detects within its neighbourhood three red faces on other elements it should change to the red state with a priority of 2. The priority value is used to choose between rules triggered simultaneously. Low values indicate high priorities. Thus the transition table provides a means of testing environmental conditions and behaving accordingly. This enables elements to 'differentiate' in a manner analogous to biological cells. When a given set of environmental conditions are met, some change in the structure of an element may be triggered to alter the way it interacts with its environment. This may be understood as a *virtual chemical reaction*.

To create many dispersed clusters of elements arranged like those discussed in section 3.2, the following transition and force tables were utilized. These tables were arrived at through experimentation, since no automated means of reverse-engineering them from the specification of a desired emergent behaviour is (yet) available.

	Inert	Grey	Green	Blue	Red
Inert	0	0	0	0	0
Grey	0	-1	-1	-1	0
Green	0	-1	+70	-30	-2
Blue	0	-1	-30	-60	-20
Red	0	0	-2	-20	+70

Table 5a. Force table for cluster formation

	Inert	Grey	Green	Blue	Red
Inert	-	-	-	-	-
Grey	-	-	-	-	-
Green	-	-	8,Red,0	-	1,Red,0
Blue	-	-	-	-	-
Red	-	-	-	-	10,Green,0

Table 5b. Transition table for cluster formation
(cell data triple: threshold, transition, priority)

The SOCA system commences with a random arrangement of polyhedra like those of the previous section. They have grey lengths and opposite end caps of green and blue. As can be seen in table 5a, green faces attract one another quite strongly, blue faces repel one another slightly less strongly. Blue and green faces repel one another around half as strongly as the blue faces repel one another. Green, blue and grey faces are all repelled weakly by nearby grey faces. So far this is similar to the membrane forming system discussed in section 3.2. In fact, to begin with this is exactly the kind of behaviour which occurs.

Unlike in section 3.2, the transition table in this case acts to trigger changes in clusters of elements. Where a green face exceeds the threshold of 8 green neighbours, it is instructed by the transition table to change state to red with the highest priority (0). The same table also says that any green face which exceeds the threshold of 1 red neighbour should become a red face itself, also with priority 0.

The effect of this state changing is that 8 green faces in close proximity all become red. The force table 5a shows that red faces are strongly attracted to one another (as were the green faces) but that red and green faces weakly repel one another. Hence, the effect is to discourage further addition of green elements to the cluster which behaves like a small membrane of section 3.2, red faces inward, blue faces outward. The rule in the bottom right most corner of the transition table ensures that a red face encountering more than 10 red neighbours, will change into a green face with priority 0. This prevents large clusters of red / blue elements forming by expelling excess bodies and changing them back into the raw blue / green state.

The result of operating this SOCA system is illustrated [Fig 5]. The clusters sit apart due to the repulsion between their blue outer surfaces. Some clusters do not reach their quota of 8 elements and so remain green on the inside. Other clusters which have undergone the green / red transition fracture to form smaller units. Still other structures form with more than 10 elements, some hovering around the green / red transition. This complexity is the nature of a fully physically based model.

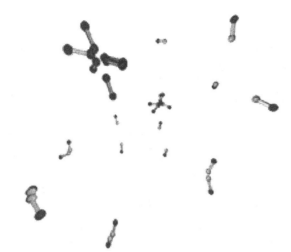

Fig. 5. Clusters of elements with red or green end caps inwards, blue end caps outwards

4 Future Work

The SOCA system is capable of simulating a vast range of emergent behaviours, far more than can be covered by this introductory paper. Work is under way to sub-assemble small groups of elements like the clusters in section 3.3, into larger groups which self-assemble into still larger configurations. Early experiments show that the SOCA elements are also capable of self-assembly into simple machines through the use of their transition tables. Elementary oscillators and rotary motors have been constructed and provide promise of further interesting results. Autocatalysis is also being investigated within the SOCA system.

5 Conclusions

A system of interacting rigid polyhedral units acting under simulated chemistry and physics has been shown to be useful for the study of self-organization and assembly. It has been demonstrated that physically based Self-Organizing Cellular Automata (SOCA) may feasibly simulate some of the basic interactions of the sub-units of living systems. Chaining, the linking of identical elements to form long, slender structures has been modelled. The formation of clusters and membrane like structures similar to liposomes has also been reproduced. The differentiation and segregation of groups of SOCA elements has been modelled by changing the state of SOCA elements according to their environmental conditions.

6 Acknowledgments

Special thanks to David Boulton, Damian Conway, Robert Dorin, Kevin Korb, Jon McCormack, Caroline McGregor, Ian Phillips and all those who have lent my passion for self-organization a sympathetic ear. Thanks also to David Baraff, Kurt Fleischer, Craig Reynolds and Karl Sims for their long-distance assistance, and to the anonymous reviewers who have helped in the fine tuning of this paper.

7 Bibliography

1. Banzhaf W., "Self-Organization in a System of Binary Strings", Artificial Life 4, Brooks & Maes (eds), MIT Press, 1994, pp109-118
2. Baraff D., "Analytical Methods for Dynamic Simulation of Non-Penetrating Rigid Bodies", Computer Graphics, Vol23, No3, ACM Press, July 1989, pp223-232
3. Beck W.S., Liem K.F., Simpson G.G., "Life, An Introduction To Biology", 3rd edn, Harper Collins, 1991, pp130
4. Burks A.W., "Essay 1 - Von Neumann's Self-Reproducing Automata" Essays On Cellular Automata, Burks (ed), Univ. Illinios Press, 1970, pp3-64
5. Cariani P., "Emergence and Artificial Life", Artificial Life II, SFI Studies in the Sciences of Complexity, Langton et al (eds), Vol 10, pp775-798
6. Dorin A., "Computer Based Life, Possibilities and Impossibilities", Proc. Information, Statistics and Induction in Science, Dowe et al (eds), World Scientific, 1996, pp237-246
7. Dorin A., Martin J., "A Model of Protozoan Movement for Artificial Life", Insight Through Computer Graphics: Proc. Computer Graphics International 1994, Gigante & Kunii (eds), World Scientific, 1996, pp28-38
8. Drogoul A., Dubreuil C., "Eco-Problem-Solving Model: Results of the N-Puzzle", Decentralized AI3, Proc. 3rd European Workshop on Modelling Autonomous Agents in a Multi-Agent World, Demazeau & Werner (eds), North-Holland, 1992, pp283-296
9. Ferber J., Jacopin E., "The Framework of ECO-Problem Solving", Decentralized AI2, Proc. 2nd European Workshop on Modelling Autonomous Agents in a Multi-Agent World, Demazeau & Muller (eds), North-Holland, 1991, pp181-194
10. Fleischer K.W., "A Multiple-Mechanism Developmental Model for Defining Self-Organizing Geometric Structures", PhD thesis, Caltech, 1995
11. Gardner M., "Mathematical Games - On Cellular Automata, Self-reproduction, the Garden of Eden and the Game 'Life'", Sci. American, Vol223 No4, 1970, pp112-117
12. Gardner M., "Mathematical Games - The Fantastic Combinations of John Conway's New Solitaire Game 'Life'", Sci. American, Vol224, No2, 1971, pp120-123
13. Goel N.S., Thompson R.L., "Movable Finite Automata (MFA): A New Tool for Computer Modeling of Living Systems", Artificial Life, SFI Studies in the Sciences of Complexity, Langton (ed), Addison-Wesley, 1988, pp317-339
14. Hosokawa K., Shimoyama I., Hirofumi M., "Dynamics of Self-Assembling Systems: Analogy with Chemical Kinetics", Artificial Life, Langton (ed), Vol1, No4, MIT Press, 1995, pp413-427
15. Ingber D.E, "The Architecture of Life", Scientific American, January, 1998, pp30-39
16. Kauffman S.A., "The Origins of Order - Self-Organization and Selection in Evolution", Oxford Univ. Press, 1993, pp289
17. Langton C.G., "Studying Artificial Life with Cellular Automata", Physica 22D, North-Holland, 1986, pp120-149
18. Lawrence D.S., Jiang T., Levett M., "Self-Assembling Supramolecular Complexes", Chemical Review, Vol95, American Chemical Society, 1995, pp2229-2260
19. Maturana H., Varela F., "Autopoiesis, The Organization of the Living", Autopoiesis and Cognition, The Realization of the Living, Reidel, 1980, pp73-140
20. McKenna M., Zeltzer D., "Dynamic Simulation of Autonomous Legged Locomotion", Computer Graphics, Vol24, No4, ACM Press, August 1990, pp29-38
21. Muller A., Reuter H., Dillinger S., "Supramolecular Inorganic Chemistry: Small Guests in Small and Large Hosts", Angew. Chem. Int. Engl. (ed), Vol34, VCH Verlag, 1995, pp2323-2361
22. Penrose L.S., "Self-Reproducing Machines", Sci. American, Vol200, No6, June 1959, pp105-114
23. Prigogine I., Stengers I., "Order out of Chaos", Harper Collins, 1985, Chpts 5-6

24. Saitou K., Jakiela M.J., "Automated Optimal Design of Mechanical Conformational Switches", Artificial Life, Langton (ed), Vol2, No2, MIT Press, 1995, pp129-156
25. Saitou K., Jakiela M.J., "Subassembly Generation via Mechanical Conformational Switches", Artificial Life, Langton (ed), Vol2, No4, MIT Press, 1995, pp377-416
26. Simon H. A., "The Science of the Artificial", 2nd edn, MIT Press, 1994, pp63-65
27. Sims K., "Evolving Virtual Creatures", SIGGRAPH 94 Conf. Proc., ACM Press, pp15-34
28. Stang P.J., "Molecular Architecture: Coordination as the Motif in the Relational Design and Assembly of Discrete Supramolecular Species - Self-Assembly of Metallacyclic Polygons and Polyhedra", Chem. Eur. J., Vol4, No1, Wiley-VCH Verlag, 1998, pp19-27
29. Steels L., "A Self-Organizing Spatial Vocabulary", Artificial Life, Langton (ed), Vol2, No3, MIT Press, 1995, pp319-332
30. Wejchert J., Haumann D., "Animation Aerodynamics", Computer Graphics, Vol25, No4, ACM Press, July 1991, pp19-22
31. Wolfram S., "Universality and Complexity in Cellular Automata", Physica 10D, North-Holland, 1984, pp1-35

Service Contract Negotiation -
Agent-Based Support for Open Service Environments

Annika Waern

Swedish Institute of Computer Science
Box 1263
S-164 29 Kista
SWEDEN
annika@sics.se

Abstract. An Open Service Architecture is a framework that supports an open set of users to subscribe to, and pay for, an open set of services. Such architectures provide an excellent application area for Agent Oriented Programming. It is useful to describe the collaboration between agents in terms of Service Contracts, that agents can form dynamically through negotiation. The negotiation of Service Contracts poses different requirements on Agent Architectures than those that current frameworks for Agent Oriented Programming address. In particular, agents must both be able to negotiate what services should be provided as well as payment schemas. I discuss the requirements on agent collaboration and communication imposed by negotiation of Service Contracts, and analyse to what extent existing approaches to Agent Oriented Programming support such negotiation.

1. Introduction

The notion of agency in computer science literature is not one uniform idea. In his introduction to the book 'software agents' [2], Jeffrey Bradshaw identifies two motivations for agent research: the search for novel interaction metaphors, and the need for new programming paradigms for large and open systems. The first has spurred work on visible interface agents that maintain a dialogue with the user, as well as software agents to which the user can delegate some of his or her more tedious tasks. The latter has concentrated on what Shoham [20,21] called Agent-Oriented Programming (AOP): techniques for constructing software architectures where the individual components are treated as if they had mental qualities such as beliefs, intentions, and desires, and collaborate with each other by communicating these.

This paper is concerned directly with the second issue: that of creating programming paradigms for large and open systems. More specifically, is deals with a specific type of such systems which we have called Open Service Architectures

(**OSA**), where an open set of users can access an open range of user services. OSAs are not necessarily agent architectures - many such systems are being built today on much simpler technology, the WWW being the chief example. But the intentional stance of the agent metaphor rhymes very well with the OSA objectives. In the KIMSAC project [6], we have investigated the use of current agent technology for developing an OSA. Although this experiment was partly successful, it showed that building truly flexible and robust OSAs is a major challenge to agent technology. In particular, current agent technology gives little support for setting up or negotiating *services* to a user or another service, as opposed to routing individual queries to a competent service.

In this paper, I first introduce the general idea of open service architectures, and exemplify by describing two different applications of agent-based OSAs. Next, I discuss the notion of service contracts in detail, and compare it to the notion of joint intentionality, which sometimes is brought up in AOP. Finally, I analyse some existing protocols for agent communication in terms of to what extent they allow agents to negotiate service contracts.

2. Open Service Architectures

An Open Service Architecture must support:
- an open set of users,

- an open set of services, and

- a means for users to access the services.

There exists of today many simple examples of OSAs, the WWW being the most successful example. The basic WWW structure is exactly this: users can access a service by navigating to it or by typing its web address. Services can be anything from pure web pages, to search engines, 'hotlists' for particular topics, or market places where vendors publish goods that users can both buy and pay for through the system.

The simple structure of the WWW has several advantages. The biggest advantage is that each information provider, vendor, or web service provider can make themselves available to users without having to negotiate with each other. But this is also the biggest drawback of the WWW architecture - if there is to be any kind of collaboration between services, it must be hand-crafted by the people developing them, and it can only be maintained if humans agree to coordinate their further development and maintenance of the services. The simplest example of this problem is stale links, but search engines, market places, and other brokering services run into more serious versions of the same problem. The problems with the WWW show that there is good reason to attempt AOP approaches to open service architectures. Below, I sketch some examples of more complex OSAs.

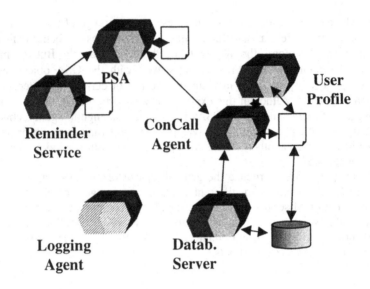

Fig. 1. The ConCall service architecture.

2.1 ConCall: An Information Service.

ConCall [13] is an information service developed at the Swedish Institute of Computer Science using AgentBase [7], a very basic shell for Agent-Oriented Programming developed in Prolog. The purpose of ConCall is to route information about calls to upcoming conferences to individual researchers, based on their interest profiles. Users can set up reminders to particularly interesting conferences, to remind them of the conference deadlines.

The conceptual architecture of ConCall is shown in figure 1. Most of the agents; the Personal Service Assistant (PSA), the Reminder Service, the User Profile and the ConCall agent are personal to the user. They hold information about the state of the current session with the user and may hold information about the user that is stored between sessions. The Personal Assistant is the user's representative in the agent architecture, and is used to help the user select services. The reminder agent and the ConCall agent are the user's personal 'copies' of generic services that other users also may subscribe to. The database agent is used by multiple users and stores no user-specific information. Agents communicate with each other by KQML messages[1], where the content is represented as ground Prolog terms. The ontologies used are application-specific. Users communicate with agents through special-purpose applets.

The ConCall service is a very good example of the kind of service architectures that we want to accomplish. All agents in ConCall have at least two interfaces: one towards users, and one towards other agents. Each agent has a span of activities that it can perform, although some of them require interaction in a particular format that may only be accessible to one type of agent (e.g. a user).

---

[1] Only the 'ask-one', 'ask-all' and 'tell' performatives are used.

The ConCall system works well in isolation, but it is not an open architecture. There is no means for users to seek for and subscribe to new services, or for the ConCall service to utilise any other reminder service than the one that is built-in. The use of application-specific ontologies means that the communication is hand-crafted for the ConCall service, and does not easily extend to new services.

In a truly open service architecture, services like the ConCall service should instead be negotiated and set up automatically or semi-automatically. The user should be able to initiate the ConCall service using something like the following procedure.

- The user instructs the PSA to contact a facilitator service to seek for a service that collects information about conference calls.

- The facilitator suggests the ConCall service, represented by a multi-user concall service agent.

- The concall service spawns a personal ConCall agent for the user. This agent proposes a service contract to the PSA (or the user), indicating what the service costs, how the service works, and what information it needs from the user in order to perform its services. In addition, it explains that it cannot keep track of reminders - a reminder service is needed for that.

- The user agrees to the deal, under the provision that the user profile cannot be passed on to other agents. (If he or she declines, the personal ConCall agent is deleted at this point.)

- The ConCall agent agrees to the deal, including the restriction on the user profile information, and provides a reference to a particular reminder service.

- The user may now register with the reminder service in the same manner, or ask the facilitator agent for some alternative service that can provide the same functionality.

2.2 Adaptation Agents: Support for User Adaptivity

Even though services should be free to design their user interaction in a manner that best suits themselves, it is useful if *some* parts of the interface is kept stable for the individual user. That way, the user is relieved from some of the burden of learning everything anew each time a new service is added. Furthermore, if parts of the interface is kept stable, services with similar functionalities can make use of a shared user model, allowing them to adapt to the user's particulars and preferences immediately, without a learning period or a tedious set-up session.

In Bylund and Waern [5], we explored the possibility of introducing separate *adaptation agents*. An adaptation agent is an agent that maintains a user model, and selects between a range of (pre-defined) adaptations, the *adaptation model*. A good application for adaptation agents are help agents, since the adaptation model for help is fairly domain independent (although the user model will require domain-specific knowledge), and the same agent potentially could be applied to a wide range of services. Figure 2 shows the role of the adaptation agent in adapting the interaction

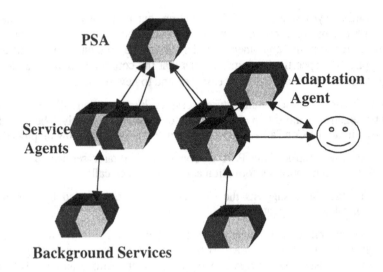

PSA

Adaptation Agent

Service Agents

Background Services

Fig. 2. A schematic graph of an open agent architecture with an adaptation agent which is shared between two services.

for two similar services. A simple adaptation agent was implemented in the KIMSAC system, see [4,6].

As opposed from the ConCall example, the adaptation agents will largely be dependent on sharing ontologies with service agents. Only services that share some ontologies with an adaptation agent that a user subscribes to, can utilise its services. In [5] we analysed the ontologies involved in setting up and executing adaptive services. These are the following.

- Elements from the user model, such as the users expertise, cognitive abilities, tasks, or preferences.
- The service context and service domain, that is, what kind of task the user currently is involved in and information about domain-specific properties of this task.
- The adaptation model - what information is to be selected and how is it going to be presented.
- Information about inference rules from the domain model that are used for user modelling.
- The *interaction schemas* used for performing adaptations. Based on work by Kühme et al. [14], we divided the process of providing the user with adapted help into four phases:
    - *Initiative* – which of the agents (including the user) is responsible for taking the initiative to an adaptation.
    - *Proposal* – which agents form proposals for how the interaction should be adapted.
    - *Decision* – which agent decides upon an adaptation.
    - *Execution* – which agent implements and executes the selected adaptation.

Of these ontologies, the two last are important for the discussions of this paper. The inference rules from the domain model must be communicated prior to the actual

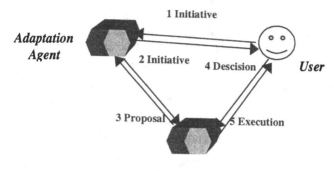

Service Agent

Fig. 3. . Interaction schema for adapting user initiated adaptive help on services (as opposed from help on the system itself).

collaboration. A service agent may for example inform the adaptivity agent about a task model for the service domain, enabling the adaptivity agent to model the user's current domain task.

The interaction schemas correspond to what is usually called *conversation policies* in Agent Oriented Programming - schemas for when agents send out certain information or information requests, and how these requests are to be routed. The converstation policies must also be negotiated before the adaptation agent services can be utilised by service agents.

One example of an interaction schema is depicted in figure 3.[2] Note that normally, service agents interact directly with the user without involving the adaptation agent, in a completely service-specific manner. To allow the adaptation agent to maintain a user model, agents must notify the adaptation agent about such user and system that will influence the user model, and this is done using the service model. The user model can in turn be communicated to several agents, to allow them to adapt their services to the user's current situation. As an example, user-initiated domain help would be implemented in the following way.

1) Whenever the user initiates a help task, the interface routes this help request to the adaptation agent, rather than the current service agent. The request contains information about the current service context, expressed in the joint - possibly quite abstract - ontology for user tasks and service domain.

2) The adaptation agent may now add information about the user profile to the request. This enables service agents to adapt their selection and/or formulation of help alternatives to user properties. The request is then re-routed to a set of service agents that have declared themselves willing and able to provide help within this part of the service model. (The adaptation agent itself may also provide 'default' help alternatives.) Normally, the service agent that the user is currently using will be one of these, but not necessarily, and neither will it always provide the best possible help.

---

[2] This particular schema was designed for the Kimsac system. In the end, it was not realized, since only system help was made user adaptive in the actual implementation.

3) The agents that are able to provide help produce help suggestions, possibly adapted to the user's profile, and route this information to the adaptation agent. This agent may again use its user profile to filter and restructure the alternatives into a help proposal to the user, possibly in the form of a menu of help alternatives.

4) The user is presented with a set of alternative help topics, from which he or she selects the most appropriate option. This triggers a request to the appropriate service agent to actually generate a help answer.

5) The service agent provides the appropriate help answer.

The notion of conversation policies is not new to Agent-Oriented programming - it is for example used in the KaOS framework (see section 4.1 below). However, this example shows that conversation policies can involve more than two agents: in this case, we need to describe conversation policies that involve the adaptation agent, an arbitrary number of service agents, and the user. Note also that the conversation policy may need to be subject for quite advanced negotiation. For example, the user may want to decide which agents should be considered as the best candidates for generating help response. The user may also want to delegate the decision to the adaptation agent, so the user is directly provided with a help answer rather than a menu of help options. Finally, agents may negotiate which types of requests should be routed via the adaptation agent and which should go directly to the current service; as some agents may contain their internal user models, and prefer to provide user-adapted answers to help requests themselves.

3. Service Contracts

One way to realise Open Service Architectures using Agent-Oriented programming, is to enable agents to collaborate by negotiating and acting within *Service Contracts*. A Service Contract is a mutual agreement between a group of agents, which describes how they collaborate. It can be partly implicit (hard-wired into the construction of agents and in the basic communication infrastructure), and partly explicitly negotiated and agreed upon. Agents may also negotiate service contracts at multiple levels: they may negotiate a service in itself, and they may negotiate how to negotiate a service. The important realisation is that each schema for negotiation is by itself a service contract, and that this object-meta level distinction need not stop at two levels.

Note that in a true Open Service Architecture, agents may always *break* service contracts, even implicit ones. Agents may be forced to break contracts due to unforeseen events. Agents may be poorly constructed and simply unable to realise the conventions. Agents may also deliberately flaunt collaboration, defecting from what was agreed to gain advantages for themselves or their owners. Furthermore, if agents engage in explicit negotiation, there is always the risk that they do not have a mutual understanding of what has been agreed. Agent architectures used to implement Open Service Architectures must contain some means of protection against several types of contract breaking, including misunderstandings, incompetent behaviour, and malevolent agents [17].

3.1 Joint Intentions, Contracts, and Emergent Behavior

Is it really necessary to introduce a notion of Service Contracts? There exist already at least two approaches in literature to handling mutual agreements between agents, the first relying on the joint planning and execution of joint intentions [12, 16], and the second dealing with the explicit negotiation of contracts [18, 22].

At a first glance, the joint intention approach seems to be a natural choice for modelling Open Service Architectues in AOP. After all, agents are often viewed as having beliefs, desires and intentions, so why not communicate these? There are several problems with this approach, however. Firstly, the full declarative formalisations of joint intentions are extremely complex. There exist of today no general agreement on how to formally describe intentions, and even less for joint intentions (see [23] chapter 6). Furthermore, to my knowledge, no communication language has been proposed that build upon the existing models of joint intentions. And still, despite the complexity of these notions, the frameworks modeling joint intentions use very weak notions of agents' desires. The desires of an agent may determine whether it decides to commit to a particular intention, but the desire itself is not a part of the agreement. Thus, the approach provides little or no support for agents bidding for contracts, agreeing to payment schemas, etc, all necessary aspects of Open Service Architectures.

An alternative approach, the Contract Net approach, has focussed on the latter issue. In the original paper by Reid Smith [22], the structure of contracts and the information these must hold was spelled out in some detail. Later work in this area has concentrated on the protocols for contracting, accommodating self-interested agents that do services for payment, and avoiding suboptimal and defect behaviours (see eg. [18, 19]). The Contract Net approach can be seen as an encapsulating framework for the discussions of this paper - whereas Contract Nets are concerned with how to negotiate Service Contracts, this paper concerns itself with what these contracts should state.

In contrast with approaches where agent agreements are made explicit, there also exist approaches to agent collaboration where no such agreements exist. The basic collaboration schema of these architecture relies entirely on individual agents' commitments (to themselves) and volunteered agent interaction, so that collaboration 'magically emerges' without explicit negotiation (see e.g. [24]). For Open Service Architectures, the approach of emergent collaboration makes little sense. After all, we will want to subscribe to services knowing roughly what these services offer to us, as well as what we are expected to do in return. I believe that explicit agreements form a cornerstone for any agent-oriented approach to Open Service Architectures.

3.2 Elements of Service Contracts

We now turn to a discussion of what Service Contracts should be able to express and how they could be defined. As discussed above, Service Contracts should be able to describe both how an actual service should be performed, methods for negotiating services, and even methods for negotiating how to negotiate services. At all these levels, it must convey sufficient information to allow all participating agents to agree upon to two critical issues,

– 'do we want to collaborate' and
– 'can we collaborate'.

The first question involves relating the contract to the desires of each of the agents involved; what is it with the contract that makes the agent willing to participate in it? The second question breaks breaks into several components, dealing with details of how the collaboration will be carried out. Here, I identify four such issues, but this list is not necessarily exhaustive - it was obtained from an analysis of the OSA examples described in section 2. The result is a list of in total five issues, that all could be subject of negotiation,

– **WHY**: Do we want to collaborate.
– **WHAT:** Do we have anything to collaborate about (do we have complementing competencies).
– **HOW:** How should we use our competencies (e.g. in the adaptation agent example in section two, service agents supply information about the task hierarchy to the adaptation agent).
– **WHEN:** What information do we need to exchange, and when.
– **LANGUAGE:** What language should we use during information exchange.

To approach more precise description of service contracts[3], let us for the moment assume that we have some way of defining agent *activities*, the things agents can do. Let *Activities* denote the domain of possible activities for agents, and *Agents* the set of all agents. To allow any kind of negotiation, agents must have a range of capabilities, which are expressed as subsets of the set of possible activities. Let *Capabilities(Agent)* denote the capabilities of the agent *Agent*. A service contract constrains how the agent can use its capabilities. Usually, it will not completely determine what an agent can and cannot do, but it will constrain what further contracts the agent can get involved in.

We can express a service contract by specifying four functions that apply to a subset of *Agents*, the agents that are bound by the contract. The functions describe how each of the agents is committed by the contract.

Actors:

> *Actors* ⊆ *Agents*

> A set of agents that are bound by the contract.

Scope:

> *Scope: Actors* --> P(*Activities*) such that

> Scope(A) ⊆ *Capabilities(A)*

---

[3] In this paper, I make no attempt to make a full formalization of service contracts. If one was sought, deontic logic would be a good candidate. This approach is used in [7]. It should be noted that in this work, sequences of actions are given a set-based semantics. This semantics forms the set of activities for that formalization of service contracts.

A service contract will not constrain everything an agent can do, but only the activities within a certain domain. Outside the domain, the agent is free to do anything it likes. The scope fall within the agent's capabilities..

Obligations:

Obl: Actors --> P(Activities), such that

$$Obl(A) \subseteq Scope(A)$$

The obligations of an agent express what an agent has contracted to do. Typically, obligations include responding to certain requests, routing messages, volunteering information under certain circumstances, etc. They must fall within the scope of the contract. The obligations state the 'what' issue, what agents collaborate about.

Entitlements:

Ent: Actors --> P(Activities), such that

$$Obl(A) \subseteq Ent(A) \subseteq Scope(A)$$

The entitlements express what an agent *may* do. The agents actual behavior will lie somewhere between its obligations and its entitlements - it must do everything within its obligations, and it may also do things that lie within its entitlements. The entitlements express the conditions under which agents are willing to collaborate, such as, how agents are entitled to use sensitive information that needs to be shared as part of the contract.

Entitlements can also be expressed negatively, a set activities that the agent is obliged to *not* do. In this case, the set of forbidden activities is instead expressed as a subset of the scope for an agent, which must be disjoint from the set of obligations for the agent.

$$Forbidden(A) \subseteq Scope(A) \text{ such that } Obl(A) \cap Forbidden(A) = \varnothing$$

Motivation:

Motivation: Actors --> {(A × Scope(A)) : A∈ Actors} such that

$$(A2, Act) \in Motivation(A1) \text{ only if}$$
$$A2 = A1 \text{ and } Act \in Ent(A1), \text{ or}$$
$$A2 \neq A1 \text{ and } Act \in Obl(A2)$$

The motivations correspond to the 'why' question, why do agents engage in a service contract. A service agent may expect to get paid for a service, or a buyer may expect that a certain high-level service is provided. An agent's motivation must fall within what is contracted; an agent's goal can either be an activity that another agent is obliged to do, or an activity that the agent itself is entitled to do. An example of the latter is an information service that agrees to provide a user with personalised information, provided that it is entitled to sell the user's interest profile to other agents.

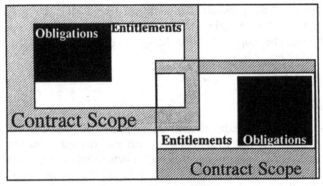

Agent Capabilities

Fig. 4. The entitlements and obligations of an agent committed to two different service contracts.

The relationships between the obligations and entitlements of an agent are shown in figure 4. The figure shows the capabilities of a hypothetical agent that is committed to two different service contracts with partly overlapping scopes. The big rectangle corresponds to the agent's capabilities. In each of the contracts, the agent has a number of activities it is committed to do - these are shown in black. Each contract also constrains the agent's activity by limiting the agent's entitlements within the scope of the contract. The activities that the agent has contracted to *not* do are shown as striped areas of the diagram. The areas left white are activities that the agent may do if it chooses to, but is not committed to do. This include both activitites within the scope of the contracts, that the agent is entitled but not obliged to do, as well as activities outside the scope of the contracts that are within the agent's capabilities.

What is an activity? We now turn to the issue of what 'a set of activities' could be. In the discussion above, the set of activities is assumed to be the set of all possible actual agent behaviours, in all contexts that possibly may occur. At this level of discussion, there is no distinction between object-level and meta-level contracts, since the activities are *instances* of agent behaviour and not descriptions thereof. However, in any kind of *descriptions* of service contracts, it is only possible to express that agents agree on certain types of activities. It is here that it makes sense to distinguish between object-level and meta-level activities.

In meta-level contracts, activity descriptions should be full service contracts. An agent may for example publish its competencies by committing itself to a contract where the agent's individual obligations constitute a set of alternative contracts, each expressing one way in which the agent can collaborate with other agents.

In object level contracts, activity descriptions should express things that agents actually do - send and receive messages, interact with external resources, draw conclusions.

It is useful to include at least two types of information in the definition of an object level activity for a particular agent.

- A set of beliefs that the activity is based upon. This does not mean that the agent need to share all of these beliefs - only that the activity is to be performed as if it did. These beliefs correspond to the 'how' issue, the sharing of information about background knowledge and domain-specific ontologies.
- A set of actions that agents may perform. These can be described as a triplet consisting of
  - A triggering condition,
  - An effect, and
  - A set of constraints (things that have to be kept true when the action is performed)

There exist a multitude of action formalisms, and several have also been used in AOP as means of communicating requests and publishing agent competencies. A simple variant is to describe the possible actions for an agent as a state-transition diagram. The triggering condition and the effects may also be expressed using either an event-based or a state-based logic for actions. If a state-based logic is used, the states can either be described by atomic names and a set of parameters (viewing agents as parameterised state automata), or in terms of beliefs, desires, and intentions (as in KQML semantics [15]). Furthermore, to allow for efficient negotiation, it makes sense to gather sets of actions into higher-level task descriptions, allowing agents to publish their competencies at a higher level than that of individual actions. If such a schema is used, contract negotiation becomes similar to hierarchic planning. Finally, actions may be modelled as atomic events or as having duration in time. In all, the choice of action formalism depends on the competencies of the agents in the service architecture, as it must be powerful enough to adequately express those competencies.

The choice of activity formalism also depends on whether it is to be used for describing a system, or to be used *inside* a system for negotiating service contracts. In formalisations that are used for negotiation, conditions and constraints should be described from the subjective perspective of agents. They cannot really relate to true states of the environment, but to facts that the actor perceives to be true. In other words, you cannot ask an agent to signal you when you have mail - only to signal you when *the agent believes* that you have mail. Within a true open service architecture, we can also expect that different agent communities communicate using several different action formalisms. Some agents will have a very small range of possible behaviours, hardwired into an agent role. These may use a simple state-based formalism to communicate their abilities and commitments. More flexible agents may communicate their motivations explicitly by stating beliefs and desires. It is then up to the 'intelligent' agents to adapt their communication to the simple state-based agents' competencies.

Breaking and flaunting contracts. The distinction between entitlements, obligations and motivations makes it possible to distinguish between several different ways that an agent can act against a contract. An agent *breaks* a contract if it does not fulfil its obligations. We can distinguish two variants of contract breaking: the case when the contract breaking makes is impossible to fulfil the motivations of the contract, and the case when the motivations of the contract still (eventually) are fulfilled. Agents can also 'flaunt' a contract - this happens when an agent exceeds its entitlements.

Finally, when service contracts are partly explicit, the possibility arises that agents interpret the same service contract description differently. This will lead them to believe that they act under a mutually agreed contract, when in reality they do not. This can lead to a conflict situation, when agents disagree on whether a contract has been violated or not, or on which party has violated the contract. Agent architectures that allow explicit negotiation of contracts should provide some means to deal with such conflicts.

4. Analysis of example AOP frameworks

Current approaches to Agent Oriented programming have not been developed to address the requirements that arise in Open Service Architectures. Consequently, there exist no framework that fully supports, or naturally extends to, the negotiation of service contracts at arbitrary levels. This is only to be expected, since the purpose of current AOP approaches has not been to support Open Service Architectures. In particular, they presuppose agent properties that cannot be expected to hold in a fully open service architecture. To illustrate these problems, I will here discuss three example frameworks, in terms of how well they support negotiation of Service Contracts; the KQML/KIF approach, Contract Networks, and Collaborate Information Agents.

4.1 Speech-Act Based Frameworks for Knowledge Sharing

A speech act is the act an actor performs by speaking, or in general, communicating [1]. A promise, for example, signals that the speaker has committed to a particular intention. The theory of speech acts underlies a number of approaches to AOP. The most widespread approaches have been developed within the U.S. *knowledge sharing effort*. These standardisation efforts encompass the communication language KQML [10], that deals with the message communication standards, the knowledge representation language KIF, and finally means for domain ontology specifications, that in turn are used to harmonise how agents understand and use domain-specific terms, rules, and definitions. The KQML/KIF approach does not require that agents are homogeneous; agents can be implemented in different techniques and exhibit different levels of intelligence or autonomy. However, agents are supposed to be sincere and benevolent, serving each new request as long as this does not conflict with the services they already have taken on. . Since agents are assumed to be benevolent, the standard performatives of KQML do not support any kind of 'why' level negotiation. KQML mainly supports two levels of negotiation: what do the agents collaborate about, and negotiation about the content ontology and language. Since KIF supports sharing of ontology definitions, it is possible for agents to tailor the competencies of one another, by communicating definitions of concepts in the domain of collaboration. However, there is no way to tie this information to a particular service - each statement is taken as literally true and incorporated into the agent's knowledge base.

A specific implementation of KQML and KIF is the Agent Communication Language, ACL, platform developed by Gensereth [11]. ACL contains a special type of agents, facilitator agents, that able to decompose information requests into simpler requests and distribute these to agents that can handle them. This means that the facilitator is able to do some run-time planning of the service contract. An alternative approach to increased flexibility is supported within the KAoS platform [3]. This architecture allows agents to choose which conversation policies they want to use. The agent that initiates collaboration does so by selecting a performative that restricts the other agents in what policies they can use.

4.2 Contract Nets

The Contract Net protocol [22] was one of the first frameworks proposed for distributed artificial intelligence. The goals were to "specify problem-solving communication and control for nodes in a distributed problem solver". This task lies very close to that of AOP, and today we would not hesitate to call the nodes in the Contract Net Architecture agents. Each of the nodes in the distributed problem solver had a particular range of competencies, and communicated by task announcements (there is this job to be done) and bids (I can do it).

In [22], task announcements were expressed as a task and a set of eligibility constraints, stating essentially how the task should be performed. These express the overall 'what' issue, what the agents should collaborate about. The Contract Net protocol is rather high level: it provides no means for negotiating details of what is to be accomplished, such as tailoring of competencies, negotiation of conversation policies, or ontology sharing. Neither does the Contract Net architecture allow for more than one level of negotiation.

The original definition of contract nets assumed that the individual nodes were benevolent. T. Sandholm has constructed versions of the Contract Net protocol that extend the protocol to collections of self-interested agents [18,19] where agents pay for services and get awarded for performing tasks. This extends the protocol to deal with the 'why' issue.

Cooperative Information Agents.

An alternative to the KQML approach to agent communication has been proposed by Frank Dignum et. al. in the *Cooperative Information Agent* (CIA) framework for agent negotiation [25]. This work also relies on speech acts, but here speech acts are modelled as the explicit offering and accepting of obligations. This way, the work much resembles the service contract approach suggested in this paper.

The CIA framework is based on a formal framework of obligations and authorizations that is given in Deontic logic [7]. This formal framework underlie the programming language CoLa (Communication and Coordination Language), in which contracts can be specified that specify how agents will collaborate. In particular, this language specifies a set of formally well-defined speech acts that can agents use in communication. The language CoLa is used as the programming language of Collaborative Information Agents, CIAs. The internal architecture and implementation of these are discussed in [25].

The formal part of this work is impressive. The work centers around a formal notion of commitments and authorizations; agents committing themselves to obligations, and agents authorizing other agents to impose obligations on them. Entitlements are not explicitly discussed, but should be possible to model using authorizations. A possible weakness is that motivations are not modeled, neither in the basic formalism nor included in the description of contracts in CoLa. This makes it difficult to model negotiation at the 'why' level.

This weakness is addressed in the CIA framework. The internal agent architecture of CIA agents contains a contract negotiation component, which currently implements contract nets. CIAs use predefined templates for contracts, so that an actual contract always is an instance of a contract template. These resemble the conversation policies used in KaOs, but are much more expressive and can involve more than two agents. The construction obtains a clear object/meta level distinction between contracts. It is not clear from the description of CIA if more than two levels of contracts can be defined, that is, if contract templates can take contracts as arguments. (The formal semantics does not support this.)

Of the three frameworks presented here, the CIA framework comes closest to providing support for arbitrary negotiation of service contracts. Where both the Contract Net and the KQML/KIF approaches limited in their support for Service Contract negotiation, CIA provides at least two levels of full negotiation. Still, CIA is not ideal for the construction of OSAs. The biggest problem is that agents are assumed to be homogeneous (implemented using the same basic architecture) and sincere. For example, if agents break their obligations, they know about it, and voluntarily pay such penalties as declared in the contract. In a true OSA, akin to the WWW, these assumptions are too strong. OSA agents may very well can break (and flaunt) contracts both on purpose and by mistake.

5. Conclusions

Open Service Architectures provide an excellent application area for Agent Oriented Programming. Agent Oriented Programming can provide mechanisms for finding services, paying for services, and most importantly, for service collaboration. It is useful to describe agent collaboration in terms of Service Contracts, that agents can form dynamically through negotiation. The rules of such negotiations are again guided by service contracts. This is an object/meta level distinction that need not stop at two levels: it could even be useful to allow arbitrary levels of service contract negotiation.

However, current approaches to agent architectures do not fully meet the requirements for Open Service Architectures. The reason is quite simply that they were not designed to deal with OSAs in mind. In this paper, we discussed three such approaches, the KQML/KIF approach, Contract Nets, and Collaborative Information

Agents, and found that all of them lacked features that are necessary to deal with OSAs. In particular, the speech-act based frameworks assume that agents are benevolent and/or sincere, properties that cannot be assumed to be true for agents in an OSA.

Future Work My research group is currently involved in the development of several adaptive information services. To support these projects, we are in the process of designing and implementing a generic, open platform for adaptive information services, based on the notion of service contracts. The work is carried out in collaboration with related work on open platforms for electronic commerce [6].

References

1. J.L. Austin. How to Do Things with Words. Oxford University Press, Oxford, England, 2nd edition (1976).
2. Jeffrey M. Bradshaw, ed. Software Agents, AAAI Press/MIT Press (1997).
3. Jeffrey M. Bradshaw, Stewart Dutfield, Pete Benoit, and John D. Woolley. KAoS: Toward an Industrial Strength Open Agent Architecture. In ed. Jeffrey M. Bradshaw, Software Agents. AAAI Press/MIT Press (1997) pages 375-418.
4. Markus Bylund. Supporting Adaptations in Open Service Architectures. Master thesis, Computing Science Dept., Uppsala University (forthcoming).
5. Markus Bylund and Annika Waern. Adaptation Agents: Providing Uniform Adaptations in Open Service Architectures. In proceedings of the 3rd ERCIM workhop on User Interfaces for All (1997), available from ICS-Forth, Crete.
6. Patricia Charlton, Yan Chen, Fredrik Espinoza, Abe Mamdani, Olle Olsson, Jeremy Pitt, Fergal Somers, and Annika Waern. An open agent architecture supporting multimedia services on public information kiosks. In Proceedings of PAAM'97, London, U.K (1997).
7. F. Dignum, j.-j. Ch. Meyer, R.J. Wieringa, and R. Kuiper. A Modal Approach to Intentions, Commitments and Obligations: Intention plus Commitment yields Obligation. in proceedings of DEON'96 Workshop on Deontic Logic in Computer Science, Lisbon, Jan. (1996), pages 174-193.
8. Joakim Eriksson, Niclas Finne, and Sverker Janson. Information and interaction in MarketSpace - towards an open agent-based market infrastructure. In Second USENIX Workshop on Electronic Commerce, USENIX (1996).
9. Joakim Eriksson, Fredrik Espinoza, Niclas Finne, Fredrik Holmgren, Sverker Janson, Niclas Kaltea, Olle Olsson. An Internet software platform based on SICStus Prolog. (Unpublished). Available as http://www.sics.se/~joakime/papers/platform-www/platform-www.html.
10. Tim Finin, Yannis Labrou, and James Mayfield. KQML as an Agent Communication Language. In ed. Jeffrey M. Bradshaw, *Software Agents*, AAAI Press/MIT Press (1997). Pages 291 - 316.
11. Michael R. Gensereth. An Agent-Based Framework for Interoperability. in ed. Jeffrey M. Bradshaw, *Software Agents*. AAAI Press/MIT Press. ISBN 0-262-52234-9. Pages 317- 345.
12. Barbara Grosz and Sarit Kraus. Collaborative Plans for Group Activities. in Proceedings of the 13th International Joint Conference on Artificial Intelligence (IJCAI), Charberry, France. Morgan Kaufmann (1993).
13. Kristina Höök, Åsa Rudström, and Annika Waern. Edited Adaptive Hypermedia: Combining Human and Machine Intelligence to Achieve Filtered Information. presented at the Flexible Hypertext Workshop at the Eighth ACM International Hypertext Conference Hypertext'97 (1997).
14. T. Kühme, H. Dietrich, U. Malinowski, and M. Schneider-Hufschmidt. Approaches to Adaptivity in User Interface Technology: Survey and Taxonomy, in *Proceedings of the IFIP*

TC2/WG2.7 working conference on Engineering for Human-Computer Interaction. Elsevier, North-Holland (1992).

15. Yannis Labrou, and Tim Finin. A Semantics Approach for KQML - A generic purpose communication language for software agents. in proc. of the third international conference on information and knowledge management, eds N.R. Adam, B. K. Bhargava and Y. Yesha, pages 447-455. New York, Association of Computing Machinery (1994).

16. H.J. Levesque, P.R. Cohen, and J. Nunes. On Acting Together. In Proceedings of AAAI-90, San Mateo, California. Morgan Kaufmann Publishers Inc (1990).

17. Lars Rasmusson, Andreas Rasmusson, and Sverker Janson. Using agents to secure the Internet marketplace - Reactive Security and Social Control. In Proceedings of PAAM'97, London, UK (1997).

18. Tuomas W. Sandholm. An Implementation of the Contract Net Protocol Based on Marginal Cost Calculations. in *Proceedings of AAAI-93*, Washington D.C. (1993), pages 256-262.

19. Tuomas W. Sandholm and Victor R. Lesser. Advantages of a Leveled Commitment Contracting Protocol. in Proceedings of AAAI-96, Portland, Oregon (1996), pages 126-133.

20. Yoav Shoham. Agent-Oriented Programming. Artificial Intelligence 60 (1993). Pages 51-92.

21. Yoav Shoham. An Overview of Agent-Oriented Programming. In ed. Jeffrey M. Bradshaw, *Software Agents*. AAAI Press/MIT Press (1997). Pages 271 - 290.

22. Reid G. Smith. The Contract Net Protocol: High-Level Communication and Control in a Distributed Problem Solver. IEEE Transactions on Computers, vol C-29 No 12 (1980).

23. Annika Waern. Recognising Human Plans: Issues for Plan Recognition in Human-Computer Interaction. Ph.D. thesis, Dept. of Computer and Systems Sciences, Royal Institute of Technology, Stockholm, Sweden (1996).

24. Adam Walker and Michael Wooldridge. Understanding the Emergence of Conventions in Multi-Agent Systems. in Proceedings of ICMAS-95 (1995).

25. Egon Verharen, Frank Dignum, Sander Bros. Implementation of a Cooperative Agent Architecture based on the Language-Action Perspective. In proceedings of the fourht International Workshop on Agent Theories, Architectures, and Languages ATAL'97 (1997).

An Awareness-Based Model for Agents Involved in Reporting Activities[1]

Bernard Moulin

Computer Science Department and Research Center in Geomatics
Laval University, Pouliot Building, Ste Foy (QC) G1K 7P4, Canada
Phone: (418) 656-5580, E-mail: moulin@ift.ulaval.ca

Abstract. As software agents are developed to achieve tasks more autonomously, they will need to provide their users with reports about their activities. In the LASOREP Project we aim to develop reporter agents capable of reporting on the activities of other agents. In this paper we present an agent model that differentiates between three components: a temporal model that simulates an agent's experience of passing time; the memory model that records the explicit mental attitudes of which the agent is aware; and the attentional model containing the knowledge structures that the agent can manipulate for its reasoning and planning activities. This agent model is the basis on which the LASOREP system is to be built.

1 Introduction

During the past five years many software agents have been developed to assist users in various activities such as information retrieval, decision support and electronic commerce (Nwana 1996). Whereas software agents will become more autonomous and complex in the years to come, end-users will still want to make important decisions and to be informed about the activities of their agents. Hence, agents will have to report on their activities in a way that their users will find natural. Considering the current trend to build conversational interfaces[2] (Microsoft 1996), we think that reports will take the form of narratives in which situations are described, agents' mental attitudes are mentioned when needed and interactions between agents are reported in the form of dialogs. In the LASOREP[3] Project, we aim at developing a software infrastructure that will enable software agents to generate reports about their activities. As in a typical multi-agent system, the agents of the LASOREP System interact with each other and with their users in order to carry out their activities. In addition, they

---

[1] This research is sponsored by the Natural Sciences and Engineering Council of Canada and FCAR.

[2] "A conversational interfaces attempts to leverage natural aspects of human dialogue and social interaction, and makes user interfaces more appealing and approachable for a wider variety of users" (Microsoft 1996, Overview).

[3] LASOREP stands for Laval SOftware REPorter

send information about their activities and interactions to a *Reporter Agent* that structures this information in order to generate a conceptual model of the report. The conceptual model of a report is built as a structure in which the context of utterance of the agents' speech acts appears explicitly in the form of a narrator's perspective and locutors' perspectives. These perspectives and temporal localizations correspond to various time coordinate systems that are needed to temporally structure a discourse (Moulin 1997a). In order to create the conceptual model of a report, the Reporter Agent chooses a strategy for creating the report structure, then filters and organizes the information obtained from the agents and aggregates the relevant information in the report structure. The conceptual model of a report is then sent to a natural language generator that produces the corresponding text.

In this paper, we will not comment upon the LASOREP architecture any further in order to focus on the characteristics of the agent's model needed to create the knowledge structures that are sent to the reporter agent. Here are some requirements for such a model. Because an agent must be able to reason about its behaviour over time, it is convenient to use branching time logic as it is done in BDI, "Belief Desire Intention" approaches (Rao et al. 1991). Such a logic provides information about the agent's internal time (processing time). In addition, we need to use another kind of temporal information which corresponds to the calendric time (dates, hours, etc.) which is the only time of interest for a user. The agent must be able to reason about situations describing the application environment and to manipulate spatial and temporal topological information that are significant to the user. The agent must be able to manipulate structures corresponding to its mental attitudes and to the attitudes it associates with other agents. However, we cannot suppose that the agent is omniscient (as assumed in BDI frameworks) and we need an operational semantics for manipulating mental attitudes. Finally, our agents must be able to reason about their interactions and to keep a trace of their conversations: interactions will be modeled as exchanges of conversational objects: agent's positionings relative to mental attitudes (Moulin et al. 1994).

On the basis of these requirements we propose a logical framework that differentiates three components in an agent's mental model: a temporal model which simulates an agent's experience of passing time (Section 2); the agent's memory model which records the explicit mental attitudes of which the agent is aware (Section 3) and the attentional model containing the knowledge structures that the agent manipulates in its current situation (Section 4).

2 An Awareness-Based Memory Model

Several different formalisms have been proposed to model and reason about mental attitudes[4] (Cohen and Levesque 1990) among which the BDI approach (Rao and Geor-

---

[4] In AI literature it is usual to call "mental states" elements such as beliefs, goals and intentions. However, we will use the term "mental attitudes" to categorize those elements. We will say that mental attitudes characterize an agent's mental model. An agent's mental

geff 1991, Haddadi 1995) is widely used to formalize agents' knowledge in multi-agent systems. Although most of these formalisms are based on a possible-worlds approach (Kripke 1963), such an approach has the drawback of exposing agents to the problem of logical omniscience. This ideal framework is impractical when dealing with discourses that reflect human behaviors, simply because people are not logically omniscient (Moore 1995). In addition, it is difficult to imagine a computer program that will practically and efficiently manipulate sets of possible worlds and accessibility relations. As a consequence, most of the practical implementations of BDI agents are only weakly related to the underlying logic (Wooldridge, Jennings 1994).

In order to overcome this theoretical problem, Fagin et al. (1995) proposed to explicitly model an agent's knowledge by augmenting the possible-worlds approach with a syntactic notion of awareness, considering that an agent must be aware of a concept before being able to have beliefs about it. They introduced a modal operator AWR_x (φ) interpreted as "agent x is aware of φ", and used it to differentiate an agent x's implicit beliefs about φ, BEL_x (φ), and its explicit beliefs $X\text{-}BEL_x$ (φ) such that: $X\text{-}BEL_x$ (φ) $<=> AWR_x$ (φ) $\land BEL_x$ (φ). Fagin et al. (1995) indicate: "Despite the syntactic nature of the awareness operator, explicit knowledge retains many of the same properties as implicit knowledge, once we relativize to awareness"[5].

In a more radical approach, Moore suggested partitioning the agent's memory into different spaces, each corresponding to one kind of propositional attitude (one space for beliefs, another for desires, another for fears, etc.), "these spaces being functionally differentiated by the processes that operate on them and connect them to the agent's sensors and effectors" (Moore 1995).

Our approach tries to reconcile these various positions, providing a practical framework composed of three layers: the agent's *inner time model* which simulates its experience of passing time; the agent's *memory model* which records the explicit mental attitudes of which the agent is aware and the *attentional model* containing the knowledge structures that the agent manipulates in its current situation.

In order to formalize the *agent's inner time model*, we use a first-order, branching time logic, largely inspired by the logical language proposed in (Haddadi 1995) and (Rao, Georgeff 1991), which is a first-order variant of CTL*, Emerson's *Computational Tree Logic* (1990), extended to a possible-worlds framework (Kripke 1963). In such a logic, formulae are evaluated in worlds modeled as *time-trees* having a single past and a branching future. A particular time index in a particular world is called a *world-position*. The agent's actions transform one world position into another. A *primitive action* is an action that is performable by the agent and uniquely determines the world

---

model evolves through time and we call an agent's mental state the current state of its mental model: For us, an agent's mental state is composed of several mental attitudes.

[5] The agent's implicit beliefs still agree with the possible-worlds approach and hence the distribution axiom is valid for them. However, the problem of omniscience is overcome for explicit beliefs since an agent must be aware of ψ before explicitly believing it to be a logical consequence of its explicit belief about φ and ($\varphi => \psi$):

$(X\text{-}BEL_x$ (φ) $\land X\text{-}BEL_x$ ($\varphi => \psi$) $\land AWR_x$ (ψ)) $=> X\text{-}BEL_x$ (ψ)).

position in the time tree[6]. CTL* provides all the necessary operators of a temporal logic. Following Haddadi (1995), we specify actions that can be performed by the agent, plans that are available to it and define several operators that apply to them. It is quite natural to model the agent's internal time using the possible-worlds approach because the future is naturally thought of as a branching structure and because the actions performed by the agent move its position within this branching structure. Our approach differs from the BDI framework in that we consider any inference drawn by the agent to be an elementary action in the same sense as communicative and non-communicative actions[7]: those inferences correspond to the manipulation of the agent's mental attitudes. Hence, the agent's successive world positions correspond to the evolution of the agent's internal mental state through time as a result of its actions (reasoning, communicative and non-communicative acts). The agent does not need to be aware of all the possible futures reachable from a given world position. This is a simple way of modeling the limited knowledge of future courses of events that characterizes people. An agent's successive world positions specify a temporal path that implements the agent's experience of passing time. This characterizes its "inner time". This inner time must be distinguished from what we call the "calendric time" which corresponds to the official external measures of time available to agents and users (dates, hours, etc.). An agent's world position can be thought of as a unique identifier of the agent's current mental state".

3 The Agent's Memory Model

The agent's mental attitudes are recorded in what we call the agent's *memory model*. Following Fagin and his colleagues (1995), we consider that the definition of the various mental attitudes in terms of accessibility relations between possible worlds corresponds to the characterization of an implicit knowledge that cannot be reached directly by the agent. An agent's implicit view of knowledge is represented in a way similar to the formalization of mental attitudes (belief, goals and intentions) using the possible-worlds BDI approach. Hence, the corresponding formal results on mental attitudes are retained relative to implicit knowledge.

---

[6] Non-primitive actions map to non-adjacent world positions. The branches of a time tree can be viewed as representing the choices available to the agent at each moment in time. As in CTL*, we can distinguish *state-formulae* (evaluated at a specified time index in a time tree) and path-formulae (evaluated over a specified path in a time tree).

[7] It is curious that specialists developing BDI frameworks have not thought about considering inferences as actions. In their frameworks we find axioms and inference applying to the various modalities (beliefs, goals, etc.), but using these inference does not appear as actions in their temporal framework. Hence, they should assume that any possible inference is always drawn at once, without the agent being aware of the inference mechanism. This is not plausible, either cognitively (reasoning requires time and energy for human beings), or computationally (a program must go through processing steps when drawing inferences). See also (Duc 1995).

At each world position the agent can only use the instances of mental attitudes it is aware of. Following Moore's proposal of partitioning the agent's memory into different spaces, the awareness dimension is captured by projecting an agent's current world-position onto so-called *knowledge domains*. The projection of agent Ag's world-position w_{t0} on the knowledge domain *Attitude-D* defines at time index $t0$ in world w the agent's range of awareness relative to domain *Attitude-D*. This is the subset of predicates contained in knowledge domain *Attitude-D* which describe the particular instances of attitudes the agent is aware of at world-position w_{t0} . The knowledge domains that we consider in this paper are the belief domain *Belief-D*, and the goal domain *Goal-D*. But an agent can also use other knowledge domains such as the emotion domain *Emotion-D* that can be partitioned into sub-domains such as *Fear-D*, *Hope-D* and *Regret-D*.

In addition to knowledge domains which represent an agent's explicit recognition of mental attitudes, we use domains to represent an agent's explicit recognition of relevant elements in its environment, namely the situational domain *Situational-D*, the propositional domain *Propositional-D*, the calendric domain[8] *Calendric-D* and the spatial domain *Spatial-D*. The *situational domain* contains the identifiers characterizing the descriptions of any relevant environmental situation that an agent can explicitly recognize in the environment. Environmental situation descriptions are categorized into *States*, *Processes*, *Events*, and other sub-categories which are relevant for processing temporal information in discourse (Moulin 1997a). These sub-categories characterize the way an agent perceives situations. A *situation description* is specified by three elements: a *propositional description* found in the propositional domain *Propositional-D*; *temporal information* found in the calendric domain *Calendric-D* and *spatial information* found in the spatial domain *Spatial-D*. Hence, for each situation description there is a corresponding proposition in *Propositional-D*, a temporal interval in *Calendric-D* and a spatial location in *Spatial-D*. Propositions are expressed in a predicative form which is equivalent to conceptual graphs (Sowa 1984). The elements contained in the calendric domain are time intervals which agree with a temporal topology such as (Allen 1983). The elements contained in the spatial domain are points, segments or areas whose properties conform to a spatial topology.

It is important to note that the agent's memory model only contains descriptions of situations that refer either to environmental situations or to mental attitudes. Hence, we only need to develop a logic that enables the agent to reason about the situation descriptions it is aware of. This is a consequence of using a syntactic approach for modeling the agent awareness capabilities. We use a unique awareness modal operator to reason about descriptions instead of using different operators to reason about each type of mental attitude, as it is currently done in BDI-approaches (see Appendix 2).

We will use the scenario displayed in Table 1 to illustrate the characteristics of our model while describing Pebot's mental model.

---

[8] Time are world identifiers and are not meaningful on their own: they characterize the agent's inner time. Dates (a date is a temporal identifier concatenating information about calendric date and time) are meaningful to agents and users. That's the reason why we provide a correspondance between time and dates.

October 20 1997, Quebec city. Pebot is Peter's personal software agent and Janebot is Jane's agent. Peter wants to show some slides to his family but he does not have a slide projector. He asks Pebot to find one. Pebot finds out that Jane possesses a slide projector. It sends a request to Janebot: "Can Jane lend her slide projector to Peter?" After few minutes, Janebot answers: "Sure! Peter can come and pick it up". Petebot replies: "Thanks! Peter will come tomorrow". Janebot answers: "I shall reserve the projector for him"

Table 1: A sample scenario

Figure 1 illustrates how worlds and domains are used to model agent Pebot's mental attitudes after it creates the goal that "Jane lends a slide projector to Peter". Worlds are represented by rectangles. These contain circles representing time indices and related to one another by segments representing possible time paths. Ovals represent knowledge domains. Curved links represent relations between world positions and elements of domains (such as spatial-D, Calendric-D, Peter's Belief-D, etc.) or relations between elements of different domains (such as Situational-D and spatial-D, Calendric-D or Propositional-D). After having discovered that Jane possesses a slide projector, we can assume that Pebot is in a world-position represented by the left rectangle in Figure 1, at time index $t1$ in world $W1$. This world position is associated with a spatial localization $Peter's.home$ in the domain Spatial-D and a date $d1$ in the domain Calendric-D, d1 being contained in the time interval named October 20 1997.

In Figure 1 we find domains representing explicit beliefs and goals: Pebot's belief-D and Pebot's goal-D. Time index $t1$ (in World W1) is related to beliefs $P.b1$ and $P.b2$ in Pebot's Belief-D. $P.b1$ is related to situation description $s1$ in Situational-D which is in turn related to proposition $p29$, to location $Peter's.home$ in Spatial-D and to a time interval $[-, Now]$ in Calendric-D. Now is a variable which takes the value of the date associated with the current time index. Proposition $p29$ is expressed as a conceptual graph represented in a compact linear form:

Possess (AGNT- PERSON:Peter; OBJ- SLIDE-PROJECTOR: *)

Belief $P.b2$ is related to situation description $s3$ which is related to proposition $p31$ (expressed as Possess (AGNT- PERSON:Jane; OBJ- SLIDE-PROJECTOR: *)), to location $Peter's.home$ and to a time interval $[-, Now]$ in Calendric-D. Notice that in Calendric-D we symbolize the temporal topological properties using a time axis: only the dates $d1$ and $d2$ associated with time $t1$ and $t2$ have been represented as included in the time interval named $Oct. 20 1997$. Pebot wants to use a slide projector: this is represented by the link between time index $t1$ and the goal $P.g1$ in Peter's Goal-D. $P.g1$ is related to situation description $s4$ in Situational-D which is in turn related to proposition $p30$ (expressed as a conceptual graph: Use (AGNT- PERSON:Peter; OBJ- SLIDE-PROJECTOR:*)) in Propositional-D.

In world $W1$, agent Pebot can choose to move from time index $t1$ to various other time indices shown by different circles in the world rectangle in Figure 1. Moving from one time index to another is the result of performing an elementary action. Pebot's reasoning module chooses the goal that Jane lends a slide projector to Peter. The corresponding elementary action is the creation of a goal *P.g2* with the status *active*[9]. In Figure 1 this is represented by the large arrow linking the rectangles of worlds *W1* and *W2* on which appears the specification of the elementary operation *Creates (Pebot, P.g2, active)*. When this elementary operation is performed, Pebot moves into a new world *W2* at time index *t2* associated with the spatial localization *Peter's.home* and date *d2*. Time index *t2* is still related to beliefs *P.b1* and *P.b2* in Belief-D, but also to goals *P.g1* and *P.g2* in Pebot's Goal-D.

In an agent Ag1's mental model certain domains may represent mental attitudes of another agent Ag2: They represent the mental attitudes that Ag1 attributes to Ag2. As an example, Goal *P.g2* in Pebot's Goal-D is related to Goal *jg6* in Jane's Goal-D which is contained in Pebot's mental model. Goal *jg6* is associated with situation description *s2* which is itself related to proposition *p32* expressed as: Lend (AGNT-PERSON:Jane; RCPT- PERSON: Peter; OBJ- SLIDE-PROJECTOR: *)).

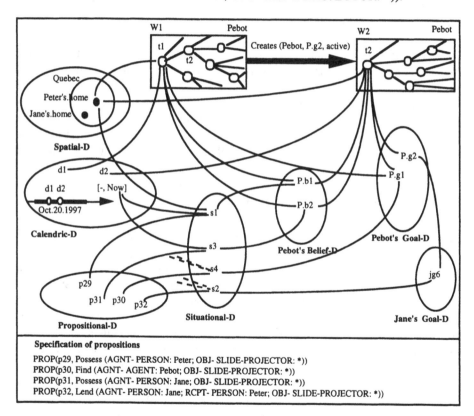

Figure 1: Worlds and Domains

---

[9] We use the same domain Goal-D in order to represent an agent's desires and intentions. We associate a status with the specification of a goal structure (goal, status). A desire corresponds to the couple (goal, desired); an intention corresponds to (goal, active). When an intention is fulfilled we have the couple (goal, success); otherwise, we have the couple (goal, failure). See Appendix 2.

Beliefs and goals are respectively expressed using the following predicates which hold for an agent Ag, a world w and a time index t:

Ag, w, t $\models$ BEL$_{bi}$ (Ag, SIT$_{st}$ (p$_h$, [d$_{h1}$, d$_{h2}$], l$_h$), belief-status)

Ag, w, t $\models$ GOAL$_{gi}$ (Ag, SIT$_{st}$ (p$_h$, [d$_{h1}$, d$_{h2}$], l$_h$), goal-status)

where b$_i$ is the belief's identifier in Belief-D, g$_i$ is the goal's identifier in Goal-D, Ag is the agent's name, SIT characterizes the situation's type, st is the situation description's identifier in Situational-D, p$_h$ and l$_h$ are respectively the identifiers of the proposition and the localization and [d$_{h1}$, d$_{h2}$] is a time associated with st. belief-status and goal-status represent the statuses characterizing these mental attitudes.

For example, Pebot's beliefs and goals at time index t2 are specified by:

Pebot, W2, t2 $\models$ BEL$_{P.b1}$(Pebot, STATE$_{s1}$(NOT p29, [-, Now], Peter's.home), active)

Pebot, W2, t2 $\models$ BEL$_{P.b2}$(Pebot , STATE$_{s3}$(p31, [-, Now], -), active)

Pebot, W2, t2 $\models$ GOAL$_{P.g1}$(Pebot, PROCESS$_{s4}$(p30, -, Quebec), active)

Pebot, W2, t2 $\models$ GOAL$_{P.g2}$(Pebot, GOAL$_{jg6}$(Jane,

PROCESS$_{s2}$(p32, -, Quebec), active), active)

This was a brief outline of the information that composes an agent's memory model. The current state of an agent's mental model is identified by a world position and gathers different elements contained in various knowledge domains associated with the corresponding world position. Formally, these associations are modeled as functions from the set of time indices of a given world to the various sets that contain the agent's explicit knowledge about situations, propositions, dates, spatial locations as well as about its beliefs, its goals and the beliefs and goals of other agents (Appendix 2).

4. The agent's attentional model

The agent's memory model gathers the elements composing the agent's successive mental states. The amount of information contained in the agent's memory model may increase considerably over time, resulting in efficiency problems. This is similar to what is observed with human beings. They record "on the fly" lots of visual, auditive and tactile information which are interpreted in terms of facts, opinions, ideas, etc. However, people usually do not consciously remember this detailed information over long periods of time. They remember information they pay attention to. Similarly in our framework, the agent's attentional model gathers knowledge structures extracted from the agent's memory model because of their importance or relevance to the agent's current activities. The attentional model is composed of a set of knowledge bases that structure the agent's knowledge and enable it to perform the appropriate reasoning, communicative and non-communicative actions. Among those knowledge bases, we consider the Belief-Space, Decision-Space, Conversational-Space and Action-Space. All the examples of this section are taken from Appendix 1 where we present the portions of those spaces for Pebot relative to the scenario of Table 1.

The **Belief-Space** contains a set of beliefs extracted from the memory model and a set of rules[10] enabling the agent to reason about those beliefs. Each belief is marked by the world position at which the agent was located when it acquired or inferred that belief. For instance, we find in Pebot's Belief Space (see Appendix 1) the belief denoted:

P.b1 $/=$ STATE$_{s1}$(NOT p29, [-, Now], Peter's.home)   pwt$_1$-active-

which means that starting at world position pwt_1, Pebot believes that situation description s1 expressed by proposition $p29$ does not hold. A simplified notation for:

Pebot, W1, t1 $|=$ BEL$_{P.b1}$(Pebot, STATE$_{s1}$(NOT p29, [-, Now], Peter's.home), active)

As another example, after Janebot says "Peter can come and pick it up", Pebot reaches the world position pwt_{10} where it infers that Jane adopted the goal to lend Peter a slide projector. That corresponds to belief *P.b4* which is a simplified notation for:

Pebot, W10, t10 $|=$ BEL$_{P.b4}$(Pebot,

GOAL$_{jg7}$(Jane, PROCESS$_{s2}$(p32, -, -), active), active)

The rules contained in the Belief-Space enable the agent to infer new beliefs. In this case, the new beliefs are added in the Belief-Space and the relevant domains are updated in the agent's memory model.

The **Decision-Space** contains a set of goals extracted from the memory model and a set of rules enabling the agent to reason about those goals. Each goal is marked by the world position at which the agent was located when it acquired or inferred that goal. For instance, we find in Pebot's Decision Space (see Appendix 1) the goal denoted:

P.g1 $/=$ PROCESS$_{s4}$(p30, -, -)   pwt$_1$-active-

which means that starting at world position pwt_1, Pebot has an active goal expressed by proposition $p30$. This is a simplified notation for:

Pebot, W1, t1 $|=$ GOAL$_{P.g1}$(Pebot, PROCESS$_{s4}$(p30, -, Quebec), active)

An agent can have a goal which refers to another agent's goal as for example Pebot's goal *P.g2* (in Appendix 1) which is a simplified notation for:

Pebot, W3, t3 $|=$ GOAL$_{P.g2}$(Pebot,

GOAL$_{jg6}$(Jane, PROCESS$_{s2}$(p32, -, Quebec), active), active)

which says that Pebot has an active goal *P.g2* that Jane adopts *jg6* as an active goal.

In the decision space there are different rules which are used to reason about goals: activation of a goal and its sub-goals; propagation of success and failure from sub-goals to higher goals; consequences of the success or failure of a goal. We do not discuss them in this paper, but see (Moulin, Brassard 1996).

Whereas the possible-world approach enables logicians to manipulate propositions and implicit mental attitudes in terms of absolute truth values, we do not suppose that our agents are aware of the absolute truth values of the descriptions of situations or of mental attitudes. Instead, we consider that an agent is aware of the status of a mental attitude between two world positions. In the agent's attentional model each mental attitude is associated with a status and the world position that held when the agent

---

[10] Usually those rules have been given to the agent by its creator or learned through experience. We do not discuss in this paper how an agent can acquire (learn) its reasoning capabilities (belief rules, decision rules, etc.), its planning capabilities (plans of actions, etc.) and its communicative capabilities (conversational schemas).

became aware of that status for this mental attitude. For a belief, the status *active* corresponds to the agent's awareness of this belief. If an agent does not consider a belief to hold anymore, this is indicated by a second world position and the status *inactive*. At different world positions goals can also take different statuses such as "active", "abandoned", "success", "failure". For instance, in Pebot's decision space, we have:

P.g3 /= PROCESS_{g5}(p33, d5, Peter's.home) pwt_4-active- pwt_9-success-

which means that goal *P.g3* became active at world position pwt_4 and was successfully achieved at pwt_9.

Considering the agent's current world position, it is easy to determine which mental attitudes have a given status: active beliefs, active goals (equivalent to intentions in BDI approach's terminology), goals successfully achieved or failed, etc. Hence, the attentional model gathers the history of the evolution of an agent's mental attitudes in an efficient way.

The **conversational space** models agents' interactions as conversations. A conversation is thought of as a negotiation game in which agents propose certain mental attitudes (such as belief, goal, emotion) and other agents react to those proposals, accepting or rejecting the proposed attitudes, asking for further information or justification, etc. We think of agents' interactions as exchanges of *conversational objects (COs)*. A CO is a mental attitude along with a positioning which an agent transfers to one or several agents during a given conversation (Moulin, Rousseau, Lapalme 1994). COs are organized into the Conversational-Space[11] that makes up a persistent memory of the conversation for the agent. COs may be related using temporal relations and/or rhetorical relations (such as CAUSE, PURPOSE, etc.). The agent positions itself relative to a mental attitude by performing actions like "proposing", "accepting", "rejecting". This is called the agent's positioning relative to that mental attitude. During a conversation, each participant agent develops its own Conversational Space which corresponds to its understanding of the semantic content of the interactions. A CO is expressed using the following syntax:

POSITIONING_{ci} (Agent1, Agent2, Mental-Attitude) wt_j

where POSITIONING denotes Agent1's positioning relative to Mental-Attitude which is conveyed to Agent2 at world position wt_j. Mental-Attitude can be any attitude that we have already mentioned (beliefs, goals, emotions, etc.). POSITIONING can be taken from a set of available actions: {PROPOSE, ACCEPT, REFUSE, INQUIRE, REPLACE, ABANDON}.

Let us comment upon some COs of our example (see Pebot's conversational space in Appendix 1) that provides a good sample of what can be modeled using our approach. CO c1 corresponds to Pebot's request: "Can Jane lend her slide projector to Peter?"

INQUIRES_{c1}(Pebot, Janebot,

BEL_{jg7}(Janebot, POSS PROCESS_{s2}(p32, -, -)), ?ST) pwt_5

The positioning INQUIRES is used by an agent in order to ask a question. Pebot's request can be categorized as a Yes/No question. Hence, the question applies to the

---

[11] In fact, COs and agents' positionings are registered in a specific Conversational Domain in the agent's memory model that we did not mentioned in Section 3 for brevety's sake.

status of the mental attitude BEL_{mg7}, which is marked by the parameter $?ST$ in the CO predicate[12]. With CO $c2$ Janebot answers Pebot's question and proposes to Pebot that she believes that situation description $s2$ holds. Then, with COs $c3$ and $c4$ Jane proposes to Pebot that Peter adopts goals $pg2$ and $pg3$. With CO $c5$ Pebot accepts those goals and with CO $c6$ Pebot expresses his feeling of gratitude. With CO $c7$ Pebot replaces goal $pg3$ by goal $P.g6$ which specifies the date of process $p34$. With CO $c8$ Janebot accepts goal $P.g6$.

The **Action-Space** records all the communicative, non-communicative and inference actions performed by the agent[13]. The agent changes its world position when it performs an action. At that time an instance of a situation description is recorded in the Situational-Domain (the agent being aware of that action at the corresponding world position) and the action is recorded in the Action-Space. As is the case for the Belief- and Decision Spaces, each action is associated with the world position at which the agent arrived when performing the action. The agent can perform several kinds of actions. We only comment upon some of them using our example.

A non-communicative action is denoted:

$DOES_{ai}$ (Ag, $PROCESS_{st}$ (p_h, [d_{h2}, d_{h1}], l_h)) pwt_n

where $PROCESS_{st}$ is the situation description of action ai.

A communicative action is performed by sending (or receiving) a CO to (or from) another agent and is denoted as in the following examples:

$SENDS_{a4}$(Pebot, TO- Janebot, CO: c1, d6, Peter's.home) pwt_5
$RECEIVES_{a5}$(Pebot, FROM- Janebot, CO: c2, d7, Peter's.home) pwt_6

A reasoning action is specified using the predicate INFERS as in the examples:

$INFERS_{a9}$(Pebot, FROM- CO: c2, BELIEF: P.b4, USING- SCH100) pwt_{10}
$INFERS_{a10}$(Pebot, FROM- BELIEF: P.b4, GOAL: success(P.g2), RULE20)

There are various ways of inferring new information, either by using rules that are available in the Belief- Decision- or Action- Spaces or conversational schemas in the Conversational Space (hence the parameter USING-SCH and RULE in the preceding predicates). We will not discuss those rules in this paper, but see (Moulin, Brassard 1996) and (Moulin 1997b). Inference mechanisms are briefly presented in Appendix 2.

5   Conclusion

An agent's attentional model gathers in the Belief-, Decision-, Action- and Conversational- Spaces most of the knowledge necessary for the agent to reason, act and com-

---

[12] For other kinds of questions introduced by interrogative pronouns such as who, which, where and when, the parameter ? would be introduced in the referent of the proper concept in the proposition associated with the mental attitude in the same way as in Sowa's notation. For example, the sentence: John asks Jane: "Who phoned you?" is represented by

$INQUIRES_{c20}$(John, Jane, BEL_{mg20}(Jane, $PROCESS_{a2}$(p54, -, -), AGNT: ?who)

with   PROP(p54, Phone (AGNT- PERSON, RCPT-PERSON: Jane)

[13] The Action-Space also gathers the rules and plans that are available to the agent. For brevety's sake they are not discussed here, but see (Moulin Brassard 1996).

municate with other agents. The attentional model provides powerful structures to declaratively specify an agent's knowledge and behavior. In a LASOREP system those structures would be sent by the agents to the Reporter agent in order to inform it about what happened during their interactions. This model is currently used to formalize agents that assist users when they exchange administrative correspondance. This is a first step toward the creation of a LASOREP system.

References

Allen, J. F. (1983). Maintaining Knowledge about Temporal Intervals. Communications of the Association for Computing Machinery, vol 26 n11.

Cohen P. R., Levesque H. J. (1990), Rational Interaction as the Basis for Communication, in (Cohen et al. 1990), 221-255.

Cohen P.R., Morgan J., Pollack M. E.(edts.) (1990), *Intentions in Communication*, MIT Press.

Duc N. H. (1995), Logical omniscience vs logical ignorance: on a dilemma of epistemic logic, in C. P. Pereira and N. Mamede (edts.), Proceedings of EPIAS'95, Springer Verlag LNAI 990, 237-248.

Emerson E. A. (1990), Temporal and modal logic, In van Leeuwen J. (edt.), *Handbook of Theoretical Computer Science*, North Holland.

Fagin R., Halpern J.Y., Moses Y. & Vardi M.Y., *Reasoning about Knowledge*, The MIT Press1996.

Haddadi A. (1995), *Communication and Cooperation in Agent Systems*, Springer Verlag Lecture Notes in AI n. 1056.

Kripke S. (1963), Semantical considerations on modal logic, *Acta Philosophica Fennica*, vol 16, 83-89.

Microsoft (1996), ActiveX™ Technology for Interactive Software Agents, http://www.microsoft.com/intdev/agent/.

Moore R.C. (1995), *Logic and Representation*, CSLI Lecture Notes, n. 39.

Moulin B. (1997a), Temporal contexts for discourse representation: an extension of the conceptual graph approach, *Journal of Applied Intelligence*, vol 7 n3, 227-255.

Moulin B. (1997b), The social dimension of interactions in multi-agent systems, Proceedings of the Australian Workshop on Distributed Artificial Intelligence DAI'97, D. Lukose, Zhang C. (edts.), to appear in Springer Verlag LNAI in 1998.

Moulin B., Brassard M. (1996), A scenario-based design method and environment for developing multi-agent systems, in D. Lukose, C. Zhang (edts.), First Australian Workshop on DAI, Springer Verlag LNAI 1087, 216 - 231.

Moulin B., Rousseau D., Lapalme G. (1994), A Multi-Agent Approach for Modelling Conversations, Proceedings of the International Conference on Artificial Intelligence and Natural Language, Paris, 35-50.

Nwana S. H. (1996), Software agents: an overview, *Knowledge Engineering Review*, vol.11, n.3, 1-40.

Pollack M. E. (1990), Plans as complex mental attitudes, in (Cohen 1990), 77-103.

Rao A.S., Georgeff M. P. (1991), Modeling rational agents within a BDI architecture, In proceedings of KR'91 Conference, Cambridge, Mass, 473-484.

Sowa J. F. (1984). Conceptual Structures. Addison Wesley.

Wooldridge M.J., Jennings N.R. (1994), Agent theories, architectures and languages, in Pre-proceedings of the 1994 Workshop on Agent Theories, Architectures and Languages, ECAI-94, 1-32.

Appendix 1

Here are presented portions of the Belief-, Decision-, Action- and Conversational-spaces of agent Pebot. We provide a list of propositions used in the different mental attitudes and conversational objects.

Pebot's Belief Space

P.b1 /= $STATE_{s1}$(NOT p29, [-, Now], Peter's.home) $\quad$ pwt_1 -active-

P.b2 /= $STATE_{s3}$(p31, [-, Now], -) $\quad$ pwt_2 -active-

P.b3 /= BEL_{jb1}(Jane, POSS $PROCESS_{s2}$(p32, -, -),) $\quad$ pwt_6 -active-

P.b4 /= $GOAL_{jg7}$(Jane, $PROCESS_{s2}$(p32, -, -), active) $\quad$ pwt_{10} -active-

P.b5 /= $FEEL_{f1}$(Pebot, Janebot, p36) $\quad$ pwt_{15} -active-

P.b6 /= BEL_{jb2}(Jane,
$\quad$ $GOAL_{g7}$(Peter, $PROCESS_{s8}$(p34, Oct.21, Quebec), active)) $\quad$ pwt_{18} -active-

Pebot's Decision Space

P.g1 /= $PROCESS_{s4}$(p30, -, -) $\quad$ pwt_1-active- pwt_{18}-success-

P.g2 /=$GOAL_{jg6}$(Jane, $PROCESS_{s2}$(p32, -, -), active) $\quad$ pwt_3-active- pwt_{11}-success-

P.g3 /=$PROCESS_{s5}$(p33, d5, Peter's.home) $\quad$ pwt_4-active- pwt_9-success-

P.g4 /=$PROCESS_{s6}$(p34, -, Quebec) $\quad$ pwt_{12}-active- pwt_{16}-replaced-

P.g5 /= $\quad$ $PROCESS_{s7}$(p35, -, Jane's.home) $\quad$ pwt_{13}-active-

P.g6 /=$PROCESS_{s8}$(p34, Oct.21, Quebec) $\quad$ replace.Pg4-pwt_{17}-active-

Pebot's Action Space

$DOES_{a1}$(Pebot, $PROCESS_{s7}$(p37, d4, Peter's.home)) $\quad$ pwt_2

$CREATES_{a2}$(Pebot, - , GOAL: active(P.g2), USING- RULE315) $\quad$ pwt_3

$CREATES_{a3}$(Pebot, - , GOAL: active(P.g3), USING- RULE320) $\quad$ pwt_4

$SENDS_{a4}$(Pebot, TO- Janebot, CO: c1, d6, Peter's.home) $\quad$ pwt_5

$RECEIVES_{a5}$(Pebot, FROM- Janebot, CO: c2, d7, Peter's.home) $\quad$ pwt_6

$RECEIVES_{a6}$(Pebot, FROM- Janebot, CO: c3, d7, Peter's.home) $\quad$ pwt_7

$RECEIVES_{a7}$(Pebot, FROM- Janebot, CO: c4, d7, Peter's.home) $\quad$ pwt_8

$INFERS_{a8}$(Pebot, FROM- ACTION: a5, GOAL: success(P.g3), RULE10) $\quad$ pwt_9

$INFERS_{a9}$(Pebot, FROM- CO: c2, BELIEF: P.b4, USING- SCH100) $\quad$ pwt_{10}

$INFERS_{a10}$(Pebot, FROM- BELIEF: P.b4, GOAL: success(P.g2), RULE20) $\quad$ pwt_{11}

$CREATES_{a11}$(Pebot, FROM- CO: c3, GOAL: active(P.g4), RULE200) $\quad$ pwt_{12}

$CREATES_{a12}$(Pebot, FROM- CO: c4, GOAL: active(P.g5), RULE200) $\quad$ pwt_{13}

SENDS-$IMPLICIT_{a13}$(Pebot, TO- Janebot, CO: c5, d9, Peter's.home) $\quad$ pwt_{14}

$SENDS_{a14}$(Pebot, TO- Janebot, CO: c6, d9, Peter's.home) $\quad$ pwt_{15}

$SENDS_{a15}$(Pebot, TO- Janebot, CO: c7, d9, Peter's.home) $\quad$ pwt_{16}

$RECEIVES_{a16}$(Pebot, FROM- Janebot, CO: c8, d10, Peter's.home) $\quad$ pwt_{17}

$INFERS_{a17}$(Pebot, FROM- CO: c8, GOAL: success(P.g1), RULE245) $\quad$ pwt_{18}

Propositions

PROP(p29, Possess (AGNT- PERSON: Peter; OBJ- SLIDE-PROJECTOR: *))
PROP(p30, Find (AGNT- AGENT: Pebot; OBJ- SLIDE-PROJECTOR: *))
PROP(p31, Possess (AGNT- PERSON: Jane; OBJ- SLIDE-PROJECTOR: *))
PROP(p32, Lend (AGNT- PERSON: Jane; RCPT- PERSON: Peter;
$\qquad$ OBJ- SLIDE-PROJECTOR: *))
PROP(p33, Contact (AGNT- AGENT: Pebot; RCPT- AGENT: Janebot))
PROP(p34, Come (AGNT- PERSON: Peter; DEST- PLACE: Jane's.home))
PROP(p35, Pick (AGNT- PERSON: Peter; OBJ- SLIDE-PROJECTOR: *))
PROP(p36, Be-Thankful (AGNT- AGENT: Pebot; RCPT- AGENT: Janebot))
PROP(p37, Retrieve (AGNT- AGENT: Pebot; THM- PROP: p31))
PROP(p38, Possess (AGNT- PERSON: Jane; OBJ- SLIDE-PROJECTOR: *)))
PROP(p39, Is.Available (PTNT- SLIDE-PROJECTOR: *))

Conversational Space

INQUIRES_{c1}(Pebot, Janebot,

$\qquad$ BEL_{jg7}(Janebot, POSS PROCESS_{s2}(p32, -, -)), ?ST) $\qquad$ pwt_5

PROPOSES_{c2}(Janebot, Pebot, BEL_{jb1}(Janebot, PROCESS_{s2}(p32, -, -))) $\qquad$ pwt_6

PROPOSES_{c3}(Janebot, Pebot,

$\qquad$ GOAL_{pg2}(Peter, PROCESS_{s6}(p34, -, Quebec), active)) $\qquad$ pwt_7

PROPOSES_{c4}(Janebot, Pebot,

$\qquad$ GOAL_{pg3}(Peter, PROCESS_{s7}(p35, -, Quebec), active)) $\qquad$ pwt_8

ACCEPTS_{c5}(Pebot, Janebot, GOAL_{pg2} AND GOAL_{pg3}) $\qquad$ pwt_{14}

PROPOSES_{c6}(Pebot, Janebot, FEEL_{f1}(Pebot, Janebot, p36)) $\qquad$ pwt_{15}

REPLACES_{c7}(Pebot, Janebot, $\text{GOAL}_{p.g3}$ BY $\text{GOAL}_{P.g6}$) $\qquad$ pwt_{16}

ACCEPTS_{c8}(Janebot, Pebot, $\text{GOAL}_{P.g6}$) $\qquad$ pwt_{17}

Appendix 2

Here, we briefly sketch the semantic of our approach relevant to representing the explicit knowledge of which an agent is aware. The universe is modeled as a time tree which is constructed as an infinite set of time indices (called world positions) and a binary relation < (transitive and backwards linear), representing all possible courses of world history: t<t' iff the time index t can be transformed into time index t' by the occurrence of a primitive action that is possible in t. The world is populated by a set of agents U_{Ag}, a set of objects U_{Obj}, a set of spatial locations U_{Loc}, a set of dates U_{dates}. The set of all possible situation descriptions is $U_{Sit} = U_{Sitenv} \cup U_{Sitment}$ where U_{Sitenv} is the set of all possible descriptions of environmental situations and $U_{Sitment}$ is the set of all possible descriptions of mental situations. The set of all possible actions is U_{Ac}. The set of all possible plans is U_P. The *domain of quantification* U is : $U_{Ags} \cup U_{Obj} \cup U_{Loc} \cup U_{Dates} \cup U_{Sit} \cup U_{Ac} \cup U_P$

The ***memory model of an agent Ag*** is represented by a model[14] M_{Ag} :

---

[14] M_{Ag} is the model of the universe as it is seen by agent Ag. Each time index represents one of Ag's potential internal state. Each arc on the tree is associated with an action that

$M_{Ag} = \langle W, T, U, <, Act, Agt, P, POS, COS, STAT, Loc, Date, Mensit, K, C, \Phi \rangle$

where W is the set of worlds; T is the non-empty set of time indices; U is the domain of quantification; $<$ (such that $< \subseteq T \times T$) is a binary relation between adjacent time indices which is transitive and backwards linear; $Act : < \rightarrow U_{Ac}$ associates a primitive action to each arc in $<$; Agt: $U_{Ac} \rightarrow U_{Ags}$ gives the agent of each elementary action; P is the set of all possible plans of agent Ag; POS is the set of possible positionings; $COS = POS \times U_{Ags} \times U_{Ags} \times U_{Sitment}$ is the set of possible exchanges of conversational objects between two agents; $STAT$ is the set of possible statuses; Loc: $T \rightarrow U_{Loc}$ gives the localisation associated with each time index; $Date$: $T \rightarrow U_{Dates}$ gives the date associated with each time index; $Mensit$ is a set of functions $Mensit_{Agi}$: $W \times T \rightarrow Powerset (U_{Sitment})$, each function gives the set of descriptions of agent Agi's mental attitudes that agent Ag is aware of at each world position w,t; The content of a mental attitude description of type Mad = {Bel, Goal, Feel} can be either another mental attitude description or the description of an environmental situation: this corresponds to $Cont_{Mad}$: $Mensit \rightarrow U_{Sit}$; The status of a mental attitude description is specified by $Stat_{Mad}$: $Mensit \rightarrow STAT$; K is an awareness modal operator; C: Const $\rightarrow$ $Powerset(U)$ is an interpretation for constants; Φ: $Pred \times W \times T \rightarrow \underset{(n \in N)}{U} Powerset(U^n)$ is an interpretation for predicates at each world position.

Each **world w** of W , called a time tree, is a tuple:

$$\langle T_W, <_W, Act_W, E_W , Loc_W, Date_W, Mensit_W \rangle \quad \text{where:}$$

$T_W \subseteq T$ is a set of time indices in world w; $<_W$ is the same as $<$ restricted to time indices in T_W ; Act_W is the same as Act restricted to the relations between time indices in T_W ; E_W : $<_W \rightarrow$ { 's', 'f' } is an arc labelling function which, for each action, maps adjacent time to either 's' (success) or 'f' (failure). $Loc_W, Date_W, Mensit_W$ are restrictions of the functions Loc, $Date$ and $Mensit$ in world w.

Semantics of mental attitude descriptions (MADs)
Here are descriptions of beliefs and goals relative to environmental situations:

$M_{Ag}, w, t \models \quad BEL_{bx}(Ag , sit_{sy} , st) \quad$ if and only if

$bx \in Mensit_{Ag} (w,t)$ and $sy \in U_{Sitenv}$ and $Cont_{Bel} (bx) = sy$ and $Stat_{Bel} (bx) = st$

$M_{Ag}, w, t \models \quad GOAL_{gx}(Ag, sit_{sy} , st) \quad$ if and only if

$gx \in Mensit_{Ag} (w,t)$ and $sy \in U_{Sitenv}$ and $Cont_{Goal}(gx) = sy$ and $Stat_{Goal} (gx) = st$

Here are descriptions of mental attitude relative to other mental attitudes:

$M_{Ag}, w, t \models \quad MAD1_{mx}(Ag, MAD2_{my}(Agi, sit_{sz} , x\text{-}st), y\text{-}st) \quad$ iff

Agi $\in U_{Ags}$ and MAD1 $\in$ {Bel, Goal, Feel} and MAD2 $\in$ {Bel, Goal, Feel} and $mx \in Mensit_{Ag} (w,t)$ and $Cont_{Mad} (mx) = my$ and $Stat_{Mad} (mx) = x\text{-}st$ and $my \in Mensit_{Agi} (w,t)$ and $Cont_{Mad} (my) = sz$ and $Stat_{Mad} (my) = y\text{-}st$ and $sz \in U_{Sitenv}$

---

is performed by Ag or another agent: the arc relates two consecutive time that are Ag's internal time positions before and after it observes the performance of the action.

This definition can be generalized to any number of embedded MADs by replacing $situation_{sz}$ by $MADk_{mk}(Agk, \ldots MADp_{mp}(Agp, situation_{sz}, p\text{-st}), \ldots, k\text{-st})$.

Since MADs are descriptions of mental attitudes, we manipulate them as propositions using a propositional calculus (this is our basis logic *MAD-C*). We define here the semantics of other *MAD-C* formulae:

$M_{Ag}, w, t \models$ NOT $BEL_{bx}(Ag, sit_{sy}, active)$ iff $M_{Ag}, w, t \models BEL_{bx}(Ag, sit_{sy}, inactive)$

$M_{Ag}, w, t \models$ NOT $GOAL_{gx}(Ag, sit_{sy}, active)$ iff $M_{Ag}, w, t \models GOAL_{gx}(Ag, sit_{sy}, abandoned)$

$M_{Ag}, w, t \models$ NOT $GOAL_{gx}(Ag, sit_{sy}, success)$ iff $M_{Ag}, w, t \models GOAL_{gx}(Ag, sit_{sy}, failure)$

$M_{Ag}, w, t \models$ NOT $GOAL_{gx}(Ag, sit_{sy}, failure)$ iff $M_{Ag}, w, t \models GOAL_{gx}(Ag, sit_{sy}, success)$

$M_{Ag}, w, t \models \varphi$ OR ψ iff $M_{Ag}, w, t \models \varphi$ or $M_{Ag}, w, t \models \psi$

$M_{Ag}, w, t \models \varphi$ AND ψ iff $M_{Ag}, w, t \models \varphi$ and $M_{Ag}, w, t \models \psi$

$M_{Ag}, w, t \models \varphi \rightarrow \psi$ iff $M_{Ag}, w, t \models \psi$ or $M_{Ag}, w, t \mid \varphi$.

Reasoning with MADs

A reasoning engine (denoted *RE*) manipulates the agent's explicit knowledge using a modal operator K and a minimal logical framework inspired by Duc's Dynamic Epistemic Logic (1995).

• *Syntax of the language.*

The atomic formulae of our dynamic epistemic logic (DE) are of the form Kp, where p is a formula of *MAD-C*. The set of *DE*-formulae is the least set which contains all atomic formulae and is closed under the usual boolean connectives ($\land$, $\lor$, $\supset$) and the following conditions: if A is a *DE*-formula, then so is $\langle F \rangle A$. We use the symbols A, B as metavariables to denote *DE*-formulae. Let At denote the set of atomic *DE*-formulae.

The formula Kp is read: p is known or agent Ag is aware of p. $\langle F \rangle A$ means "A is true after some course of action" and $[F] A$ means "A is true after any course of action". In our framework, F represents the processing steps that agent Ag's reasoning engine must perform in order for formula A to appear in Ag's attentional model. Those processing steps make up the elementary action that makes Ag go from one internal state (world position w, t) to another. Remember that inferences are thought of as actions in a similar way as communicative and non-communicative actions.

• The logic *BDE* (*Basic Dynamic Logic*) has the following axiom schemata[15]:

A1. All classical tautologies of the language DE

A2. $[F] (A \supset B) \supset ([F]A \supset [F]B)$

A3. $[F]A \supset [F] [F]A$

A4. $Kp \land K (p \rightarrow q) \supset \langle F \rangle Kq$

A5. $Kp \supset [F] Kp$

A6. $\langle F \rangle Kp$, where p is a tautology of the language *MAD-C*

---

[15] We use the symbols $\land$, $\lor$, $\supset$ and to represent the usual boolean operators manipulated by the reasoning engine. These symbols must be distinguished from the boolean operators used in the *MAD-C* basis logic: AND, OR, $\rightarrow$.

The rules of inference are:

R1. Modus ponens: if A and $A \supset B$ are theorems, then B is a theorem.

R2. Necessitation: if A is a theorem, then so is $[F]A$.

A1, A2, A3, R1 and R2 axiomatize a minimal temporal logic of transitive time. A4 says that the reasoning engine is capable of using modus ponens. A5 says that the engine does not forget what it knows. A6 says that the engine is able to use the theorems of classical logic. The notions of a proof, a theorem, and a consistent formula or set of formulae are defined as usual, relative to the system BDE.

- Duc (1995) provides a list of provable formulae:

1. $Kp \wedge \langle F \rangle K (p \rightarrow q) \supset \langle F \rangle Kq$ 5. $K(p \text{ AND } q) \supset \langle F \rangle Kp \wedge \langle F \rangle Kq$
2. $Kp \supset \langle F \rangle K (p \rightarrow q)$ 6. $K(p \text{ AND } q) \supset \langle F \rangle (Kp \wedge Kq$
3. $Kp \wedge Kq \supset \langle F \rangle K(p \text{ AND } q)$ 7. $Kp \supset \langle F \rangle K(p \text{ OR } q)$
4. $Kp \wedge \langle F \rangle Kq \supset \langle F \rangle K(p \text{ AND } q)$ 8. $Kq \supset \langle F \rangle K(p \text{ OR } q)$

- Those formulae show that bringing about new knowledge in the agent's attentional model requires some effort: the processing steps symbolized by the $\langle F \rangle$ operator. In that way our agent is not logically omniscient nor logically ignorant.

Models for BDE

- For each world w of W we have a temporal frame $(T_w , <_w)$ on which we can define a valuation V_w which is a function from T_w to the set of subsets of At. The function V_w is defined on DE-formulae of the form Kp and is isomorph to the function $Mensit_w$ which specifies the content of the agent's memory model at the various of world w.

- A BDE-model consists of a temporal frame and a valuation function V_w satisfying the following conditions:
  - For all $s \in T_w$, if $Kp \in V_w(s)$ and $s < t$ then $Kp \in V_w(t)$
  - For all $s \in T_w$, if $Kp, K(p \rightarrow q) \in V_w (s)$
          then $Kq \in V_w(t)$ for some $t \in T_w$ with $s < t$
  - If p is a tautology of the language MAD-C, then for all $s \in T_w$, there is a $t \in T_w$ such that $s < t$ and $Kp \in V_w(t)$.

- For any temporal model MR associated with the reasoning engine RE, we can recursively define the relation "the formula A is true at state s in MR" for each $s \in T_w$ as follows:
  - $MR, w, s \models Kp$ iff $Kp \in V_w(s)$ for any atomic formula Kp
  - $MR, w, s \models \neg A$ iff $MR, w, s \mid A$
  - $MR, w, s \models A \supset B$ iff $MR, w, s \models B$ or $MR, s \mid A$
  - $MR, w, s \models \langle F \rangle A$ if there is some t such that $s < t$ and $M, w, t \models A$

- Duc (1995) showed that a BDE system is sound and complete.

$\mathcal{GISM}$
A Language for Modelling and Designing Agent-Based Intelligent Systems

Hongxue Wang and John Slaney

Automated Reasoning Project
Australian National University
Canberra, ACT 0200, AUSTRALIA

Abstract. In this paper we report $\mathcal{GISM}$[1], a constraint-based and object-oriented language for modelling and designing agent-based intelligent systems, including an introduction to the theory behind, the essence of the language, the control mechanisms for intelligent systems modelled in $\mathcal{GISM}$, and an application example. The language is quite general, declarative, high level, and naturally concurrent supported. It takes advantages of different programming paradigms and knowledge representation schemes.

1 Introduction

In recent years, the idea of an agent has been intensively used in AI both conceptually and technically. At conceptual level, agent has been successfully used to present traditional AI algorithms and techniques [7]. At technical level on the other hand, agent-based methodologies and techniques have made modelling and design of large scale very complex systems possible [5,6]. Why are agents so important and powerful in AI? We suggest an answer for it from our ontological investigation on generalities of intelligent systems. We outline some of our investigation results as follows.

[Goals of AI] Though for individual researchers their goals may vary and change over time, Artificial Intelligence as a discipline, has only two major goals to achieve: to understand intelligence and to construct useful intelligent systems [2].

Since intelligence can be generally explained as behaviours of intelligent systems, it is most important to understand what intelligent systems are.

[Intelligent System] An intelligent system is an integration of agents with models of their worlds in which they are situated, or will be situated, such that, every agent is able to act in some way; every agent can access necessary knowledge and/or information for it to act properly; at least some of the agents are aware of their own abilities, responsibilities and goals, and those of other agents, to ensure that, every

---

[1] Though $\mathcal{GISM}$ is often called $\mathcal{G}$eneral$\mathcal{ISM}$ or $\mathcal{GISM}$o, it stands actually for $\mathcal{G}$eneralised $\mathcal{I}$ntelligent $\mathcal{S}$ystem $\mathcal{M}$odeller.

agent in the system can not only play its own roles, but also cooperate with others if necessary, to achieve its goals.

The knowledge that an agent may use resides in two places: agents and world models. The Knowledge residing in the former is normally more generic, while the knowledge in the latter is more domain dependent or task oriented.

[**Agent**] An agent is anything that can purposely act either physically or mentally within a designated environment, on behalf of the designer, the owner or the user, which might be another agent.

By the above definition, agents can be many different things such as computers, robots, human operators, or even wind, if the God is the owner of it.

In an intelligent system, an agent may be as small as a micro chip, or as big as another intelligent system. In defining an intelligent system however, a given agent may only interest others in the following aspects: (1) What actions it can take. (2) Within what time frames it can act, so tasks can be scheduled for it. (3) How fast it can work on a specific task. (4) What conditions have to be satisfied before it can take any specific action. (5) What aspects of the environment will be affected by taking a specific action.

For an individual agent itself on the other hand, it should know: (1) What actions it has to take for being an agent in the system. (2) Within what time frames it should take and complete each required action. (3) Are all preconditions set for it satisfied?

[**Agent World**] For an agent in an intelligent system, the environment it will be situated in and act on, as well as other agents that it will cooperate with, is together called an agent world or world for simplicity.

[**Model of World**] A model of an agent world is a set of descriptions from which the agent can access necessary knowledge of its world in order to act properly.

Generally speaking, in order to make an agent to act, the following aspects of a world should be modelled for it: (1) *components* of the world. (2) *properties* of the world. (3) *actions* it can, should or has to take. (4) its *beliefs* in the world. The large portion of such knowledge is the relationships between components and properties. (5) *plans* for achieving its goals at a time. Such knowledge is usually in form of relationships between actions, such as in what order some actions should be taken. (6) *schedules* that set agent actions in specific timeframes. (7) its *responsibilities* in the system. Such knowledge usually tells the agent in what situation it should do what. (8) *goals* to be achieved. Although an intelligent system should have some kind of goals, not every agent in the system has to know or have its own goals. (9) *rules of cooperation and coordination* with others. As in a society, there should be some laws or principles, to ensure that all the agents can act in a harmonious mannar. (10) *tenses, modalities* of the above knowledge.

Our investigation shows that technically, all these aspects of agent worlds can be put into the following three categories: *Objects*, including components and properties of agent worlds; *Actions*, describing what an agent can do, what are required to do, and what have been scheduled to do; *Constraints*, depicting relationships between objects and actions. Knowledge such as beliefs, responsibilities, intentions and goals can all be formalised as some kind of constraints.

This analysis leads to the establishment of a generic knowledge representation scheme, called Constrained Object Hierarchies ($\mathcal{COH}$s), for modelling various agent worlds.

Definition($\mathcal{COH}$) *A constrained object hierarchy is a structure $< O, A, C >$ in which, O is a set of $o_1, o_2, \ldots, o_m$ where each o_i is either a constant object such as an integer and previously defined $\mathcal{COH}$, or a reference to such an object; A is a set of $a_1, a_2, \ldots, a_n$ where each a_i specifies an agent action which can be understood and taken by an agent; C is a set of $c_1, c_2, \ldots, c_q$ where each c_i is a constraint on objects and actions.*

By this definition, it should be clear that though some agent worlds could be modelled using data structures such as *record* in PASCAL, *struct* in C, and *class* in C++, $\mathcal{COH}$ itself can serve more naturally for the purpose of modelling agent worlds.

[Object Reference, Variable] For an agent in a world, mentally, every object has to be referred by a name, called object reference. Any agent action will be eventually on or through object references. Object references are often called variables traditionally.

With any object reference, three things are most essential for an agent to act properly: *domain, state* and *categories*.

[Domain of Object Reference] A domain is a multiset of objects which can be used to indicate what object can or can not be referred by an object reference.

A domain dx can be attached to an object variable x in three ways: x:dx, x-:dx and x+:dx. If a domain dx is attached to x as x:dx, only objects in dx are allowed to assign to x. In addition to that of x:dx, x-:dx requires the manipulation agent to remove the object from dx afterwards. Unlike x:dx and x-:dx, x+:dx indicates the manipulation agent to add the unified object to dx, regardless whether the object is in dx or not. Such mechanisms are essentially useful in resource-related agent actions.

[State of Object Reference] At any time, an object reference has to be in one of the following five states: (1) *not assigned and not assignable because domain is empty,* (2) *assignable but not assigned,* (3) *assigned but no consistency checking is carried out yet,* (4) *locally consistent,* (5) *the current assignment is the only choice unless backtracking.*

[Categories of Object Reference] In modelling an agent world, an object reference may belong to the following specific categories: (1) *feature object reference* is that which decides the properties of the world or problem, similar to the role of the coefficients playing in mathematical programming [11]. In a world, feature object references may vary in accordance with the task being carried out or the goal being achieved; (2) *passive object reference* is that to which an agent can never assign an object by just choosing one from attached domain; (3) *constant object reference* is that once it has been assigned a value, any further change to it will be prohibited; (4) *perceptive object reference* is an interface to other agents outside the current world. If an object reference is categorised as perceptive one , some agents inside the world may watch for changes to it, and react on such changes.

[**Classification of Agent Actions**] In a world model $\mathcal{COH}$, actions are further classified into *doable actions, Required actions* and *scheduled actions. Doable actions* define what agents can do within the world, that is, their abilities. *Required actions* indicate what agents are required to do for achieving a specific goal such as in a plan. *Scheduled actions* detail when, where and who should take a specific action.

[**Properties of Agent Actions**] In many situations, it is necessary to make assertions on agent actions. To do so, the following properties of agent actions need to be addressed: *States of actions*, such as whether it is started, ended and in-progress; *Scheduled timeframes* indicate scheduled starting time, ending time or duration; *Actual timeframes* record actual started time, actual ended time; *Repetition* tells how many times the action can be repeated; *Duplication* tells how many copies of the actions can be taken concurrently; *Resources required* tell what resources, in form of objects, are required for an agent to carry out this action; *Environments affected* tell that by carrying the action, what aspects of the world will be affected or changed; *Destination of produced object* tells where the objects produced by this action should be put, if the action is an object producer.

[**Kinds of Constraints**] Our research shows that there are three different kinds of constraints in terms of the roles they play in deciding agent behaviours. These three kinds of constraints are: (1) *Identity Constraints* describe agent beliefs in its world or the identities of the world. A unified logic framework, called $\mathcal{UniLog}$, has been developed to fully formalise different aspects of such beliefs [14]; (2) *Trigger Constraints* tell agents when some specific actions should be taken. A trigger constraint can be formalised as:
$$(F_1 \wedge F_2 \wedge \ldots \wedge F_n) \Rightarrow \{actions\};$$
Where F_i is a $\mathcal{UniLog}$ formula; (3) *Goal constraints* tell agents what should be achieved. In many situations, having a goal is important for an agent to act. A goal constraint can be a $\mathcal{UniLog}$ formula, or representation $minimise(expr)$ or $maximise(expr)$, where $expr$ is a numerical expression.

Based on the above discussion, a complete model of an intelligent system can be sketched as:

<descriptions of agents> + <models of agent worlds>

To make such a multi-agent intelligent system model work, there must be, at least, one super agent[2] which can understand the above definition in order to: (1) call all involved agents; (2) be sure that in every world an agent can be in charge if necessary.

---

[2] Such a super agent does not have to be one of the agents in the system. Humans, such as personnel officers in an organisation are usually such super agents.

In doing so, the corresponding intelligent system will be set up. Fig. 1 shows the topology of such a system, where a link $W_i \to W_j$ between world W_i and W_j represents that W_i is part of W_j, while a link $A \to W$ between agent A and world W denotes agent A is in charge of world W.

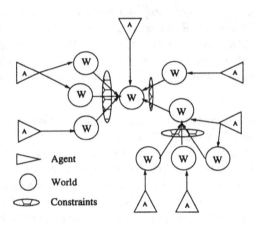

Fig. 1. The topology of a multiagent intelligent system

When such a system functions, it could be in either a stabilised or un-stabilised state. By stabilised state, we mean that both its identity and goal constraints are satisfied, and no action can be triggered off at the time.

2 Modelling Intelligent Systems in $\mathcal{GISM}$

Based on the generic theory of intelligent systems and the $\mathcal{COH}$ world modelling scheme outlined above, a modelling language $\mathcal{GISM}$ for generalised intelligent systems has been derived and implemented. As pointed in the theory, a model of an intelligent system consists of two kinds of descriptions at top level. One is declarations of agents to be involved in the system. The other is models of the agent worlds. In the following, we first show how an agent can be depicted in $\mathcal{GISM}$, and then show how agent world can be modelled in $\mathcal{GISM}$.

2.1 Depicting Agents

Descriptions of agents are to be used by agents to know each other for control, communication and cooperation. The following is the structure of agent description in $\mathcal{GISM}$ as a special type of objects or worlds viewed and manipulated by agents at higher level:

```
Agent <agent-local-name> [of <type-id>|<agent-id>] {
    <agent-id>;
```

```
<available-timeframes>;
<profile for doable-actions>; // abilities.
<profile for required-actions>; // such as plans.
<profile for scheduled-actions>; // schedules.
<general requirement>; // resources and tools.
}// end of agent depiction.
```

In addition to information on scheduled timeframes, preconditions as well as postconditions, a profile for an agent action could also include detailed description about how the action should be taken. Some actions, such as instructions of CPU chips, are primary, generic and lower level, and can be defined in an agent structure. Other agent actions are usually higher level and world or task-oriented, so it is convenient to define them within agent world models.

2.2 Modelling Worlds for Agents

Following the $\mathcal{COH}$ knowledge representation scheme, the syntax of an agent world in $\mathcal{GISM}$ is centred at three concepts: object, action and constraint. The following code shows the structure of agent world in $\mathcal{GISM}$.

```
world <world-name> [extended <proto-worlds>] [for <agent-id>] {
   <local agents>; // a special kind of objects.
   <objects or sub-world models>; // ordinary objects.
   <doable actions>; // what the agent can do.
   <required actions>; // what are required to do.
   <scheduled actions>; // exactly when, how and who does a job.
   <identity of the world>; // identity constraints.
   <triggering conditions on actions>; // trigger constraints.
   <the goal for the agent to achieve>; // goal constraints.
}// end of an agent world.
```

In $\mathcal{GISM}$, a domain can be referred by a name. In addition to default domains of Int for integers, Real for reals, Char for ASCII characters, String for literal strings, a new domain can be defined in several different ways such as enumeration, recursion, constraint and composition. The following are some examples:

```
domain IntDomain=[1,2,5..12,45];
domain DomByConstraint={$[*]:[1..1000];$[*]%2=0};
domain RecursiveDomain={1,2,3|$[n]=$[n-1]+$[n-2]};
domain SomeEven={(* i:[0..9])($[(i)]=2*i)};
```

Inside a world model, an object reference can be declared in two ways:

- *referring* is to declare a new name and let it refer to object in a defined domain, or a copy of a defined $\mathcal{COH}$:
  ```
  Int ix; or Int days:[1,2,3,4,5,6,7];
  ```

– *Composing* is to define a new world model and get a name for it. The new world model can be either completely new or extension to some defined world models:

```
world Computer {
  Monitors monitor;
  Keyboards keyboard;
  Cases case:[desktop, minitower, mediumtower];
} // end of Computer world definition.
```

To put an object reference into a specific category, one can simply prefix the following tokens to the reference name: *identity, passive, const* and *perceptive.*

2.3 Defining Agent Actions

The definition of an agent action inside a world model tells agents for a given action name what the action is, and/or what to be done with the action. To capture these two kinds of knowledge of agent actions, we have developed a unified scheme to define agent actions, as a special type of objects or worlds. The following code is the structure of definition of agent actions in $\mathcal{GISM}$.

```
action makeAtrip() for Driver {
  /* declarative section describes properties of the action
     such as starting time, completing time,
     preconditions, postconditions as UniLog formulas, etc. */
  CODE {
    /* imperative section contains a  piece of program in
       an understandable language, which tells how to act. */
  }
}//end of defining action make a trip.
```

2.4 Defining Constraints

As in $\mathcal{COH}$, there are three kinds of constraints: identity, trigger and goal constraints. In the current implementation, these three kinds of constraints are put separately into three constraint stores: identity constraint store, trigger constraint store and goal constraint store. What actions agents can autonomously take in an intelligent system are mainly decided by the trigger constraints. During their actions, agents try to satisfy the goal constraints while keeping consistency of identity constraints. In $\mathcal{GISM}$, these three kinds of constraints are all built from $\mathcal{UniLog}$ formulas but in programming style: use && for $\wedge$, || for $\vee$, for $\neg$, -> for $\rightarrow$, <- for $\leftarrow$, <-> for $\leftrightarrow$, => for $\Rightarrow$. ";" is used in constraint stores to separate constraints.

In contrast with ordinary first order logic where a predicate is purely a symbol, one can define new relations between objects in $\mathcal{GISM}$, and use defined relations as predicates. This makes constraint formalisation very declarative. The definition of a new relation can be either declarative or imperative. The former only describes what the relation is, while the latter tells how such piece of constraint can be resolved by giving a piece of program in a language. The following is an example:

```
relation inCircle(Point p; Circle c) {
  /* declaratively describe in what condition a point p is
     inside circle c. Provide a Point is represented by x, y,
     a circle is represented by a centre of Point and a
     Real number r*/
  (c.centre.y-p.x)^2+(c.centre.y-p.y)^2=(c.r)^2;
  CODE {
    /* imperative section tells how to resolve such a piece
       constraint that formalised using this relation. */
  }
}//end of defining relation inCircle.
```

In defining such a relation, one can even indicate if it is a symmetric, transitive or reflective relation, by prefix *symm*, *trans* or/and *refl* to keyword *relation*.

3 Manipulation and Control

By now, we shall be able to set up models for a given intelligent system in $\mathcal{GISM}$. Through parsing such models, corresponding intelligent systems will be built up, if the required agents are available and targeted environment can be interacted with. In this section, we deal with how agents can, and should act in such intelligent systems.

3.1 What Agents Can Do

Basically, in a world an agent can do only three atomic things: reading the state or value of an object reference, changing the state or value assigned, and evaluating mathematical or logic formulas. These three basic actions have been used to program computations in conventional programming languages. As a language for programming intelligent systems, $\mathcal{GISM}$ offers a set of higher level actions which can be used to implement many different intelligent with $\mathcal{COH}$s. The following are some of such higher level agent actions: (1) *toSat()* is to satisfy the constraints in one or two or all three constraint stores. (2) *lookUp()* is to look up the current states and values of some variables listed. (3) *lookSat()* is to satisfy the constraints, and look up the states and values of some variables listed. (4) *toPlan()* is to make plans, as lists of required actions and temporal constraints on these actions, for agents to achieve a specific goal at a specific time. (5) *toSchedule()* is to schedule required actions for agents involved, in accordance with relevant constraints in the constraint stores. (6) *keepSat()* is to keep all constraints of a world satisfied while reacting on the changes from outside.

3.2 The General Control Flow

In an intelligent system developed from its $\mathcal{GISM}$ model, the control of agent activities are generally based on by what task the system was initially activated. There are three different types of tasks: (1) *transformational tasks*, which are used to find right output for a given input. (2) *lookup tasks*, which are used to find out internal state or values of the worlds. (3) *reactive tasks*, which require the agents to live in the worlds and react to changes.

Fig. 2 shows the overall control flow of agent activities in an intelligent system.

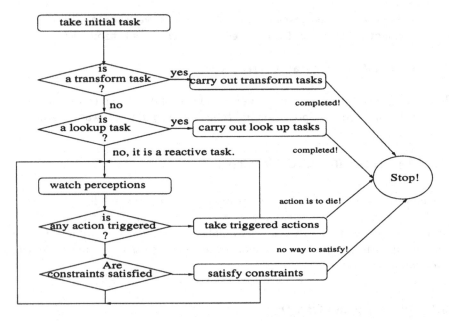

Fig. 2. The overall control flow of intelligent system

3.3 How an Intelligent System Can Be Activated

An intelligent system could be activated when an agent is asked to, or autonomously takes a doable action. In a sense of system control, it is not very interesting if an intelligent system is activated by transformational or lookup tasks, even though the tasks might be very computationally expensive such as solving equations involving thousands of variables, or other constraint satisfaction problems. In these two cases, all activities of agents are deterministic.

When an intelligent system is activated as reactive system, agents have to react to their environment by taking proper actions. What is more interesting is how those actions should be reactively started and successfully completed. Generally, in a reactive intelligent system, agent actions are centred at keeping their identity constraints satisfied while doing their best to achieve their goals. Suppose an intelligent system was activated at time t_0. By taking various actions, the system is progressively stabilised at time t_1. That is, the identity constraints have been satisfied, the goals have also been achieved, and no actions could be triggered off through trigger constraints. In such a progressively stabilised world, all perceptive object references are being watched by some responsible agents. Now suppose a change to some perceptive object reference has been made, the following actions will be taken by responsible agents in the system, in order to stabilise the systems again: (1) Read changes to perceptive object references. (2) Check if any trigger constraint can be fired up. If so, take fired action. (3) Try to revise the identity and goal constraints for consistency. If there is any inconsistency, to re-satisfy the constraints, with care of the trigger constraints.

By repeating these actions, the system may become stabilised again at time t_4. As time goes on, the system goes from un-stabilised to stabilised, and to un-stabilised again because of the changes to the system. This process can be pictured as in Figure 3.

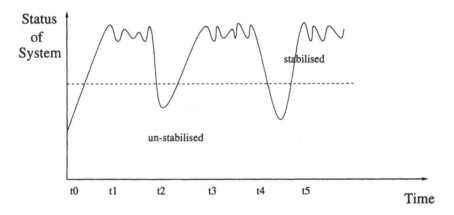

Fig. 3. An intelligent system goes in a circle

3.4 Planning to Achieve a Goal

At a specific time, actions to be taken next usually vary in accordance with the goal to be achieved. Planning is a process of finding out what agent actions are required to achieve a specific goal in an agent world, and to set up temporal relationships between agent actions so that a goal can be reached by agents in the intelligent system, from a given state of the world [8]. In planning, only orders of agent actions are concerned. No exact time slots are filled for an agent with actions. In $\mathcal{GISM}$ term, planning, as a meta-task, is to find out required actions and put into the list of *required actions*, and to work out temporal constraints between required actions and put such constraints into *identity constraint store*. By default, a generic agent action toPlan() can be taken in any well established world, to develop a plan of agent actions so that the system can reach its goal state from the current one. By well established, we mean that there are enough information about the state of the world, the goal state and doable actions to change the world.

3.5 Scheduling Agent Actions

Scheduling deals with allocation of resources over time for some agents to perform a collection of tasks or actions. It is an important and even crucial task for agents in an intelligent system to be able to act or to achieve their goals. In $\mathcal{GISM}$ terms, to make schedules for agents in a world is to develop a set of scheduled actions for each individual agent, based on required actions and constraints on the actions, such that the constraints on agents and the worlds can be satisfied. Importantly, scheduling also produces preconditions for each scheduled action and may put them into the *trigger constraint store*. Taking the advantages of integrated expressive power, various smart scheduling algorithms are allowed to be coded in $\mathcal{GISM}$ to make scheduling. By default, any implementation of such scheduling algorithm will override a generic scheduling action toSchedule(), which is also a meta-task implemented in $\mathcal{GISM}$.

3.6 Social Contract for Agents to Cooperate and Coordinate

When more than one agents exists in an intelligent system, cooperations and coordinations are necessary. The following are some laws that all agents should obey: (1) *respect sovereignty*: an agent has the right to access its own world and below, but has no right to access the other worlds. (2) *respect privacy*: although an agent has the right to access its sub worlds, it can do so only if either it is also the agent in charge of the sub-worlds, or something has been declared accessible for it. (3) *be responsible*: whenever an action has been triggered off, the designated agent has to manage to carry it out. (4) *be informative*: an agent should check designated perceptive variables regularly. Whenever a message is detected, it should make response as soon as possible.

There are also some commonsense rules that an agent should comply with when it act. For an example, when taking an action, an agent should take its responsibility to set the actual starting time, and the actual ending time when it completes the action.

4 Application of $\mathcal{GISM}$ to Intelligent System Design

In this section, we consider how to model and design an intelligent taxi network as an application example of our theory and techniques introduced above. The taxi network is organised as follows:

There are a finite number of taxis connected to the central station by some means such as telephone or computer network, while customers log their booking through telephones. An operator in the central station monitors information about the taxis and customer bookings, and is also responsible for scheduling which taxi(s) to complete which customer booking(s), while taxi drivers are doing their own planing on how to make a specific trip. The goal of the system is to (1) maximise the number of completed customer booking in a unit time. (2) minimise the average customer waiting time.

According to our intelligent system theory, two things have to be done in designing an intelligent system. One is to choose competent agents. The other is to set up world models of the environment for agents. These two things are usually interwoven with each other in designing a complex intelligent system. In the taxi network example, there are two types of agents: operators at central station and taxi drivers. These two type agents could be declaratively defined in $\mathcal{GISM}$ as follows:

```
agent Operator { // do not have to be a human.
  Name name;
  Int oid;
  /* other relevant details, such as available time,
     if operators need to be scheduled. */
} // end of agent type Operator definition.

agent Driver { // do not have to be a human too.
  Name name;
  Int tid;
  TimeWindow timewindows[]; // a pair of time points.
} // end of agent type Driver definition.
```

We would not treat customers as agents here, since our taxi network is not interested in any aspects of their worlds, but only messages from them to make, change or cancel bookings. We even do not care how they send messages to the central station, but only the messages.

Now let us model drivers' world as Taxi which may include a traffic map, and the operator's world as TaxiNet. There are also two sub-world models for communications between the operator and the customers, and communications between the operator and the drivers. We will not discuss them in detail here, since it is easy to figure out what needs to be passed to the central station from a customer, and what needs to be passed between the central station and a taxis driver.

```
world Taxi for Driver {
  perceptive OperatorMessage operatormessage[];
  // Such a message contains a job description.
  DriverMessage drivermessage; // to be read by operator.
```

```
identity Address currentposition;
State state; // State holds two values: BUSY and FREE.
Path drivingroute[]; /* a path contains from where to where
                        through which way.*/
action makeTrip() { // for agent Driver by default.
  Name passenger[]; Address departure, Address arrival;
  Time requireddeparturetime, requiredarrivaltime,
       realdeparturetime, realarrivaltime;
  CODE {
    /* if we use a human driver, no action code is needed but
       just follows the driving plan in  drivingroute developed
       by toPlan().
       if we employ robot drivers, a piece of code has to be
       sent for every single job, together with description.*/
    }// end of CODE section of an action.
  }

action makeTrip() jobs[];//jobs to be assigned by operators.

action toPlan(Address goals[]) { // a list of address to go.
  /* to make plan for the next trip. A plan consists of a set
     of triple <starting point, road name, reached point>,
     will be put into  drivingroute. */
}
//  some identity constraints are omitted.
trigger constraint {
  (operatormessage[].size()>0)=>{ queueJobs(); };
  (jobs[].size()>0 && state=FREE) =>
     { state:=BUSY;
       toPlan(jobs[0].departure, jobs[0].arrival);
       jobs[0](); jobs[].pop(); state:=FREE;
     };
  }
}
```

The whole taxi network can be then modelled as:

```
world TaxiNet for Operator {
  identity constant Real alpha, delta;
  /* the weights of profit and average waiting time,
     which are part of identity of the taxi company. */
  passive Real profit;
  passive Real awt; //average waiting time.
  Taxi taxis[]; //  models of  taxis viewed by Operator.
  action Taxi.makeTrip() requiredaction[]; // jobs to be created.
  action Taxi.makeTrip() scheduledaction[]; // scheduled jobs.
```

```
perceptive CustomerMessage customermessage[];
/* this is another way to claim object reference.*/
perceptive taxis[...].drivermessage;
action dealingJob() {
  CODE {
    /* used to create or delete an entry in requiredaction,
       based on information contained in a customer message. */
  }
}
identity constraint {
  taxis[].size()>0;
}/* For a real taxi network, there are many other identity
    constraints to be satisfied for the net running.*/
trigger constraint {
  (customerMessage[].size()>0) => { dealingJob(); };
  (requiredaction[].size()>0) => { toSchedule(); };
  ((! i)isAssigned(taxis[i].drivermessage))=>
      {checkTaxiInfo(i);};
  (scheduledaction[].size()>0) => { sendJobs(); };
}// end of trigger constraints.
goal constraint {
  maximise(alpha*profit+delta/awt);
}/* For a given number of customers, suppose the operator can
    calculate the profit and the average waiting time, then
    the goal at the time can be described as above.*/
}// end of operator's world.
```

Modelled as above, taxis are sub-worlds of TaxiNet. Operators communicate with taxi drivers through two types of perceptive object references: *operatormessages* and *drivermessages*. Customers are connected with the taxi network by perceptive object reference *customermessage*. In a real taxi network, operator agents need to maintain a list of customer worlds on the fly, but in this simple version, relevant information on customers is modelled into jobs for simplicity.

It should be pointed out that, we do not specify here how the constraints are to be resolved, since our present intention is rather in the problem representation. We allow that special purpose constraint solvers, or general CSP or linear algebra modules may be used as appropriate.

5 Conclusions

We have reported in this paper a powerful language for modelling, and designing various agent-based intelligent systems. $\mathcal{GISM}$ is so generic that many different systems can be modelled in terms of agents and $\mathcal{COH}$s, and their behaviours can then be simulated, evaluated and understood. Most importantly, our success in gaining generalities has not sacrificed the practical values of the language.

Our experience shows that there is no difficulty to implement either $\mathcal{GISM}$ or a specific intelligent systems in $\mathcal{GISM}$. However, to such a generic agent-based intelligent system modelling language, there are certainly many issues at both theoretical and technical level. In the future, we are going to investigate various large scale applications of the theory and the language.

References

1. Boutilier C., Shoham Y. and Wellman M., *Economic principles of multi-agent systems*, Artificial Intelligence 94(1997), pages 1-6, Elsevier, 1997.
2. S.J. Russell, *Rationality and intelligence*, Artificial Intelligence 94(1997), pages 57-77, Elsevier, 1997.
3. Park T. J. and Gelder A. V., *Partitioning Method for Satisfiability Testing on Large Formulas*, CADE-13: 13th International Conference on Automated Deduction, New Brunswick, New Jersey, Page 748-762, July/August 1996.
4. Jérôme Gensel, *Integrating Constraints in an Object-Oriented Knowledge Representation System*, in Mafred Meyer (ed.) Constraint Processing, pages 67-83, Springer, 1995.
5. Kinny D. and Georgeff, *Modelling and Designing of Multi-Agent System*, in Jörg P. Müller et al. (eds.) Intelligent Agent III, Springer-Verlag, LNAI 1193, pages 1-20, 1993.
6. Wilfred C. Jamison, *ACACIA: An agency based collaboration framework for heterogeneous multiagent systems*, in Chengqi Z and Lukose D. (eds.) *Multi-Agent Systems – Methodologies and Applications*, Lecture Notes in Artificial Intelligence (LNAI-1286), Springer Verlag Publishers, 1997.
7. S.J. Russell and P. Norvig, *Artificial Intelligence — A Modern Approach*, Prentice-Hall, Englewood Cliffs, 1995.
8. N.R. Jennings, *Controlling cooperative problem solving in industrial multi-agent systems using joint intentions*, Artificial Intelligence 75(1995), pages 1-46, Elsevier, 1995.
9. B. Grosz and S. Kraus, *Collaborative plans for complex group activities*, Artificial Intelligence 86 (1996), Elsevier, 1996.
10. Jaffar, J. and Lassez J.-L, *Constraint Logic programming*, in proceedings of the fourteenth ACM Conference on principles of programming languages. Munich. Association for Computing Machinery,1987
11. Frederick S. Hillier et al., *Introduction to Operations Research*, McGraw-Hill Publishing Company, 1990.
12. Wang H., *Constrained Object Hierarchies – An Architecture for Intelligent Systems*, doctoral consortium abstract, in Proceedings of Fifteenth International Joint Conference on Artificial Intelligence, Morgan Kaufmann Publishers, 1997.
13. Wang H., *On Generalities of Intelligent Systems*, Technical Report TR-ARP-05-98, Automated Reasoning Project, the Australian National University, 1998.
14. Wang H. and Slaney J., *UniLog: A Unified Logic Framework*, presented at the 1998 Australasian Association for Logic Conference, abstract published in a bulletin of Australian Society of Logic, 1998.

Programming Internet Based DAI Applications in Qu-Prolog

Keith Clark[1], Peter J. Robinson[2], and Richard Hagen[2]

[1] Dept. of Computing,Imperial College,London, England, U.K.
klc@doc.ic.ac.uk tel: +44 171 594 8211 fax:+44 171 581 8024
[2] Software Verification Research Centre, The University of Queensland,
Brisbane, Australia.
{pjr,rah}@csee.uq.edu.au tel: +61 7 3365 3461 fax: +61 7 3365 1533

Abstract. This paper presents the unique collection of additional features of Qu-Prolog, a variant of the AI programming language Prolog, and illustrates how they can be used for implementing DAI applications. By this we mean applications comprising communicating information servers, expert systems, or agents, with sophisticated reasoning capabilities and internal concurrency. Such an application exploits the key features of Qu-Prolog: support for the programming of sound non-clausal inference systems, multi-threading, and high level inter-thread message communication between Qu-Prolog query threads anywhere on the internet. The inter-thread communication uses email style symbolic names for threads, allowing easy construction of distributed applications using public names for threads. How threads react to received messages is specified by a disjunction of reaction rules which the thread periodically executes. A communications API allows smooth integration of components written in C, which to Qu-Prolog, look like remote query threads.
Keywords: Prolog, internet agents, distributed symbolic programming, KQML information servers

1 Introduction

Qu-Prolog [1, 2] is an extension of Prolog designed initially as an implementation and tactic specification language for interactive theorem provers, particularly those that carry out schematic proofs. Qu-Prolog has built-in support for the kinds of data structures typically encountered in theorem proving activities such as object variables, substitutions and quantified terms. Qu-Prolog is the implementation language of the Ergo theorem prover [3], which has seen substantial use in development of verified software, both directly [4] and indirectly through the prototyping of a program refinement tool [5].

As part of our ongoing efforts to scale up our formal development tools, we are interested in developing multi-user versions of these tools. In particular, we are interested in implementing a multi-threaded, multi-user version of Ergo where a collection of people and autonomous provers for specialised subproofs can work together to produce a large formal program verification. The architecture of the application will be that of co-operating, distributed agents interacting with both human Ergo users and automated prover agents to coordinate and realise a team program verification effort. We anticipate that many of the agents will be personal agents with a primary role of coordinating the human verification effort, providing an agent based CSCW environment. However, other agents, knowledgeable about proof tactics for specialised types of theorems, will be autonomous agents substituting for human agents.

As a preliminary step to this multi-user Ergo, we have recently augmented Qu-Prolog to support multi-threading and high-level inter-thread communication between Qu-Prolog threads running anywhere on the internet. We believe that this new version of Qu-Prolog is a promising language for implementing DAI applications comprising communicating agents or intelligent information sources with sophisticated reasoning capabilities and internal concurrency. This paper describes the unique collection of features that Qu-Prolog has over standard Prolog, and we sketch how they can be used to rapidly implement DAI applications.

In another case study we have implemented a concurrent OO extension of Qu-Prolog in which objects, implemented as threads, have both a knowledge base and methods that are invoked by sending messages to the object. The Qu-Prolog language is freely available (contact Richard Hagen), and we would like to see it widely used within the DAI community.

IC-Prolog [6] and BinProlog [7] are two other Prolog's that provide support for multi-threading and high-level communication. Neither IC-Prolog nor Bin-Prolog have extra support for implementing theorem provers. IC-Prolog uses mailboxes, which are similar to message buffers but they are separate constructs from threads. A thread is created without a mailbox, and several threads can share the same mailbox. Neither threads nor mailboxes have an internet wide naming mechanism. BinProlog uses Linda tuple spaces for high-level communications between threads. Thread naming can be achieved by embedding names within tuples but, in general, more communications are required than in Qu-Prolog for communicating between threads.

1.1 Sketch of how agents can be implemented in Qu-Prolog

In broad terms, a Qu-Prolog internet agent typically comprises a collection of Prolog query threads running within a Qu-Prolog application. The application runs as a single Unix process on some host. Each of the agent threads has an IWI (internet wide identity) and a single message buffer of pending messages (rather like an email inbox). Messages can be sent to a thread T from another thread, running anywhere on the internet, using T's IWI. Threads can be given public names, which are Prolog symbols, as can Qu-Prolog applications.

A thread will typically react to a received message by asserting or deleting facts from the Qu-Prolog dynamic database, by forking new threads, and by sending messages to other threads, both local and remote. Often a response message is also sent to the thread that sent the message. How a thread reacts to messages in its message queue is specified by a disjunction of message reaction rules of the form:

```
message_choice(
message_pattern1 -> action_conjunction1;
message_pattern2 -> action_conjunction2;
....
message_patternk -> action_conjunctionk)
```

All the threads comprising an agent A execute concurrently (as POSIX threads). All the agent's threads can access and update the dynamic database of the Qu-Prolog application within which they are executing. This acts as the belief repository of the agent.

In addition to an interface thread, which usually has a public name, an agent may have a learning component that constantly monitors and generalises assertions added to the dynamic database by the other agent threads. Another can be a background inference component, finding and asserting interesting consequences of assertions added to the dynamic database, and handling issues of truth maintenance of these asserted consequences when their supporting assertions are withdrawn.

In addition, some of the agent's threads will be temporary threads forked to handle a particular request from another agent. Conversations between agent's can thus be handled by temporary, conversation specific threads within each agent. This means that agents can concurrently engage in multiple conversations with any number of agents. Each conversation thread within a particular agent only needs to remember the current state of one conversation. It also only needs to be able to handle messages for its type of conversation.

Qu-Prolog threads can be programmed to automatically suspend until a clause of a certain form is added to or deleted from the dynamic database. This allows the straightforward implementation of belief store demons. The learning and consequence finding threads can gracefully suspend when they have finished processing the current belief store, to be automatically awakened when a new clause of interest is asserted or deleted by some *other* thread of the agent.

The above is our sketch of the potential of Qu-Prolog for implementing multi-agent applications. We must confess that we have only just begun to explore its DAI use and we have not yet built any realistic applications. What we hope to do in this paper is to introduce the key features of Qu-Prolog and to whet the appetite of the DAI community to what we belief is Qu-Prolog's eminent suitability as a programming tool for DAI.

The organization of the rest of the paper is as follows. In section 2, we describe the multi-threading and inter-thread communications features in more detail. In Section 3 we illustrate the use of these features by sketching the implementation of KQML [9] style information server that uses just Prolog inference to answer queries. We show how, by defining special meta predicates, we can extend Prolog so that both queries and rules can transparently access remote information servers. In effect, we show how the KQML information servers can be used to implement a distributed deductive database in Qu-Prolog. In section 4 we just summarise the Qu-Prolog features that support the implementation of more complex inference systems because they are more fully described elsewhere [1]. They can be used to enrich the information servers with support for a wide range of logics and inference styles.

2 Threads and Thread Communication

The support for multiple query threads means that Qu-Prolog can concurrently execute several queries against its static and dynamic database of clauses. When a Qu-Prolog application starts, it has only one query thread, but this thread can fork any number of child threads, which in turn can fork further threads. The threads execute concurrently. They may suspend waiting for a message of a certain form to be added to their message queue, or waiting for a clause of a certain form to be asserted to the Qu-Prolog dynamic database.

Information sharing by threads. Threads running *within* a single Qu-Prolog application share the dynamic memory of that application. When a thread executes an **assert** or a **record** the data is added to the data area accessible by all the local threads. An asserted clause can later be accessed by another local thread using **clause** or **retract**. By executing either of these calls as arguments to a special **thread_wait** meta-call predicate, we can make the clause accessing call suspend (rather than fail) if their is no current matching clause. Suspension of the clause accessing call suspends the thread, which resumes when a matching clause is asserted by another local thread. Using this mechanism we can implement dynamic database demons as threads that execute a simple recursive program of the form:

```
demon(DemonTrigger) :-
   thread_wait(clause(DemonTrigger)),
   (OtherDemonCond1 -> DemonAction1 ;
    OtherDemonCond2 -> DemonAction2 ;
```

```
    ..... ;
  DefaultAction),
  demon(NewDemonTrigger).
```

Each demon thread suspends until a clause matching `DemonTrigger` is asserted by another local thread. It then executes the nested conditional, checking for certain other conditions. If any of these succeed it executes a corresponding action conjunction which can assert more clauses (causing other local demon threads to become active) and communicate messages to other, usually remote, threads. The communicated messages can in turn cause assertions to be made within other Qu-Prolog applications, perhaps causing the firing of remote demons.

Message communication between threads. The dynamic database offers blackboard style communication between threads within a single Qu-Prolog application. In addition, such threads can explicitly communicate with one another by sending messages, which are Prolog terms. Message terms can be sent not only to local threads - those executing within the same Qu-Prolog application - but to non-local threads executing in a Qu-Prolog application *anywhere* on the internet[1]. This is the only method[2] of communication between threads in different Qu-Prolog applications. Each Qu-Prolog thread has a unique internet wide identity. The same message-send primitive is used to send a message to a thread irrespective of its location. Each thread has a message buffer of received but unprocessed message terms. By executing special message queue access primitives a thread can either extract the first message in the queue, or search for and extract a message unifying with one or more message patterns. A thread trying to access a message from its message queue will automatically suspend if the queue is currently empty, or if no message is found that satisfies any of the message patterns it is looking for. In each case the thread will be automatically resumed when a new message is received from another thread. It will immediately resuspend if the message does not satisfy any of the message patterns it is seeking.

Public names for threads. To send a message to another thread the communicating thread must know the identity of the target thread. A parent thread always knows the identity of all its offspring threads because the thread fork primitives either return a system generated identity or they allow the parent thread to give the thread a symbolic name when it is forked. Thread identities can also be sent in messages and the recipient of a message always has access to the identity of the sender of the message. However, if we have a distributed application comprising of several Qu-Prolog applications we need a way of bootstrapping the inter-thread communication between the applications. This is achieved

---

[1] The target thread can also be a C application. Using a Qu-Prolog communications API any C application can be engineered to receive Prolog terms from, and to send them to, Qu-Prolog threads or other C applications using the communications API.

[2] Apart from file sharing in a shared file system.

by giving each Qu-Prolog application a public symbolic name, such as **agents** or **database**. All that is required is that this name is different from the name of any other Qu-Prolog application (or application using its communications API) running on the same host machine. Thus, we can have Qu-Prolog applications with the name **database** running on any number of different machines.

Suppose now that a thread is forked within the **agents** application and explicitly given the symbol name **archive_agent**. If the application is running on the machine with internet name **everest.it.uq.edu.au** then

```
archive_agent@agents:'everest.it.uq.edu.au'
```

is the public internet unique identity of this thread. The name can be used to send a message to the thread from a Qu-Prolog thread running on any other internet host, including **everest.it.uq.edu.au**.

A thread is given a symbolic name by executing the call

```
thread_set_symbol(archive_agent)
```

within the thread, or by being forked with the call

```
fork_named_thread(Goal,archive_agent)
```

where **Goal** is the call that the new thread will execute. When this goal terminates the thread will terminate.

Typically, the main or initial thread of an application is in charge of forking extra threads. If this is an information server application this initial thread is usually programmed as a top level repeat/fail loop, or a tail recursion, that executes a disjunction of reaction rules for the initial messages that can be sent to it from some client application thread. We shall give an example of this later. For some of these 'queries' messages, the main thread may fork one or more child threads to process the 'query' or to engage in a conversation with the client. The client, in turn, can fork a thread for each such conversation. This enables peer to peer, or agent to agent application programming, rather than just client/server programming.

Sending messages. As we have said, a Qu-Prolog thread running in any Qu-Prolog application on any host, can send a message to another thread running on any other internet host, providing it knows the threads unique internet identity. The message is *any* Prolog term. It is sent using the message-send library predicate **>>**:

```
Msg_term >> Thread_ID
```

This puts **Msg_term** at the end of the message buffer for the destination thread. If the thread is local, running in the same Qu-Prolog application, this enqueuing of the message is almost immediate. If not, there is a slight delay as the term is byte encoded, sent using TCP/IP, and decoded within the destination application. The communication is asynchronous, the sender does not delay until either the message is read or enqueued at the destination. It immediately continues with the execution of its next call.

The form of the term `Thread_ID` depends on whether the sending and receiving threads are in the same application or same machine.) The full internet wide identity of the destination thread can always be used and must be used when the destination thread is running on another host machine. So:

`Msg_term >> archive_agent@agents:'everest.it.uq.edu.au'`

can be used to send a message to the `archive_agent` thread, in the application `agents`, on the host machine `everest.it.uq.edu.au` from anywhere on the internet. In general, a message-send has the form:

`Msg_term >> ThreadName@ApplicationName:HostName`

where `TheadName` and `ApplicationName` are bound to the atom names of a thread and a Qu-Prolog application, respectively, and `HostName` is bound to the (usually) quoted atom name of an internet host machine.

As with email communication, the global name can be shortened for local communications. The shorter `ThreadName@ApplicationName` can be used for a communication to a thread running on the same machine, and just `ThreadName` can be used to send a message to another thread running within the same application. Thus, `ApplicationName` is a thread name domain and a `HostName` is an application name domain. The communication middle-ware that ensures messages are correctly transfered between different machines, and different Qu-Prolog applications, relies both on internet domain names servers for resolving machine names to IP addresses, and special Qu-Prolog application name servers for resolving application names to communications ports. Name tables for thread names are maintained within each Qu-Prolog application. Further details of the Qu-Prolog communications system are given in [8].

Reading messages. A thread reads the *first* message in its buffer (if there is one) by executing the call:

`Msg << Sender`

This removes the first message term from the threads message buffer, unifies it with `Msg`, and unifies the global identity of the thread that sent the message with `Sender`. (The sender's global identity is automatically included in a special message wrapper of each message term.) The call fails if either unification fails. The call and the thread suspend if the message buffer is empty. Both are resumed when a message arrives. If `Sender` is an unbound variable it will be bound to the sender's global identity. This can then be used to communicate with the sender using a:

`ReplyMsg >> Sender`

communication.

Actually, two thread global identities are always attached by the Qu-Prolog inter-thread communications system to every message term. These are the identity of the sender and the identity of the thread to which any reply to the message should normally be sent. By default, the reply thread is the sender, but the sender can explicitly change this to be another thread. It does this using the variant message-send:

```
Msg >> Thread_ID reply_to Other_Thread
```

Because the reply-to address attached to a message may have been explicitly changed in this way, a thread receiving a message can use the message receive variant:

```
Msg << Sender reply_to ReplyTo
```

This accesses both the sender and the reply-to identities. The sender of a message cannot change the sender identity attached to a message, so the receiver always accesses in the **Sender** argument the identity of the thread which sent the message. However, being able to explicitly set the reply-to field of the message wrapper allows a thread to forward a message *on behalf of* another thread. To make sure a message has not been forwarded, a thread can use:

```
Msg << Sender reply_to Sender
```

Searching for a particular message. A thread can *search* its message buffer for a message that unifies with a given message pattern, or which is sent from some particular thread, or has a particular reply thread identity, using:

```
Msg <<= Sender        Msg <<= Sender reply_to ReplyTo
```

If there is no message in the buffer that both unifies with **Msg** and satisfies any required constraints on **Sender** or **ReplyTo**, this call, and the thread that executes it, suspend. Both are resumed when a new message is added to the message buffer of the thread. The call succeeds only when a message is eventually found that satisfies all the required conditions. This message is then removed from the message buffer. The next call on **<<=** will rescan from the front of the message buffer.

For example:

```
ask(Q) <<= Thread@agents:'everest.it.uq.edu.au'
```

will search the message buffer for a message of the form **ask(Q)** from any thread in the **agents** application running on **'everest.it.uq.edu.au'**. It will suspend until such a message arrives.

Reaction rules for messages. The most powerful form of message-receive is the **message_choice** disjunction of message reaction rules. This has the form:

```
message_choice (
    MsgGuard1 -> CallConj1
  ;
```

```
MsgGuard2 -> CallConj2
    .
    .
MsgGuardn -> CallConjn)
```

where each **MsgGuard** has the form:

```
MsgPtn << S reply_to R :: Test
```

The **reply_to R** and `:: Test` are optional. This will scan the message buffer testing each message, in turn, against the sequence of alternative message guards. When a message **M** is found that matches the **MsgPtn << S reply_to R** of one of the message guards, *such that* the associated **Test** call succeeds, the message is removed from the buffer and the corresponding **CallConj** is executed. The **Test** call can be an arbitrary Qu-Prolog call. Typically it tests variable values given by the unification of the message **M** with **MsgPtn << S reply_to R**

As with the single message search operator **<<=**, the **message_choice** call will suspend if the end of the message buffer is reached. It will be automatically resumed when a new message is added. We can also set a limit on the time the **message_choice** call and the thread that executes it should suspend. By adding:

```
timeout(T) -> TimeOutCall
```

as a new last alternative of the message choice we will limit the time that the thread spends searching for an acceptable message to **T** seconds. When the time limit is reached, and no acceptable message is in the current message buffer, the thread executes **TimeOutCall**.

Programming reactive components. The publically named interface thread of an agent or information source is typically its reactive component. Its role is to react to external messages, delegating any extended processing to forked threads, so as to be able to quickly react to other messages. Such a thread will execute a goal, say **reactions**, defined by the single Qu-Prolog clause of the form:

```
reactions:-
  message_choice (
    MsgPtn1 -> Action1 ;
    ....
    MsgPtnk -> Actionk),
  reactions.  % tail recursive call
```

3   Implementing a KQML style information source

In this section we illustrate the use of multi-threading and message communication by showing how we can set up a publically named information source that accepts KQML [9] style query and update messages. We assume familiarity with the basic concepts of KQML.

KQML message as a Prolog term. A KQML message has the form:

```
(performative :keyword1 value1 :keyword2 value2 ......)
```

where the number of keyword/value pairs is variable and can be given in any order. This can be mapped into the Prolog term:

```
performative([keyword1(value1), keyword2(value2), ......])
```

where the performative and each keyword become Prolog functors and the sequence of attribute value pairs becomes a Prolog list of unary terms. For example, the KQML message:

```
(ask-one :reply-with q123 :language prolog
   :content ''price(ford,mondeo,X)'')
```

becomes:

```
ask_one([reply_with(q123),language(prolog)
   ,content(price(ford,mondeo,X))])
```

KQML has :sender, :receiver and :replyto fields but we do not need to have them within the message. The Qu-Prolog communications system puts them in the message wrapper.

Let us assume that we launch a series of information server applications on different hosts, giving each the application name kqml_server. Within each such application, we will have a main thread which will be given the symbolic name listener. We therefore communicate with the server by sending KQML messages to listener@kqml_server:machine. We will give the reaction rules to enable the listener thread to respond to the KQML messages: ask-if, ask-all, stand-by of a stream-all, tell, untell. For simplicity we assume that all the queries use the content language prolog. The program executed by the listener thread is given below.

Note that an ask_all message is handled by executing a findall within the main query thread. However, the stand_by(stream_of) message causes a new thread to be started, with identity I, executing the call ans_gen(Q,R). Here, Q is the query and R is the address of the thread to which answers are to be sent - the client. The identity I of the forked query thread is sent to the client in a generator message. The client will now interact with this temporary thread, which lazily generates the sequence of answers to Q, in response to next messages from the client.

The ans_gen program finds the first solution instance of Q (if any), and then waits for a next or discard message from the client R. Receipt of a next message causes it to respond with a reply(Q) message, or a reply(Q) message, or a reply(fail) message when there are no (more) solutions. In the former case it then backtracks to find the next solution to Q. Receipt of a client discard message causes it to terminate.

```
listener_loop :-
    message_choice (
      ask_if(AttList) << _ reply_to R ::
                (member(content(Q),AttList),
                 member(reply_with(Lab),AttList))
        ->
          (Q -> tell([in_reply_to(Lab),content(yes)]) >> R
            ; tell([in_reply_to(Lab),content(no)]) >> R
        ;
      ask_all(AttList) << _ reply_to R ::
                (member(content(Q),AttList),
                 member(reply_with(Lab),AttList))
        ->
          findall(Q,Q,Ans),  % Ans becomes list a solution
                             % instances of Q
          tell([in_reply_to(Lab),content(Ans)]) >> R
        ;
      stand_by(stream_all(AttList)) << _ reply_to R ::
                member(content(Q),AttList)
        ->
          thread_fork(ans_gen(Q,R),I),
          generator(I) >> R
        ;
      tell(content(A)) -> assert(A)
        ;
      untell(content(A)) -> retract(A)
    ),
    listener_loop.

ans_gen(Q,R):-
   call(Q), % get next answer to query Q
   message_choice ( % now wait for a next or a
                    % discard message from R
      next << R -> reply(Q) >> R,
                   % if next, send solved Q as reply
                   fail
                   % now fail to get next sol. to call(Q)
        ;
      discard << R -> thread_exit). % terminate on receipt
                                    % of discard message
ans_gen(Q,R) :- % this clause used when no more sols to Q
   message_choice (
      next << R -> reply(fail) >> R, thread_exit
        ;
      discard << R -> thread_exit).
```

Remote calls to such an information server. If the client is a Prolog thread, it can use the following meta-call predicates, declared as operators, to transparently send remote queries to the information server. A call of the form C..QS sends an **ask_if** message to the query server QS. C?QS sends an **all_of** message to the query server QS, waits for the list of solutions from the server, and then uses **member** to locally backtrack over the solutions as required. A call of the form C??QS sends a stand_by(stream_of(...)) message to QS, waits for the thread ID to be returned in a **generator** reply message, and then uses deal_with_ans to process the reply and to manage any subsequent backtracking.

```
Call..Q_S :-
  gen_label(Lab),
  ask_if([reply_with(Lab),content(Call)]) >> Q_S,
  tell(L) <<= Q_S,
  member(in_reply_to(Lab),L),
  member(content(yes),L).  % a no answer causes Call..Q_S to fail

Call?Q_S:-
  gen_label(Lab),
  ask_all([reply_with(Lab),content(Call)]) >> Q_S,
  tell(L) <<= Q_S,
  member(in_reply_to(Lab),L),
  member(content(AnsList),L),
  member(Call,AnsList).

Call??Q_S :-
  stand_by(stream_of([content(Call)])) >> Q_S,
     % send stand_by stream_of query to Q_S
  generator(QTh) <<= Q_S, % wait for id of new query thread
  next >> QTh,         % request first answer from this thread
  reply(Ans) <<= QTh,     % wait for the reply from QTh
  deal_with_ans(Ans,Call,QTh).

deal_with_ans(fail,_,QTh) :-   % answer is fail message
   !, fail.                     % cause Call??Q_S to fail
deal_with_ans(Call,Call,_).    % unify Ans with Call
deal_with_ans(_,Call,QTh):-
  next >> QTh, % request next Ans for Call
  reply(Ans) <<= QTh,
  deal_with_ans(Ans,Call,QTh).
```

Note that C?QS is an eager remote call. All answers to C that can be found against the information in QS are returned to the client thread that executes the ? call as a list AnsList of instantiations of C. Client backtracking through successive solutions to C is achieved by unifying C with the returned instantiations in AnsList, one at a time.

In contrast, C??QS is an lazy remote call. Solutions are only returned to the thread that executes the call on demand. The demands, **next messages**, are generated by local backtracking within the C??QS call.

The above meta calls hide the KQML protocol of message exchanges with the remote query server. They can be used as normal Prolog calls in queries and in clauses in the Prolog databases of each information server. So a user query to one server can result in a chain of remote queries being sent over the network of query servers. The initial information server thus serves as an interface to the entire network of information servers [3].

As an example, the query:

```
employee(X)?IS1,disabled(X)?IS2
```

finds the employees recorded in remote information source IS1, perhaps a company information source, that are disabled according to the information source, IS2. The rules for **disabled** in IS2 might itself involve remote subqueries. For example:

```
disabled(X):-
    has_physical_defect(X,D),
    considered_disabling(D)?IS3.
```

4 Programming richer inference systems

The KQML information source of the previous section using standard Prolog evaluation to answer the queries it receives. This is Horn clause resolution augmented with the negation as failure rule. In fact, since Qu-Prolog does the occur check in unification, each information source uses sound inference to answer queries. The reasoning is, however, limited. In particular, we may want agents to be able to reason about their own beliefs and the beliefs of other agents, or to do temporal reasoning in order to plan. Using the extra support that Qu-Prolog provides for implementing formal proof systems, we can much more easily implement more complex inference systems than in a normal Prolog. In this section we summarise the features of Qu-Prolog specific to this purpose. They are more fully described and their use exemplified in [1, 2].

Qu-Prolog extends the syntax of Prolog to include support for quantified terms, object variables and substitutions. Object variables use the same syntax as atoms but are distinguished from atoms by declaration. Atoms that are used as quantifier symbols are declared in the same way as atoms are declared as operators.

---

[3] There is a slight problem with the above implementation of remote querying. If a query or clause executes a cut (!) after a C??QS call, but before all the solutions have been requested and returned, the temporary thread created by QS will not be exited, and will be left as an orphan. A slight elaboration of the query server and the ?? program will ensure that all query threads that are spawned in order to answer a remote lazy query will be sent a **discard** message. Details are given in [8].

Given appropriate declarations of x and y as object variables and `all` and `ex` as a quantifier symbols then the following are syntactically correct Qu-Prolog terms.

```
all x ex y f(x,y)     all X Y      !!sum(Lo,Hi) x f(x)
```

In the second example the normal Prolog variable X stands for a list of object variables and in the last example the quantifier is a compound term, `sum(Lo,Hi)`, a summation quantifier, applied to object variable x. In this case the `!!` declares `sum(Lo,Hi)` as a quantifier.

Qu-Prolog also provides a notation for substitutions. The term `[A/x]B` represents the term obtained by replacing all free occurrences of object variable x in B by A, with any necessary change of bound variables so that no free occurrences of an object variable, say y, in A is caught by an explicit quantification that happens to use the object variable name, y, in B. Any such quantification on y can be changed to a quantification on a different object variable, say y1, that does not appear free in A. For example:

```
[g(y)/x]all y f(x,y)
```

becomes

```
all y1 f(g(y),y1)
```

not

```
all y f(g(y),y)
```

The unification algorithm of Qu-Prolog carries out substitution evaluation where possible and attempts to make terms α-equivalent (that is, identical up to change of bound variable). During substitution evaluation it will automatically rename bound variables where necessary. For example, the terms `all y f(y)` and `all z f(z)` are already α-equivalent and therefore unify without instantiation. The terms `all y Y` and `all z f(z)` unify by instantiating Y to `f(y)` as is required to make the terms α-equivalent.

The data structures and unification algorithm of Qu-Prolog provide built-in support for expressing and correctly applying inference rules for a wide range of logics and inference styles. For example, the following clauses express the $\forall$-introduction and $\exists$-introduction rules for a sequent calculus.

```
rule(all_intro, H --> all x G, [H --> G]) :-
    x not_free_in H.
rule(exists_intro, H --> ex x G, [H --> [B/x]G]).
```

where `-->` is the sequent arrow.

The features of Qu-Prolog described above support efficient implementations of theorem provers that might, for example, be used as the inference engine of complex KQML information servers. They can also be used to program agents that do modal or temporal reasoning using appropriate formal logics.

5 Conclusion

In this paper we presented the multi-threading and message communication capabilities of Qu-Prolog, and its features that support the programming of richer proof systems. We illustrated these by showing how we could implement a distributed deductive database system of heterogeneous provers that communicate using KQML style messages.

Our thesis is that the combination of multiple threads and high-level communication using symbolic addresses supported by Qu-Prolog provides application writers with simple and powerful techniques for implementing a wide range of intelligent distributed systems, possibly opening up new application areas for logic programming.

References

1. Peter J. Robinson. Qu-Prolog 4.2 User Guide. Technical Report No. 97-12, Software Verification Research Centre, School of Information Technology, University of Queensland.
2. Peter J. Robinson and Richard Hagen. Qu-Prolog 4.2 Reference Manual. Technical Report No. 97-11, Software Verification Research Centre, School of Information Technology, University of Queensland.
3. Holger Becht, Anthony Bloesch, Ray Nickson and Mark Utting. Ergo 4.1 Reference Manual, Technical Report No. 96-31, Software Verification Research Centre, Department of Computer Science, University of Queensland.
4. C. Fidge, P. Kearney and M. Utting. Interactively Verifying a Simple Real-time Scheduler. In P. Wolper, editor, *Computer Aided Verification*, Lecture Notes in Computer Science 939, pages 395-408, Springer Verlag, 1995.
5. David Carrington, Ian Hayes, Ray Nickson, Geoffrey Watson and Jim Welsh, A Tool for Developing Correct Programs by Refinement. *Proc. BCS 7th Refinement Workshop, Bath, UK*, (ed. He Jifeng), Electronic Workshops in Computing, Springer, 1996, 1–17.
6. Yannis Cosmadopoulos and Damian Chu, IC-Prolog II Reference Manual, Imperial College, 1993, http://www-lp.doc.ic.ac.uk/LocalInfo/prolog.html
7. P. Tarau, BinProlog 5.75 User Guide, Technical Report 97-1, Département d'Informatique, Université de Moncton.
8. K. L. Clark, P. J. Robinson and R. Hagen Multi-threading and Message Communication in Qu-Prolog Technical Report No. 98-11, Software Verification Research Centre, University of Queensland. (Also http://www-lp.doc.ic.ac.uk/ klc/qp.html)
9. T. Finin, Y. Labrou and J. Mayfield KQML as an Agent Communication Language *Software Agents*, (ed J. Bradshaw), AAAI/MIT Press, 1997

Design of an Agent-Based, Multi-user Scheduling Implementation

Andrew Scott   Karen Jenkin   Rye Senjen

Telstra Research Laboratories
Box 249, Rosebank MDC
Clayton 3169, Australia

{a.scott, k.jenkin, r.senjen}@trl.telstra.com.au

Abstract

The meeting scheduling domain in a large, geographically distributed corporation is characterised by scenarios where position in the corporate hierarchy and frequent rescheduling and cancellation of meetings plays a large role in determining the outcome of the scheduling task. We highlight these important issues, and describe in detail both a mathematical model and scheduling implementation designed to address the distributed meeting scheduling problem in this domain. The design of the implementation deals with the need for privacy, scalability, user control, reasonable meeting times, and trust. The implementation itself is written using conventional DAI tools, such as KQML and CLIPS. A small-scale qualitative survey was performed which indicated alignment of the design with the needs and expectations of users.

1. Introduction

The use of agents to address the problem of scheduling meetings in a multi-user environment has long been a popular approach within the field of distributed artificial intelligence (DAI). The reasons for this popularity are clear:

- using an agent for each participant in the scheduling problem, and restricting the form of communication between agents goes some way to ensuring privacy of meeting information,
- participants can perform customisation of their interfaces and algorithms at a local level, rather than by influencing a central server,
- distributing the process of negotiation through agents discourages the formation of a "communications bottleneck" in a solution,
- similarly, distributing this process allows computation to be evenly spread across a number of hosts in a network, and
- agents provide an obvious abstraction of the personal assistant to represent a person in negotiating a meeting, and so is a model of the real-world solution to the problem.

Previously, we examined the problem of computing the importance of meetings in the schedule of a busy person, in a large, geographically distributed organisation [6]. We concluded that many existing approaches to scheduling meetings did not address the issues of company hierarchies and location information when deciding when to add a new meeting. Another limitation of existing approaches were that they did not acceptably handle the situation of busy people, where there is little or no free time, and appointments are regularly cancelled or re-scheduled.

In this paper, we build on our previous approach, and describe a multiple user scheduling approach and its implementation. In section 2, we summarise the problem of meeting scheduling and extend the definitions of importance from our earlier work. Section 3 covers the implementation of our meeting scheduling system. In section 4 we analyse this scheduling system and detail the results of a small-scale survey on meeting scheduling. In section 5, we describe directions for future work, and in section 6 draw conclusions on the suitability of using both our model of meeting importance as well as our system for negotiating meetings.

2. Problem Overview

Our problem domain is that of a large, geographically distributed corporation. Within such a domain it is possible for meetings to be: initiated by managers who expect their staff to drop everything to attend; organised in different locations, where substantial travel time must be allowed for between meetings; and regularly rearranged, due to the schedules of busy people.

The Secretaries' Nightmare problem [5] is a complex scenario involving four people meeting and many constraints on possible solutions. The scenario was proposed for analysing different meeting scheduling approaches, however it is inadequate for assessing solutions designed for our problem domain. It does not include, in particular, cases where attendee's positions in the company hierarchy would affect scheduling decisions (as all its attendees are from different organisations), or the outcome of being forced to cancel or reschedule an existing meeting due to the final scheduling of the new meeting.

The problem domain of a single, large organisation best fits the Closed Scheduling System paradigm, as defined by Ephrati *et al.* [1]. A Closed System is characterised by a particular scheduling mechanism being imposed on the members of the system, i.e. the attendees of the meeting. Alternatively, in an Open System, the individuals involved in organising a meeting are not in any way required to meet with each other, nor to accomplish this task in a particular way. Scheduling meetings in a Closed System is possibly easier than in an Open System as we can guarantee that the value systems used by the participants in a meeting will be compatible for the purpose of comparing the relative suitability of meeting times.

Even though the domain is a Closed System, there is still an important issue of privacy. Who, where, and for what purpose people meet with others is valuable corporate information. It is desirable that this information does not leave the computer of the user, or remains within a secure system. Even free time information may be valuable, especially if a request for a meeting is refused.

This suggests that all calendar information cannot be stored on a single server. Not only would a nefarious person compromising the server cause valuable schedule details to be compromised, but all attendees of any meetings organised by the server would have to completely trust the organisation that owned and administered the server. For instance, a company server could not be used to organise a meeting where one of the attendees was not an employee of the company, or if it was used, it might not be completely effective.

As a result of this strong privacy requirement, automated scheduling must be accomplished in a distributed fashion, where no agent needs access to any other agent's scheduling details.

Another strong requirement in a large corporation is that of scalability. This has two important aspects: processing load and communications load. The fact that there are potentially tens of thousands of employees with calendars means that no single server would be able to perform the task of automated scheduling.

The natural reaction is to design an architecture where each of a meeting's attendees' agents shares the processing load between them evenly. This would mean that each agent would have to communicate with each other agent. For N attendees there would be $O(N^2)$ communication paths. This is not ideal for large meetings.

Another response is to give the agent of the person who initiates the meeting the whole processing load. This would distribute most of the processing in the network amongst those agents who initiate meetings, and have all agents communicate only with this agent, requiring only $O(N)$ communication paths. However, this gives a large amount of control to the initiating agent, and also requires the machine that the initiating agent resides on to be powerful enough to cope with the task.

We now define the aspects of meeting scheduling in our domain as follows.

A proposed meeting M of duration d may occur sometime within a period of time T. The terms *meeting* and *appointment* are used interchangeably. A timeslot t is a period of time that the meeting may conceivably occur over, in other words t is of duration d, and consists of time only within T. Two timeslots t_1 and t_2 may overlap. There are finitely many timeslots, and they are common to all attendees of meeting M. Note that for different meetings, the duration and various starting times of timeslots may be different. The agents within a particular implementation should abide by a timeslot policy to ensure that agents may compare timeslots. One such policy might be that timeslots are evenly spaced, starting every fifteen minutes, and have duration equal to the length of the appointment in question, rounded up to the next fifteen minutes.

The importance of a meeting M, written $I(M)$, may take integral values in the range $\{1,...,100\}$. The importance is either chosen by the user from a list ('normal' = 50, 'high' = 70, 'irrelevant' = 5, etc.), or if the user specifies, computed in software.

We looked at ways of representing the cost to a person of rescheduling, and chose one that would provide our representation of convenience (see below) with suitable properties. We define the cost to a person of rescheduling meetings overlapping a given timeslot t to accommodate a new meeting M, over the range $[1,2]$ as

$$C_R(M,t) \quad = \quad \sqrt{2\left(\frac{98+I_{max}(t)}{98+I(M)}\right)}$$

where $I_{max}(t)$ is the maximum importance of any existing meeting overlapping timeslot t (or 1 if there are no such meetings). The cost of rescheduling a meeting for one that is equally important is hence $\sqrt{2}$.

We will define a person's d_{home} to be the distance in kilometres from their home location (wherever that is) to the location of M. The distance ratio for this person travelling to a meeting M at timeslot t is defined as

$$D_R(M,t) \quad = \quad \frac{1+d_{std}}{1+d_{actual}}$$

where d_{std} is the distance in kilometres of the return trip from the home location (wherever that is) to the location of M (in other words $d_{std} = 2 * d_{home}$), and d_{actual} is the sum of the distance to travel from the location of the last meeting before timeslot t to the location of M (or d_{home} if there is no such meeting) plus the distance to travel from the location of M to the first meeting after timeslot t (or d_{home} if there is no such meeting).

We define the gain made in travel for a person by scheduling the meeting M at t, over the range $(0,1]$ as

$$G_T(M,t) \quad = \quad \left(\frac{D_R(M,t)}{5}\right)^{\frac{1}{2}\log_5 2} \qquad \text{where } D_R < 5.0 \;{}^{\bullet}$$

$$= \quad 1.0 \qquad\qquad \text{otherwise}$$

When there is no gain to be made over performing a return trip, then the gain made in travel will be $1/\sqrt{2}$. We are justified in limiting the effect of the distance ratio to be no more than five times, as any advantage in distance beyond this makes no reasonable difference, and hence this allows us to restrict the range of the travel gain (which would otherwise be unbounded).

For example, if a meeting is at a location that is 40 km from the home location, then assuming an average car speed of 80 km/h, this will take 30 mins. If there are

---

${}^{\bullet}$ The general form $(\frac{1}{n}x)^{\frac{1}{2}\log_n m}$ gives a curve with respect to x, that passes through the points $(0,0)$, $(1,\sqrt{m})$ and $(n,1)$.

meetings either side of this meeting in locations that are 8 kms away from that location (ie. 6 mins at that car speed), then G_r would be 1.0, but G_r would be 1.0 as well if those meetings were all in the same location.

The convenience to a person of scheduling a meeting M in a timeslot t is expressed as

$$C(M,t) \quad = \quad \frac{G_T(M,t)}{C_R(M,t)}$$

Convenience is defined over the range (0,1], where a convenience of 1.0 is the most convenient a given timeslot could be, 0.0 would be least convenient, and a convenience of 0.5 is the level of convenience if the person had to reschedule an equally important meeting which is in the same location as the new meeting.

The definitions for G_T and C_R have been altered from those presented previously [6]. These new definitions have been chosen because they enable convenience to be defined as above, with a restricted range, and a well-defined meaning for the start, end, and middle points of that range. This is necessary because the conveniences of different attendees are combined, as will be seen in the following section, and this requires a uniform scale.

3. Agent Architecture

The architecture is designed so that each person or place has a single Meeting agent, and although there may be multiple Facilitator agents, only one is used in scheduling any particular meeting. Meeting agents are responsible for knowing the priorities of their users. Facilitator agents make decisions about which timeslots to schedule meetings for. An Agent Name Server (ANS) is used to keep a register of all active agents and their addresses. A representation of the architecture is given in Figure 1.

In our current implementation, all agents are written in a modified version of CLIPS v6.04 and communicate using KQML messages. A company-specific Corporate Directory is accessed via an LDAP gateway, and the Calendar Database is accessible via Oracle database routines that we have incorporated into CLIPS. People interact with their Meeting agents via web browsers.

The basic process for organising a meeting is as follows:
1. The initiator of a meeting contacts their Meeting agent to organise a meeting given a number of constraints, such as the period of time that the meeting may occur within, duration of the meeting, time available to spend organising the meeting, location of the meeting, and attendees of the meeting. The initiator also provides some information to assist with scheduling, such as the description of the meeting, importance of the meeting, and importance of each attendee.
2. The initiator's Meeting agent uses this information and sends messages to the Facilitator agent requesting it to organise a meeting with the given attendees in

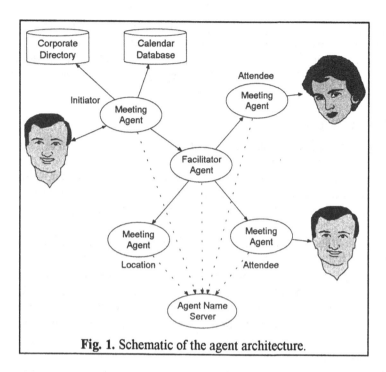

Fig. 1. Schematic of the agent architecture.

the given location, and provides a number of timeslots, each with an associated convenience value.

3. The Facilitator agent contacts the Meeting agent representing the location (if there is one) and finds out when there are free spaces in its calendar.
4. The Facilitator agent then contacts the Meeting agent for each attendee of the meeting (if there are any) and finds out what their convenience values are for the timeslots.
5. Using all of the information it has gathered, the Facilitator agent then selects a timeslot and informs all Meeting agents of the result.
6. Each Meeting agent then stores an appointment in their calendar database records and informs their user (for those agents representing humans).

The important aspects of the process are:

- There is no iterated negotiation - the only opportunity for an agent to reject the decision is at the end of the process.
- The number of communication paths is roughly proportional to the number of attendees, since the only other agent that an agent communicates with is the Facilitator.
- The agent that decides when to have the meeting (the Facilitator) does not know the contents of anyone's calendar nor does it have access to their calendar database, nor even the corporate directory.
- Hence, the Facilitator needs to be trustworthy to carry out the process without bias.

- No details about existing meetings, or even free time, are communicated across the network, only the convenience of different times.
- The final decision may cause an overlap with a previously organised meeting, and therefore cancellation or rescheduling of an existing meeting may be necessary.

3.1 The Meeting Agent

There is a Meeting agent for each person or place that is to be involved in automatic meeting negotiation. The Meeting agent has two tasks: to initiate a meeting request from the user, and to respond to a meeting request from the Facilitator. Both of these tasks involve computing the conveniences of timeslots in a given period, but the former task also involves computing the importance of all attendees.

Meeting agents that represent locations differ from other Meeting agents in that they never initiate meeting requests. At present, they are not strictly involved in meeting negotiations either, as they simply take the conveniences of timeslots supplied by the Facilitator from the initiating Meeting agent and return them to the Facilitator, filtered so that timeslots overlapping existing appointments have a convenience of 0. Eventually, negotiation will be a two-step process of gathering conveniences from multiple locations, and these will be combined with the conveniences of multiple attendees, where the final choice of meeting time may cause a meeting booked at a location to be rescheduled. This is possible in an automated world, as the previously booked meeting can be immediately rescheduled, although such a process would be unworkable in a typical human personal assistant environment, as the personal assistants would spend all their time scheduling and rescheduling.

Initiating Meetings

The Meeting agent receives details of a proposed meeting from the user via some interface (at present, this is a web page). The details consist of the period the meeting may occur within, the meeting duration, the time available to spend organising the meeting, the location of the meeting, the description of the meeting, the importance of the meeting, the attendees of the meeting, and the importance of each attendee.

The set of all possible timeslots within this period is created. Timeslots are created following the policy of beginning timeslots at fifteen minute boundaries past the hour (e.g. 6:00am 6:15am, 6:30am, etc.) or thirty minute boundaries past the hour, depending on meeting constraints, with durations equal to the length of the meeting.

For each timeslot, a number of proposals for its convenience might be generated, such as a convenience based on the function described in section 2, a convenience based on a user-specific daily profile, and other rules as appropriate. The convenience set for a timeslot is equal to the minimum convenience out of all the proposals for that timeslot.

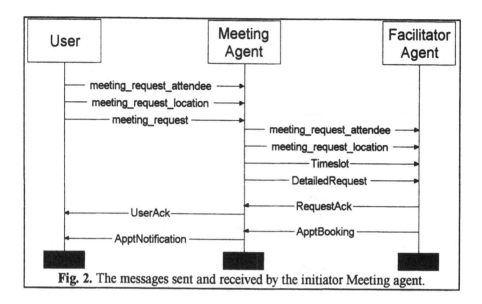

Fig. 2. The messages sent and received by the initiator Meeting agent.

The daily profile models a typical Monday, Tuesday, etc. for that user, and takes the form of a "night-time" convenience and a "day-time" convenience, with a two-hour changeover period between them. A user can configure the times that the model changes from night-time to day-time and visa versa, but not the conveniences themselves, which are set at a convenience of 0 for the most inconvenient time (whether it is night-time or day-time), 1 for the most convenient time, and 0.8 during the changeover period. The value of 0.8 was chosen to be sufficiently convenient for this free time to be chosen than to cancel most appointments. A decay of convenience across the changeover period would probably be more representative of human behaviour, although a fixed value was chosen for simplicity of implementation.

The Meeting agent has a set of known Facilitator agents that it trusts to organise appointments. This set might be expanded by allowing the user to add the names of other trusted Facilitator agents, or by keeping track of Facilitator agents used when other Meeting agents have organised meetings with its user as an attendee. One Facilitator agent from the set is chosen to be Facilitator for this meeting.

A subset of the timeslots (e.g. the most convenient 30 timeslots) or ideally all of the timeslots are sent to the Facilitator, as well as the attendees with their importance according to the user (or the agent's estimate of importance, if they were not specified), the desired location, and finally the description and the other constraints for the meeting in a DetailedRequest message. This is acknowledged by the Facilitator via a RequestAck message. When the meeting negotiation has finished, the Meeting agent will receive an ApptBooking message, and will subsequently notify the user. This process can be seen in Figure 2. Note that although only a single message is shown of each type, multiple messages may actually be sent.

Attending Meetings

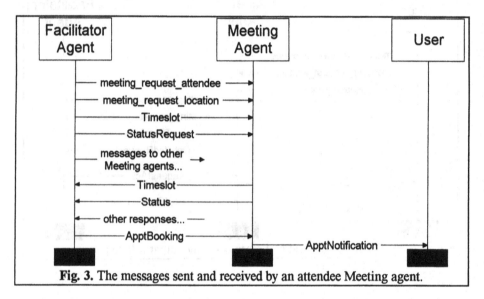

Fig. 3. The messages sent and received by an attendee Meeting agent.

Meeting agents of users attending a proposed meeting perform many of the activities that an initiating Meeting agent performs. When a StatusRequest message is received, the Meeting agent computes the convenience of a number of timeslots (which must include those received from the Facilitator, plus any others within the period being considered), and returns these to the Facilitator. Like the initiating Meeting agent, when the negotiation is finished, the attendee Meeting agent will receive an ApptBooking message. This process can be seen in Figure 3. A sample message is shown in Figure 4.

```
(tell :sender Facilitator :receiver MeetingAgent4242 :language
clips :content (StatusRequest (meeting-id aaa.1) (initiator
"Mister Burns") (tStartLimit 897519600) (tEndLimit 897951600)
(tDuration 1800) (szDescription "Project XYZ brainstorming
discussion") (tUrgency 89760600) (timeslot-messages 60)
(attendee-messages 2) (location-messages 1) ))
```

Fig. 4. An example of a KQML message sent to a Meeting agent.

If a Meeting agent is sent an ApptBooking that requires an existing meeting to be cancelled in order to accommodate it, then a cancel message would be sent to the Facilitator agent in order to contact the attendees and organise for rescheduling.

3.2 The Facilitator Agent

The Facilitator agent is responsible for responding to meeting requests from any initiating Meeting agent. It does this by coordinating the communication with the Meeting agents representing the meeting location and meeting attendees (if there are any), and then combining the convenience values received from the Meeting agents to choose the best timeslot. Finally, it informs all the Meeting agents involved in the negotiation process of the allocated appointment time.

Figures 2 and 3 show the messaging protocol, which has already been explained in section 3.1. The Facilitator agent waits until it receives all Timeslot and Status messages from the attendees' Meeting agents before proceeding to the scoring mechanism for finding the best timeslot. This mechanism is described below.

Timeslot Scoring

For a meeting, there is a list of attendees (including the initiating user), $\{a\}$, each with their assigned importance level (which is either chosen by the user or computed by the Meeting agent), written $I(a)$. Importances range from 1 to 99, with 99 being the highest importance (e.g. the CEO). Also, for each attendee there is a set of convenience values for all timeslots in the allowed period, $\{c(a,t_n)\}$, where t_n is the nth timeslot. Timeslots not explicitly sent to the Facilitator agent by a Meeting agent are set to a default convenience value, provided to the Facilitator within the Status message from the Meeting agent.

To ascertain the most convenient timeslot, it is simply a question of calculating a combined convenience score for each timeslot, utilising the conveniences from each attendee and the attendee's importance. It has been suggested [1] that maximising the product (rather than the sum) of individual conveniences guarantees a relatively fair outcome, however this is not suitable when the importance of an attendee is included (i.e. the negotiation process is not necessarily fair for users with a lower priority in an organisation). Hence, the basic method for calculating the score of the nth timeslot is expressed as

$$S(t_n) \qquad = \qquad \sum_a c(a,t_n)I(a)$$

However, in order to provide some flexibility to the system, the above method was enhanced to allow for the ability to weight the relevance of attendee importance in scoring timeslots, as well as the ability to model the preference for earlier rather than later times in the period being considered, i.e. to schedule meetings for as soon as possible. These functions are discussed below.

Rather than always using the attendee importance measure, there is benefit in weighting the relevance of importance in choosing the most appropriate timeslot, to control the extent to which these importances influence the result. So, we introduced an importance weighting factor, W_A, with a range $[0,1]$. The adjusted attendee importance becomes

$$I^*(a) \qquad = \qquad 1 + \frac{W_A I(a)}{99}$$

So, if the weighting factor is equal to 0, no relevance is placed on the importance of attendees (i.e. all adjusted importances are equal to 1). On the other hand, if the weighting factor is equal to 1 the attendees' importances are given maximum relevance and the adjusted importances lie in the range (1, 2].

To address the preference for earlier alternatives (rather than waiting for more distant alternatives) within the period under consideration, a time decay was introduced. As with attendee importance, weighting the relevance of this decay provides more control over the configuration of the system. To introduce an exponentially decreasing timeslot preference, the decay is written as

$$D(t_n) \qquad = \qquad e^{W_D(1-n)}$$

where W_D is the decay weighting factor, with a range [0,1], and n represents the nth timeslot. So, if the weighting factor is equal to 0 no relevance in placed on the preference for earlier timeslots (i.e. the decay is equal to 1 for all timeslots). A relatively conservative value for W_D is employed, otherwise the decay is extremely rapid and dominates the scoring method.

In consolidating these enhancements, the score of the nth timeslot becomes

$$S(t_n) \qquad = \qquad e^{W_D(1-n)} \sum_a c(a,t_n) I^*(a)$$

and the timeslot chosen for the meeting is the one with the highest score. If this score is below a pre-set threshold value, then the Facilitator agent sends a "failed" status within the ApptBooking message that is sent to all Meeting agents.

4. Analysis of the Implementation

We conducted qualitative email interviews with 40 people from within a large organisation (personal assistants, executives and non-executives, both male and female, and from a broad range of age groups) to elucidate their priorities in relation to: meeting cancellation, the importance of people attending the meeting, and meeting time availability. These interviews were set in the context of either an agent-based system or a Personal Assistant performing a proposed scheduling arrangement.

Analysis of the responses indicates that meeting scheduling in large organisations is dominated, in order of importance, by: a person's position with respect to others, the meeting topic, and time availability. Who initiated/requested the meeting was often given as the most important factor by the interviewees, as this affected the outcome of the interaction. Few of the interviewees, when presented with a case where the scheduling task was performed by an agent-based system, commented on this fact. Foremost on everybody's mind was the hierarchical position the person with whom they were proposed to meet occupied. How and by whom the meeting time was found was completely irrelevant. This was an important finding, as we had expected to encounter some negative reaction to agent-derived meeting times.[†]

Our implementation competently produces meeting time proposals based on positions in the hierarchy (via the attendee importances based on the corporate directory, and supplied to the Facilitator agent), time availability (taking into account possibility of rescheduling), and to a limited extent, meeting topic. It was up to users to assign an importance to a meeting based on the topic.

Other salient points of this implementation that were not assessed were:
• its high degree of privacy protection with regard to meetings and free time,
• its scalable design in terms of communications and processing load, and
• the ability for users to control the importance of people and meetings.

This last point is worth emphasising. Haynes *et al.* [2] similarly perceived the value in giving users a strong level of control over both the amount of information the user has to enter and the information itself. Kelley and Chapanis emphasise the need to be able to support a "large amount of diversity" for scheduling systems to be effective [3]. For importances, we allow the user to specify the details, or the system will automatically calculate them based on information, such as in the corporate directory. By providing the facility for users to take control, a greater level of trust in the system is obtained.

Another view of trust is that of the agents' trust: can any agent deceive the others to produce a resulting meeting time in their favour? The answer is yes, but this is minimal due to factors both internal and external to the system. The initiating Meeting agent has a large degree of control over the outcome. The period over which a meeting can occur, and the importance of the attendees are specified by this agent. However, as long as these constraints are realistic, the result produced by the Facilitator agent should be reasonable.

Internally, the period is likely to be as large as is reasonable, since artificially restricting the period to only a couple of timeslots increases the likelihood that there will not be good overlap between free times in the different calendars. If there isn't a mutually convenient time, then the score calculated by the Facilitator agent may fall beneath the pre-set threshold and the meeting may not get scheduled.

Also, the importance of the attendees is not likely to deviate too wildly from reality, as these importances are broadcast by the Facilitator agents to the attendee Meeting agents. This information may be revealed to the users of those Meeting agents. If

---

[†] Maes and Kozierok state the conventional wisdom [4] that an agent that does not gradually build a trust-relationship may leave a user "with a feeling of loss of control and understanding."

those users are upset or insulted by the importance that they have been assigned, they might not attend the meeting. The case where this would matter is where the users are more important than the Facilitator agent has been informed.

Regardless of the above internal issues, external factors will dominate in ensuring reasonable requests. The contents of someone's schedule is not a rigid contract, and they may need to cancel for one reason or another. If meeting times are consistently unfair to attendees then it is unlikely that they will be able to attend the meetings.

One last point to consider about the implementation is its robustness. An agent-oriented approach helps in ensuring the robustness of the process, but the robustness of the algorithm is even more important. Unfortunately, our current implementation may possibly enter infinite loops when organising meetings where at least one of the attendees is very busy.

5. Future Work

An important direction for future work is to remove the possibility of loops. These occur because of two factors: The calculation of convenience of a timeslot may be greatly skewed by factors not related to the contents of the schedule (e.g. travel time), and there is nothing to prevent a cancelled meeting being rescheduled in the same timeslot it was cancelled from if every other timeslot is far less convenient.

To address the first factor, the G_T factor should be incorporated into the importance of a meeting, rather than scaling the convenience of a timeslot. Also the weighting on the importance of existing appointments should be increased.

The second factor requires more extensive changes. The Facilitator agent cancels a meeting request if its best score is less than a pre-set threshold. Every Meeting agent should send the Facilitator a threshold that it believes represents the level where its user would not find it worth having a meeting. The Facilitator agent would compare these thresholds to the final score before choosing to reject a proposal. Also, if a meeting is cancelled, a Meeting agent should increase its threshold to ensure that a meeting of convenience lower than the existing meeting does not oust it.

In addition to alterations in the implementation, we intend to conduct more extensive quantitative interviews of people to judge the acceptability of the solutions produced by the implementation in a large corporation.

6. Conclusion

In this paper, we have highlighted the important issues in the domain of meeting scheduling in a large, geographically distributed corporation, and detailed both a mathematical model and scheduling implementation designed to address the distributed meeting scheduling problem in this domain.

The design of the implementation addresses the level of need for privacy, scalability, user control, reasonable meeting times, and trust. The implementation itself is written using conventional DAI tools, such as KQML and CLIPS. The automated meeting scheduling system appears to be ideally suited to organising meetings in the domain.

A small-scale qualitative survey was performed which indicated alignment of the design with the needs and expectations of users. An important result was that the opposition to agent-based systems may not be as large as imagined. Future research in this area will concentrate on obtaining quantitative results on the acceptability of agent-based scheduling systems to users in large corporations.

7. Acknowledgments

The permission of the Director, Telstra Research Laboratories, to publish this material is hereby acknowledged. We would also like to thank Brad Starkie, Telstra Research Laboratories, for his involvement in designing and implementing the prototype.

8. References

[1]   E. Ephrati, G. Zlotkin, and J. S. Rosenschein. A non-manipulable meeting scheduling system. In *Proceedings of the Thirteenth International Distributed Artificial Intelligence Workshop*, pages 105-125, Seattle, Washington, 1994.

[2]   T. Haynes, S. Sen, N. Arora, and R. Nadella. An automated meeting scheduling system that utilizes user preferences. In *Proceedings of the First International Conference on Autonomous Agents*, pages 308-315, Marina del Ray, California, 1997.

[3]   J. F. Kelley and A. Chapanis. How professional persons keep their calendars: implications for computerization. *Journal of Occupational Psychology* 55, pages 241-256, 1982.

[4]   P. Maes and R. Kozierok. Learning interface agents. In *Proceedings of the Eleventh National Conference on Artificial Intelligence (AAAI-93)*, pages 459-465, Washington, DC, 1993.

[5]   C. Petrie. The Secretaries' Nightmare. In *Proceedings of the CAIA Workshop on Coordinated Design and Planning*, San Antonio, Texas, 1994.

[6]   B. Ward, A. Scott, and R. Senjen. Using agents to schedule meetings between busy people. In L. Cavedon, A. Rao, and W. Wobcke, editors, *Proceedings of the AI'97 Workshop on the Theoretical and Practical Foundations of Intelligent Agents and Agent Oriented Systems*, Perth, Australia, 1997.

A Team of Agents
Cooperating for Intelligent Tutoring

Ruddy Lelouche

Département d'informatique
UNIVERSITÉ LAVAL
Québec G1K 7P4 CANADA

Tel.: (+1-418) 656 2131, ext. 2597
Fax: (+1-418) 656 2324
e-mail: lelouche@ift.ulaval.ca

Abstract

This paper presents how the tutoring knowledge in an ITS, in particular in a domain involving problem-solving skills in addition to conventional domain theory, can be designed and organised as a team of cooperating intelligent agents. After a brief description of the domain knowledge and a generic functioning framework for ITSs in problem-solving domains, we introduce how the tutoring knowledge is modelled as pedagogical agents. We then show how these agents are designed to interact with one another and with the student, and discuss about techniques which may help an agent to decide to intervene in the process in order to fulfil a given pedagogical function, henceforth making pedagogical interactions smoother and hopefully more efficient. To illustrate our point of view, we then present and comment, in a particular application domain, a problem-solving exercise and a possible tutoring dialogue based on that exercise. Finally, referring to that example, we show a few techniques by which such a dialogue can be achieved. Such a cooperative-agent-oriented model should both facilitate the implementation of the tutoring knowledge in an ITS and help improve the student's comprehension through more efficient pedagogical interactions.

Introduction

For a few decades, computers have been used in the development of educational systems, were it for programmed instruction (Skinner [33]), for computer-assisted instructional and tutoring systems, or for "intelligent" AI-based systems (Lelouche [21]). This last category has evolved during the recent years, being successively called intelligent computer-assisted instruction/learning (ICAI/ICAL) systems (Barr & Clancey [3]), intelligent tutoring systems (ITSs) (Sleeman & Brown [34]), or more recently intelligent/interactive learning environments (ILEs). In the first projects, research has been focused on representing and dealing more with the domain knowledge (e.g. SCHOLAR [7], SOPHIE [6], BUGGY [5]) than with the tutoring knowledge (e.g. QUADRATIC [29] [30], WUSOR [18]). In many of the first experimental systems, pedagogical procedures have been integrated to the domain knowledge (e.g. GUIDON [8]). However, the interest for an explicit representation of tutorial knowledge has been continuously growing since the first endeavours towards "intelligent" computer-aided instruction (ICAI) systems. For example, concepts such as the student model (Fletcher [13]), the pedagogical diagnosis (Ohlsson [28]), and the tutoring expertise (Macmillan & Sleeman [25]) have been widely discussed since their respective introduction into the ICAI vocabulary as fundamental knowledge engineering principles. Most AI representation paradigms have been used, like production rules, networks, frames, etc. More recently, in order to facilitate the assignment of pedagogical tasks in a tutoring session context, the multiagent-system concept has been adapted to ITSs, giving the idea of an agent-based approach to represent the pedagogical knowledge and its use in a tutoring context (Masthoff [26]).

In that context, while working on the domain knowledge representation in a specific ITS in a discipline called cost engineering (Galibois [16], Lelouche & Morin [24]), we also conducted our reflections about how to help both the system to easily and efficiently generate simple and meaningful pedagogical interactions and the tutoring knowledge to be as general and portable as possible — which is the endeavour of most ICAI researchers nowadays. While developing a knowledge representation suitable in cost engineering, we came up with the concept of know-how domains or KH-domains, i.e. domains in which the student is supposed to acquire, besides domain theoretical elements, some kind of problem-solving skills in that domain. We then applied the KH-domain concept to ITSs, yielding KH-ITSs (Lelouche & Morin [23]). The goal of this paper is to present the foundations of an agent-based representation of the tutoring knowledge within a KH-ITS. More precisely, the paper emphasizes the system–student interactions and the agent–agent interactions, but only gives a first look at the architectural design.

We first briefly present the structure of knowledge in a KH-domain and generic operating modes based on this structure (section 1). Next, we introduce our tutoring knowledge model using the concept of pedagogical agents (section 2), and present some general albeit fundamental characteristics of these tutoring agents (section 3). We then give an excerpt of what could be a problem-solving tutoring session based on this approach, using a cost-engineering problem as example (section 4). Finally, we give a few types of architectures suitable for allowing all this multiagent world to work together for the student's benefit (section 5).

1 Knowledge representation and operating modes

This section introduces some background elements useful for presenting our tutoring agent approach. In section 1.1, we establish the distinction between domain knowledge and problem-solving knowledge in a KH-domain. We then use that distinction in section 1.2 to define four generic operating modes of a KH-ITS.

1.1 Domain knowledge and problem-solving knowledge

In this section we deal with the knowledge to be acquired by the student, usually called domain knowledge. However, in the particular case of KH-domains, the domain to be taught clearly encompasses both domain theoretical elements and practical problem-solving skills. We therefore think that knowledge to be taught in a KH-ITS ought to be divided in the same way (Lelouche & Morin [23]).

In a KH-domain, we thus restrict the name *domain knowledge* (DK) to the first type of knowledge, i.e. that part containing all theoretical and factual aspects of the knowledge describing the domain to be taught to the student. Although its specific structure can be varied, it typically may include concepts, entities, relations (Brodie & al. [4]), possible use restrictions, objects (Kim & Lochovsky [19]), semantic networks (Kowalski [20]), facts, rules (Clocksin & Mellish [9]), etc.

By opposition, the *problem-solving knowledge* (PSK) is specific to KH-domains, henceforth to KH-ITSs. It contains all computational and inferential dynamic *processes* used to solve a problem, i.e. a practical situation based on the domain knowledge (Kowalski [20], Patel & Kinshuk [31]).

1.2 Generic operating modes

In any ITS, depending on what he wants to do with the system, the student can choose one of two ways of using it: either he wants to learn something new, or he wants to check the correctness of what he thinks he has learnt. These correspond to two fundamental *pedagogical missions* of the system. In the former case, the knowledge he wants to acquire is obviously transferred from the system to the student. In the latter case, the student provides the system with the knowledge (supposedly acquired) that he wants it to assess: knowledge is thus transferred from the student to the system. Besides, as that of a human tutor in a KH-domain, the objective of a KH-ITS is to help the student master both DK and PSK knowledge. Therefore, for whichever reason the student wants to use the system, the involved knowledge may be either essentially factual and theoretical (DK) or essentially practical and applied to a problem (PSK). As a result, these orthogonal considerations yield altogether four distinct *generic operating modes*, which are briefly presented in table 1 (see details in Lelouche & Morin [23]).

Student's goal		*To learn new material*	*To assess his learning*
Knowledge transfer		System → Student	Student → System
Main type of knowl- edge in- volved	*Domain knowl- edge*	*Domain-presentation mode:* The student asks the system some information about a domain element, and the system reacts by transferring to the student the required information or knowledge.	*Domain-assessment mode:* The system basically prompts the student to develop a domain element and the student thus expresses his understanding of that element.
	Problem -solving knowl- edge	*Demonstration mode:* The student asks the system to solve a practical problem or to show him a given resolution step while he solves such a problem.	*Exercising mode:* The system prompts the student to solve a practical problem; he solves it step by step, showing what he understands of the involved problem-solving knowledge and of the associated domain knowledge.

Table 1: Operating modes in a KH-ITS.

In any of the four operating modes, some tutoring activities have to take place, so that the selected mode may attain the student's goal. In particular, in order to sustain the student's learning or motivation, or to help him understand a difficult topic in an alternate way, some tutoring activities may involve interactions usually associated with another operating mode, i.e. may trigger a temporary *mode shift* (Lelouche & Morin [23]). All this brings us now to the tutoring knowledge.

2 Tutoring knowledge as tutoring agents

In order to present our modelling of tutoring knowledge, we first recall its definition and purpose in ITSs (section 2.1), then present how we introduce it in KH-ITSs as tutoring agents (section 2.2).

2.1 Definition and purpose of the tutoring knowledge

Tutoring knowledge (TK) contains all tutoring entities enclosed in the ITS. It is not directly related to DK or PSK, for it is not to be taught to the student. Instead, it is there to help the student to understand, assimilate, and master more efficiently the knowledge included in DK and PSK (Gagné & Trudel [15]). Because of its reusability, we expect the tutoring knowledge to be the same for a wide variety of KH-domains.

The main system activities using TK are thus:
* ordering and formatting the topics to be presented to the student;
* monitoring a tutoring session, i.e., triggering the various tutoring processes according to the system tutoring goal and the student's actions; such monitoring may imply giving explanations, asking questions, changing to another type of interaction, etc.;
* in a KH-domain, while the student is solving an exercise, monitoring the student's problem-solving activities as required by the student or by the tutoring module: understanding and assessing these activities, giving advice to correct or optimise them, giving hints or partly solving the exercise at hand, etc.;
* continuously analysing the student's progress in order to optimise the tutoring process.

2.2 Introduction of tutoring agents

Because of its dynamic nature, like the problem-solving knowledge, the tutoring knowledge will be made of process-like entities. However, unlike PSK, the tutorial processes cannot be predetermined, because of the need for adaptive reactions to the student's actions. Moreover, in order to maintain the student's attention within a tutoring session, the tutor must be able to use a variety of different stimuli, to present a topic in multiple ways, and to vary the explanations provided to the student. This is why we think that the concept of *tutoring agents* (TAs), able to interact and cooperate with the student, is appropriate to model the tutoring knowledge.

As we see it, the goal of every TA is to perform a given *tutoring function* (we use the term *function* to distinguish it from a problem-solving *task*) for the student's benefit. Some of these functions are:
* to present a subject element,
* to explain a subject element,

- to give an example,
- to answer a student's question,
- to evaluate the student's answer to a system-asked question,
- to diagnose a student's behaviour.

A tutoring function is ultimately defined by its specification, i.e. the data, given as input, that it processes or on which it operates, and the output that it provides to the student as a result of this process. To each TA we may thus initially associate one tutoring function and to each tutoring function one interaction with the student.

Some examples of TAs in a KH-ITS may thus be the following, named after the tutoring function they are expected to perform:

- *Domain presenter*: presents a domain topic (a DK element or group of elements);
- *Domain assessor*: assesses the student's understanding of a given domain topic (within DK);
- *Problem solver*: solves a given problem (a complete demonstration);
- *Exerciser*: assesses the student's domain mastering through an appropriate exercise (refers to PSK and subsidiarily to DK);
- *Question asker*: asks the student a question about DK or PSK;
- *Problem selector*: selects or generates a problem to be given to the student;
- *Topic chooser*: chooses a topic or a subtopic to focus on;
- *Problem-step solver*: shows a resolution step (a partial demonstration — to be distinguished from the problem solver);
- *Explanation provider*: explains a domain topic or a problem-solving technique.

3   More about tutoring agents

The fundamental reason for introducing agents as tutoring knowledge elements is their capabilities of communication and interaction. We first show how the modularity in the tutoring functions leads us to redefine interactions between agents (section 3.1), while keeping their respective scope under control (section 3.2). We then show how specific agents can be defined to account for the system variety of stimuli (section 3.3) and how a given agent takes control of the interaction with the student (section 3.4).

3.1 Interactions between tutoring agents

As suggested by the terms "tutoring" and "agent", TAs are entities whose ultimate purpose is to *communicate with the student* in order to efficiently fulfil their respective tutoring function, as part of the pedagogical mission of the system. However, associating one agent to every possible tutoring function would duplicate the similarities between two functions, and thus unduly augment the memory used by the tutoring knowledge and complicate the maintenance of that knowledge. Besides, some functions may be too complex to be clearly exhaustively described and fulfilled by only one agent. This is why we shall modularise the tutoring complex functions into simpler ones, and eventually into elementary functions.

As a result, supposing that each TA is still specialised in a particular tutoring function, it may have to count on other agents specialised in different functions, then used as *service functions*, in order to perform its own tutoring function and produce its expected "pedagogical output". Given this extension, an agent may thus be put forward either by a student's action/behaviour (initial design) or by a higher level function performed by another agent (extended modular design). For the same reason, the result of an agent's action may be used either by the student (pedagogical output of the corresponding tutoring function) or by the higher level agent that used it (normal output of the corresponding service function).

In the case of a KH-ITS, we then have three types of agents:
- *Tutoring agents* are the ones which interact directly with the student and perform a real tutoring function; typical tutoring agents are the problem solver, the domain presenter, the domain assessor, and the exerciser, each one in charge of one of the fundamental operating modes.
- *Service agents* perform service functions on behalf of other agents; they may or may not interact with the student; the question asker, the problem selector, and the topic chooser are service agents because their sole action cannot be a student-related tutoring function.
- Finally, *mixed agents* may be triggered in either way depending on the circumstances; such are the problem-step solver and the explanation provider.

The four tutoring agents may also help one another, in particular when mode shifts take place (see section 3.3); however, because of their essentially student-oriented nature, and because of the fundamental operating modes of the system, we basically maintain them in a separate category. Our division of TAs in three categories is very close to the one used between agents in the cognition-based architecture (Arcand & Pelletier [2]).

3.2 Scope of agents

When a TA takes control, both the scope of the subject matter covered and the level of the data processed by that agent must be kept under control. In other words, when an agent takes charge of the subtask of another, that subtask must be of a lower level than that of the task of the relieved agent. This principle is similar to the one used in algorithmics, where a procedure may call only lower-level or lower-scope procedures, although here an agent must be responsible for its own level and scope. Therefore, the function performed by an agent may be associated to an *abstraction level*, which is defined by the level of the entities on which it operates. This abstraction level is also that of the agent's output, i.e. the result of its action.

It is important to note that the notion of scope of an agent, based on the abstraction and complexity levels, although a non trivial one, will or can be used as a general foundation to circumvent the possible problem of infinite recursive calls between agents (Lelouche & Morin [22]). Indeed, since each delegated agent fulfils a lower-scope function, a delegation must eventually be made to an agent which will not delegate anything, i.e. which will fulfil its function alone. This recursive approach is in fact close to Tambe's [35].

3.3 A variety of agents for a variety of stimuli

In a traditional tutoring session, a teacher must be able to keep the attention and motivation of his students in order to transfer his knowledge efficiently. A way to do so is to vary the stimuli, like using various audio-visual aids, varying the tone or stress of the voice, walking to a different part of the room, etc. Similarly, a tutoring system should use a sufficient variety of stimuli in order to keep the student's attention. A possible way to do so is to have as many TAs to create these stimuli on demand as the number of stimuli types that the system is expected to use. Such an approach will allow the system to run, no matter which stimuli-related agents are implemented.

But that endeavour for variety can be more interestingly applied to the different pedagogical behaviours and tactics employed by the tutor, to the explanations provided, and even to the generic functioning modes. As seen in section 1.2, each mode indeed represents what the student globally wants to do with the system, and is associated to a main TA to fulfil the corresponding tutoring function. However, when the broad system wants to use another type of interaction in order to help the student to better understand a given topic, it will use another main TA, normally associated to another operating mode. This is the *mode shift* principle, discussed in detail in (Lelouche & Morin [23]).

With such a variety of stimuli, it becomes easy for a teacher, henceforth for the tutoring module of an ITS, to vary its tutoring tactics in order to avoid having the student bored by a monotonous page-turning-type lecture. For example, in a tutoring session in the domain-assessment mode, if the student has difficulty answering a system's question, the system may give him various hints and clues, e.g. by showing him a solved problem, by presenting him a paragraph of theory, or even by asking him another theoretical question, naturally having a narrower — and expectedly easier — scope than the initial one (see section 3.2). All these possible hints or clues will then be provided by as many possible other agents (section 4.2 gives several examples of such agent cooperation).

3.4 How an agent takes control

If a tutoring system is to vary the types of its interactions with the student, it should also be able to make wise decisions about what kind of interaction to choose and when to apply it. A first means to progress towards this goal is to keep track of the interactions of the current session. For example, if the system has to explain a topic to the student and detects it has already done four theoretical presentations (associated to the domain-presentation mode), it might purposely choose another type of interaction to fulfil its own task, and that will be done by a different agent.

Keeping track of the past interactions may, of course, go much farther than the current session — for example, by building and maintaining a student model (Fletcher [13]). Building a student model is obviously one of the deepest and longest-term means of keeping track of the student's evolution. Indeed, the student model is an incremental interpretation of the student's behaviour whose purpose is to reproduce not only the current state of his knowledge but also his learning profile, with its strengths and weaknesses, and possibly his learning preferences (tutoring strategies that are likely to work best). The system can thus use its general model of the student's knowledge status and preferences to guide its interactions, which may become very efficient when enough data about the student have been gathered into the student model and can be adequately processed.

4 An application domain example

In this section, we want to give a more concrete flavour to our work. Our application domain is cost engineering (Galibois [16]), which consists of mathematical and computational tools for the engineer to evaluate the worth of engineering projects. We first briefly present the separation between DK and PSK (section 4.1), then a problem-solving example based on our approach (section 4.2). We can then use it to present an excerpt of a problem-solving tutoring dialogue between a student and an ITS (section 4.3). We then summarise the roles of the various TAs involved in that dialogue (section 4.4). Finally, we present (section 4.5) some knowledge elements upon which TAs may base themselves to interact, and we show how these elements are (or are likely to be) taken into account in the tutoring session excerpt.

4.1 Separation between the domain knowledge and the problem-solving knowledge

Cost engineering is a KH-domain. It is therefore modelled as two parts (see section 1.1). The domain knowledge is essentially modelled as concepts and relations, while the problem-solving knowledge is modelled as processes and subprocesses. That model is detailed in (Lelouche & Morin [24] [23]); here we only give the elements necessary to understand the example.

In the *domain knowledge, concepts* are entities like investment, interest, investment duration, present and future values, compounding period, number of compounding periods, interest rate, or annuity. They are linked to one another by *relations* like *kind of, part of*, or numerical relations. For example,

$$F = P \times (1 + i)^n \qquad (1)$$

is a quaternary relation $R(F, P, i, n)$ which, given the present value P of an investment over n periods at rate i, expresses the corresponding future value F of the investment. Such relations, or formulae like (1), lead to the notion of *factor*, a pedagogical concept:

$$\Phi_{PF,i,n} = (1 + i)^n = F/P \qquad (2)$$

$$\Phi_{FP,i,n} = (1 + i)^{-n} = P/F \qquad (3)$$

Factors like $\Phi_{PF,i,n}$ or $\Phi_{FP,i,n}$ allow us to distinguish their algebraic definition from their possible uses in the application domain. Similarly, there exists a factor $\Phi_{AP,i,n}$ to convert a periodic series of identical amounts A into a unique present value P. Another factor, $\Phi_{PA,i,n}$ does the reverse process.

The *problem-solving knowledge* is modelled as various domain-specific processes and subprocesses that may be used to solve various types of cost-engineering problems. Rather than presenting them *in abstracto*, let us move directly to the problem to be solved, and we shall then explain the processes used to solve it.

4.2 A problem-solving example

Let the exercise to be solved be as follows (e.g. as presented to the student):

"Determine the present value of a five-year annuity of $1,000 starting at the end of year 1, plus an extra revenue of $500 at the end of year 3, plus an expense of $1,500 at the end of year 4. The annual interest rate is assumed to be 10%."

The normal processes used by an engineer, a tutor, or a good student to solve this exercise are the following:

1. *Identify and instantiate the given problem data:*
   - annual interest rate $i = 10\%$;
   - ($n_1 = 5$)-year annuity $A_1 = 1,000$;
   - future value amount $F_2 = 500$ at end of year $n_2 = 3$;
   - future value amount $F_3 = -1,500$ at end of year $n_3 = 4$.

2. *Identify and instantiate the expected result:* some present value P equivalent to the sum of all above amounts.

3. *Build a temporal diagram:*
   - a time line encompassing five years;
   - the arrows corresponding to the above described given amounts, upward for an income and downward for an expense;
   - a bold arrow representing the expected result P.

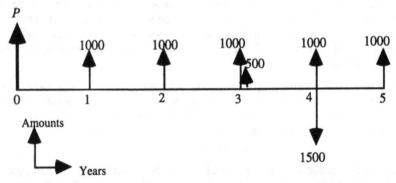

This diagram shows the data identified above and the result sought after. The solving process basically consists in adding all the arrowed amounts to get their equivalent present value P. But these amounts, situated at different dates, cannot be added directly. We must thus decompose that activity into lower-level ones.

4. *Choose a common reference date* towards which all the amounts will be moved. Since we are looking for the present value P of this set of amounts, the simplest common reference date is naturally the present moment, that is, year 0.

5. *Deal with each element individually:* the annuity, the extra revenue at year 3, and the expense at year 4:
   a. The annuity is composed of a series of five annual $1,000 amounts. If we take advantage of the Φ_{AP} factor mentioned earlier in this section, we may compute their present value directly: $P_1 = 1,000 \times \Phi_{AP,10\%,5}$.
   b. Since the amount of $500 at the end of year 3 must be moved back three years, its present value is $P_2 = 500 \times \Phi_{FP,10\%,3}$.
   c. Similarly, the expense of $1,500 at the end of year 4 must be moved back four years, but with an opposite sign. Therefore, its equivalent present value is $P_3 = -1,500 \times \Phi_{FP,10\%,4}$.

6. *Add the obtained present values:*

$$P = P_1 + P_2 + P_3$$

7. *Replace all factors by their numerical values*, either by computing them or from a factor table:

$$P_1 = 1,000 \times \Phi_{AP,10\%,5} = 1,000 \times 3.79079 = \$3,790.79$$

$$P_2 = 500 \times \Phi_{FP,10\%,3} = 500 \times 0.75131 = \$375.66$$

$$P_3 = -1,500 \times \Phi_{FP,10\%,4} = -1,500 \times 0.68301 = -\$1,024.52$$

$$P = P_1 + P_2 + P_3 = 3,790.79 + 375.66 - 1,024.52 = \$3,141.93$$

and, therefore, the expected answer is $3,141.93.

4.3 Tutoring session excerpt based on that problem

To illustrate the generation and development of tutorial processes by the TAs in TK, we now attempt to show how system–student interactions take place during a tutoring session, and how the TAs may intervene. To mimic the session progress and make the interactions clear to the reader, we assume that they are conducted in natural language; the corresponding dialogue is shown in italics, with the student's input preceded by ** (e.g. system prompt). Each dialogue intervention is identified by a "(Dx)" marking on the right. We indent our explanations about the dialogue in order to visually distinguish them from the dialogue itself; moreover, only the major intervening agents are mentioned here.

For our sample session, let us suppose that:
* the student has selected the exercising mode;
* the system has given him the cost-engineering problem shown and solved in section 4.2 (we then refer to the normal solving processes shown in that section);
* the student has correctly identified and instantiated the problem data (process 1) and expected results (process 2); he is now drawing the temporal diagram (process 3).

The session might then proceed as follows:

> The tutoring agent A, a problem-solving assessor, is in control of the exercising mode and monitors the student's actions.

** *Where should I put the arrows of the annuity? In columns 0 to 4 or 1 to 5?* (D1)

> Agent A detects that the student does not clearly understand how to position annuity arrows in a temporal diagram. Among various possibilities, the student is given a short theoretical reminder (temporary shift to an interaction usually associated with the domain-presentation mode), which is provided by the tutoring agent B, a domain presenter.

Remember what you learnt about annuities. By default (like here), the arrows are placed at the end of their respective years. Therefore, the first arrow will be placed at the end of the first year (column 1), and so on. (D2)

** *OK, I think I understand now.* (D3)

> The student claims he understands the pedagogical output provided by B. Control thus returns to agent A and to the standard exercising mode.

[...] (D4)

> Let us skip a few steps, and suppose that the student has finished drawing the temporal diagram. He is now adding together the involved amounts (process 5).

** *We have 1000 * FAP(0.10, 5) + 500 * FFP(0.10, 3) + 1500 * FFP(0.10, 4).* (D5)

The student has correctly understood how to calculate the annuity and the $500 income, but he mistakenly adds the $1,500 expense (see process 5c).

Almost... (D6)

This time, the student is asked a domain question (temporary shift to a domain-assessment interaction). This is done by another agent, a domain assessor, called C.

... What did you learn about the difference between incomes and expenses? (D7)

** I don't understand where my error is. (D8)

The theoretical domain question failed. Agent A', another problem-solving assessor, then gives as a clue to the student a short mathematical question (of much narrower scope than that of the initial question driven by agent A).

For example, if you receive $5,000 and spend $1,500, how much will you have? (D9)

The interaction produced by agent A' is associated with the exercising mode, but still in the context of the intervention of agent C.

** $3,500. (D10)

The student has correctly understood and answered the question of agent A', which may return a success acknowledgment. But agent C takes control back and elects to rephrase its own question.

So, what is your deduction upon this clue? (D11)

The student applies it to the initial problem.

** I think I got it: + 1500 * FFP(0.10, 4) should be – 1500 * FFP(0.10, 4). (D12)

The student has understood the point regarding the expense sign. But his answer is local, i.e. he has corrected his mistake without integrating it into the complete answer. So agent A comes back at the highest level.

You are right. Now you can formulate the complete answer. (D13)

** 1000 * FAP(0.10, 5) + 500 * FFP(0.10, 3) – 1500 * FFP(0.10, 4). (D14)

The student has now given the expected complete computation layout (process 6).

Very good. (D15)

The dialogue would then proceed with the numerical computation (process 7).

4.3 Roles of tutoring agents in that excerpt

There are several agents intervening in the above dialogue.
- Agent A, a *problem-solving assessor*, is in control of the exercising mode (one of the four fundamental functioning modes). It globally drives the solution of the problem, and it monitors and assesses the student's actions. To help him, it lets other agents take some subtask in charge whenever needed, here agents B and C.
- Agent B, a *domain presenter*, intervenes to present a domain element.
- Agent C, a *domain assessor*, asks the student a domain theoretical question. Since he is unable to answer it, C lets agent A' help him resolve this student impasse.
- Agent A', another *problem-solving assessor*, takes over agent C to ask the student a problem-solving question. The small exercise presented by A' is completely different from the problem at hand supervised by A, and its scope is much narrower.

Agent change from A to B	Centralised control	Distributed control
How the change takes place	Call from A to B, then return to A.	Delegation by A, or interruption by B.
Who makes the decision	The calling agent A.	The newly intervening agent B.
Conflict possibility	NO (one decision-maker A)	YES (several possible interveners B_1, B_2, ..., or A)

Table 2: Comparison of central control and distributed control.

During various exchanges with the author, some people argued that, for a single student, a single agent might do a better job, while others, when the author then defended a central control, were in favour of a true multiagent environment as presented here! Table 2 briefly compares central and distributed controls. Certainly, there is little difference between central control and a monoagent system, since the notion of "calls" applies equally well to (sub)agents or to (sub)programs. Similar to this situation is a multiuser environment where every student would deal with a personal clone of the single agent. On the other hand, a distributed control like the one presented here allows a much greater flexibility to experiment with various tutoring strategies or even with various learning theories, independently of the number of simultaneous users.

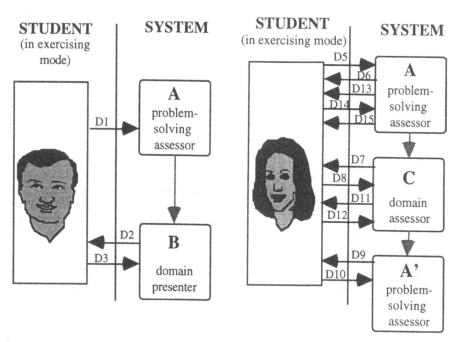

First part of the excerpt   *Second part of the excerpt*

Figure 1: Diagram of the agent interactions.

Figure 1 summarizes the student–agent and agent–agent interactions taking place in the above example. The involved agents have triggered various tutoring processes: ask a question, answer a student question, make a decision regarding the type of interaction to enable, temporarily change the interaction type, all while monitoring the session in order to keep track of the student's progress and to understand and influence its evolution throughout the problem-solving session. The knowledge used to actually trigger these processes is outlined below, while its organisation is presented in section 5.

4.5 Student-related knowledge involved in agent interactions

A TA may refer to various types of contextual knowledge elements to decide to intervene and generate a terminal student–system interaction or to let another TA take control. Some such knowledge elements are:

* the student's current knowledge state (or the current state of the student model),
* the student's primary goal (recall that he has the choice of the leading tutoring mode),
* the session log (provides, in particular, information about the knowledge acquired by the student and the past interactions),
* the points where the student stumbled (helpful to determine the gravity and nature of the encountered errors and misconceptions),
* the student's motivation and physical state (tired, in good shape, etc.).

For instance, in interaction (D1), the student hesitates on where to place the annuity arrows. This may be due to the fact that he is not very acquainted yet with annuity-related factors. If there have been some errors before, or if the student shows some tiredness, agent A may try to lighten his work by letting another agent directly answer his question, which is done in (D2).

In (D5), the student appears to be confused about incomes and expenses. However, this may as well be a mere lack of attention. This time, the system tries to capture his attention by asking him a question (D7). And since his error is quite basic (the abstraction level is much lower than that of, for example, understanding how to use a factor), the system may want to address the student about the theory itself rather than by way of an exercise. This is done by a domain assessor, agent C.

The student's answer in (D8) shows that the question asked in (D7) is not enough to make him properly understand his error. Is the student simply too tired? Or does he have real difficulties? To cope with these possibilities (which are beyond the "exact" contents of a computer-based student model) and to help the student to get through the problem, another exerciser, agent A', takes control and asks a question about the same topic as agent C, but differently (namely an appropriate exercise); this is done in (D9).

This time, the student seems to understand (or to wake up if the error was an accidental slip!), so the task of agent A' is completed. Moreover, since the student answers the question at a higher level (D12), that of the primary exercise (asked by A), the function of agent C is also over.

Thus, agent A is back and asks the student to integrate his answer (now correct) into the global exercise solution (D13). The student does so in (D14). Everything seems to be properly understood by now, so the tutoring session may proceed.

5 How can this cooperation be achieved

Without presuming about our definitive implementation, we think that the blackboard architecture is a suitable approach for describing how such a cooperation between TAs can be achieved (section 5.1). However, some other architectures described in the literature can also give us useful clues (section 5.2).

5.1 Description using the blackboard architecture

Our design of TAs and the way they interact during a tutoring session (see sections 3 and 4) led us to envision the blackboard architecture (Englemore & Morgan [11], Erman & al. [12], Nil [27]) as a good model for our approach.

- The *blackboard* itself would include all the necessary knowledge about the session environment, i.e. essentially:
  - the session history and state (equivalent to the session log in a more traditional system), with relevant statistics about the various interactions;
  - all relevant knowledge about the student, either in the long range (his knowledge of DK and PSK, the points where he stumbled, etc.) or in the shorter session range (his currently chosen operating mode, his motivation and physical state, etc.); alternatively, this student-related knowledge could be adequate pointers to the learner model, if one is present.
- The *knowledge sources*, obviously, would be the various TAs.
- The *control knowledge* would be knowledge about the overall tutoring system strategy; that knowledge would refer to the knowledge base of the tutoring module containing available strategies, but also include parameters or variables about which ones are favoured; indeed, the system tutoring strategy, like the control knowledge in a blackboard system, is responsible for activating the right knowledge sources (here TAs) at the right time, as well as for controlling access to the blackboard.

5.2 Other suitable architectures

Other architectures described in the literature can also provide us with some agent-oriented functions quite adequate in an ITS context, thus complementing the traditional blackboard architecture.

A multiagent architecture close to ours is the cognition-based architecture (Arcand & Pelletier [2]). Although this architecture is essentially geared at network-based multi-agent architectures (which is not necessarily our case), the authors' distinction between a senior intelligent agent, a junior intelligent, and a facilitator parallels ours between a full-fledged TA, a mixed agent, and a service agent (see section 3.1).

If we now look at single agent modelling, Tambe and Rosenbloom's approach to agent tracking [36] will provide us the mechanisms allowing each TA to know what other TAs are doing, thus conveniently cooperating with them to achieve the overall system pedagogical mission in conjunction with the student-chosen operating mode. Besides, their work, like ours, is based on Anderson's [1] model tracing technique for tracking student actions.

Finally, another interesting contribution worth mentioning is Gmytrasiewicz's recursive modelling method [17]. His utility maximising action is indeed close to what we call the achievement of the pedagogical mission of the system, in order to decide which action to have executed by which agent. Thus his approach to recursive reasoning seems to adequately complement Tambe's [35].

Conclusion

In this paper, we presented how tutoring knowledge can be modelled, in a general way, in terms of tutoring agents. We first presented some basics related to KH-ITS, namely the domain knowledge, the problem-solving knowledge, and the four generic operating modes that we defined upon this division of the knowledge to be taught. We then introduced the tutoring knowledge, supposedly common to all ITSs, through an agent-based approach, and we gave some KH-ITS-based examples. We then presented some general principles regarding the interactions between agents, their respective scope in such an interactive context, their variety, and how an agent takes control to fulfil a given task within a tutoring session. We then presented a cost engineering problem and its solution, which we then used in a sample tutoring session integrating all these notions. Finally we presented several architectural approaches suitable to realise this cooperation between tutoring agents in order to provide a better service to the learner.

As to exploring the potential of agent-based architectures in learning environments, we think that the various concepts regarding tutoring agents presented in this paper, how they are defined and characterised as well as how they can be differentiated from one another, should help an ITS designer to find out a relatively easy and efficient way to model the tutoring knowledge required to fulfil the pedagogical mission of his tutoring system. Moreover, the tutoring agent concept might be extended to more general pedagogical agents; such agents, for example, could assure the maintenance of the student model and, possibly, take care of the interface management. Certainly, much progress still has to be made towards reaching a complete model.

Acknowledgments

The authors wants to thank his graduate student Jean-François Morin for his valuable inputs into this work, and an anonymous referee for suggestions which helped improve the first version of this paper.

References

[1]   Anderson J. R., C. F. Boyle, A. T. Corbett & M. W. Lewis (1990) "Cognitive modelling and intelligent tutoring". Artificial Intelligence, vol. 42, p. 7-49.

[2]   Arcand J.-F. & S.-J. Pelletier (1996) "Cognition-based multiagent architecture". In [37], p. 267-282.

[3]   Barr Avron & William J. Clancey, eds. (1982) "Chapter IX: Application-oriented AI research: Education". In The Handbook of Artificial Intelligence, volume 2 (Avron Barr & Edward Feigenbaum, eds.). HeurisTech Press (Stanford, CA) & William Kaufmann (Los Altos, CA), p. 223–294.

[4] Brodie Michael L., John Mylopoulos & Joachim W. Schmidt, eds. (1984) *On Conceptual Modelling, Perspectives from Artificial Intelligence, Databases, and Programming Languages*. Springer Verlag (New York).

[5] Brown John Seely & Richard R. Burton (1978) "Diagnostic models for procedural bugs in basic mathematical skills". *Cognitive Science*, vol. 2, p. 155–192.

[6] Brown John Seely, Richard R. Burton & Alan G. Bell (1974) *SOPHIE: a sophistocated instructional environment for teaching electronic troubleshooring*. BBN Report no. 2790, Bolt, Beranek and Newman Inc. (Cambridge, MA).

[7] Carbonell Jaime R. (1970) "AI in CAI: an artificial intelligence approach to computer-aided instruction". *IEEE Transactions on Man–Machine Systems*, vol. MMS-11, no. 4, p. 190–202.

[8] Clancey William J. (1983) "GUIDON". *Journal of Computer-Based Instruction*, vol. 10, no. 1, p. 8–14.

[9] Clocksin William F. & Christopher S. Mellish (1981) *Programming in Prolog*. Springer-Verlag (Berlin).

[10] Díaz de Ilarraza Sánchez Arantza & Isabel Fernández de Castro, eds. (1996) *Computer-Aided Learning and Instruction in Science and Engineering*, Proceedings of the *Third International Conference, CALISCE'96*, San Sebastian, España, 29–31 July 1996. LNCS 1108, Springer (Berlin).

[11] Englemore R. & T. Morgan, eds. (1988) *Blackboard Systems*. Addison-Wesley Publ. (Reading, MA).

[12] Erman L., F. Hayes-Roth, V. Lesser & D. Reddy (1980) "The Hearsay II speech-understanding system: integrating knowledge to resolve uncertainty". *ACM Computing Surveys*, vol. 12, no. 2, p. 213-253.

[13] Fletcher J. Dexter (1975) "Modeling of learner in computer-based instruction". *Journal of Computer-Based Instruction*, vol.1, p. 118–126.

[14] Frasson Claude, Gilles Gauthier & Alan Lesgold, eds. (1996) *Intelligent Tutoring Systems*, Proceedings of the *Third International Conference, ITS'96*, Montréal, Canada, 12-14 June 1996. LNCS 1086, Springer (Berlin).

[15] Gagné Denis & André Trudel (1996) "A highly flexible student-driven architecture for computer-based instruction". In [14], p. 66–74.

[16] Galibois André (1997) *Analyse économique pour ingénieurs*, 2nd edition. Éditions AGA (Sainte-Foy, Canada).

[17] Gmytrasiewicz P. (1996) "On reasoning about other agents". In [37], p. 143-155.

[18] Goldstein Ira P. (1982) "WUMPUS". In *The Handbook of Artificial Intelligence*, volume 2 (Avron Barr & Edward Feigenbaum, eds.). HeurisTech Press (Stanford, CA) and William Kaufmann (Los Altos, CA), p. 261–266.

[19] Kim Won & Frederick H. Lochovsky, eds. (1989) *Object-Oriented Concepts, Databases, and Applications*. ACM Press, Addison-Wesley Publ. (Reading, MA).

[20] Kowalski Robert (1979) *Logic for Problem Solving*. North-Holland (Berlin).

[21] Lelouche Ruddy (1998) "The successive contributions of computers to education: a survey". *European Journal of Engineering Education*, vol. 23, no. 3.

[22] Lelouche Ruddy & Jean-François Morin (1997) "Use of abstraction and complexity levels in intelligent educational systems design". Proceedings of the 15th *International Joint Conference on Artificial Intelligence* (IJCAI-97), Nagoya, Japan, 23–29 August 1997, p. 329-334.

[23] Lelouche Ruddy & Jean-François Morin (1997) "Knowledge types and tutoring interactions in an ITS in a problem-solving domain". Proceedings of the 10th *Florida Artificial Intelligence Research Symposium* (FLAIRS-97) — Special Track on ITSs, Daytona Beach, Florida. 10–14 May 1997, p. 62–66.

[24] Lelouche Ruddy & Jean-François Morin (1996) "The formula: a relation? Yes, but a concept too!". In [10], p. 176–185.

[25] Macmillan Stuart A. & Derek H. Sleeman (1987) "An architecture for a self-improving instructional planner for intelligent tutoring systems". *Computational Intelligence*, vol. 3, no. 1.

[26] Masthoff Judith F. M. (1997) *An agent-based interactive instruction system.* Ph.D. thesis, University of Technology Eindhoven (Netherlands), 222 pages, ISBN 90-386-0319-3.

[27] Nil H. P. (1986) "Blackboard systems". *AI Magazine*, vol. 7, no. 2, p. 38-53 and vol. 7, no. 3, p. 82-106.

[28] Ohlsson Stellan (1987) "Some principles of intelligent tutoring". In Lawler Robert & Masoud Yazdani (eds.) *AI and Education: Learning Environments and Intelligent Tutoring Systems.* Ablex Publishing (Norwood, NJ).

[29] O'Shea Tim (1979) *Self-improving Teaching Systems: an Application of Artificial Intelligence to Computer-aided Instruction.* Birkhauser Verlag (Basel, Switzerland).

[30] O'Shea Tim (1979) "A self-improving quadratic tutor". *International Journal of Man–Machine Studies*, vol. 11, p. 97–124 (Reprinted in [34].)

[31] Patel Ashok & Kinshuk (1996) "Applied artificial intelligence for teaching numeric topics in engineering disciplines". In [10], p. 132–140.

[32] Rickel Jeff & W. Lewis Johnson (1997) "Steve: An animated pedagogical agent for procedural training in virtual environments", IJCAI-97 *Workshop on Animated Interface Agents*, Nagoya, Japan, 23–29 August 1997.

[33] Skinner Burrhus F. (1968) *The Technology of Teaching.* Appleton–Century–Crofts (New York).

[34] Sleeman Derek H. & John Seely Brown, eds. (1982) *Intelligent Tutoring Systems.* Academic Press (London).

[35] Tambe Milind (1995) "Recursive agent and agent-group tracking in a real-time dynamic environment". *Proc. of the First International Conference on Multiagent Systems (ICMAS 95)*, San Francisco, CA, June 1995.

[36] Tambe Milind & Paul S. Rosenbloom (1996) "Architectures for agents that track other agents in multiagent worlds". In [37], p. 156-170.

[37] Wooldridge Michael, Jörg P. Müller & Milind Tambe, eds. (1996) *Intelligent Agents II: Agent Theories, Architectures and Languages.* Proc. IJCAI'95 Workshop (ATAL), Montreal, Canada, August 1995. LNAI 1037, Springer (Berlin).

Secure Information Gathering Agent for Internet Trading

X.F. Wang[1], X.Yi[2], K. Y. Lam[1], E.Okamoto[2]

[1]Department of Information System and Computer Science
Faculty of Science, National University of Singapore
Lower Kent Ridge Road, SINGAPORE 119260
E-mail:{wangxiao,lamky}@iscs.nus.edu.sg
and
[2]School of Information Science
Japan Advanced Institute of Science and Technology, Japan
E-mail: {xyi, okamoto}@jaist.ac.jp

Abstract. With the proliferation of commercial information on the Internet, intelligent agent becomes an effective implement to collect information for conducting trading. However, great security threats also exist under this scenario. Since agent will be executed by the host, it seems inevitable to expose its codes and data to host's attacks. In this paper, we propose a security system to protect information gathering agent from malicious hosts. The encryption technique and detection object will be taken to sense any illegal manipulation to the agent body. Distributed login data base (LDB) is introduced to assure any destructor will be easily dug out. Therefore, Internet trading under the framework of this system enable agent to conduct commercial information gathering among hosts freely and securely.

Keywords: Electronics commerce, information gathering agent, detect object, public-key cryptosystem and hash function, non-repudiation

1 Introduction

Electronic commerce on the Internet has quickly grown in recent years in view of its low expense and high efficiency. However, the amount of business information available on the Internet is so large that it becomes nearly impossible for customers and merchants to visit each site on the networks, analyze the information and make sound business decisions as to the trade of goods or services. So far, one of the best solutions [1] is utilising intelligent trade agents to trade for humans.

Mobile agent has the ability to migrate itself across nodes of a network to accomplish its mission autonomously. Under the scenario of Internet trading, an information gathering agent (IGA) roams through the different sites on the web, filters the commercial information according to its domain knowledge and user preferences, and brings back well tailored materials to support user's commercial decision. This provides a greatly flexible and efficient alternative to conduct Internet trading.

However, mobile agent's potential benefits must be weighed against the security threats they pose. Since its codes are executed by a host, an information gathering agent has to expose its data and codes to the host environment. Therefore, a malicious host can always scan the agent for information, alter the agent states and codes, even kill the agent. Current consensus is that it is computationally impossible to protect agent from a malicious host. Instead of tackling the problem from a computational (difficult) point of view, most researches [2] are looking at sociological means of enforcing good host behavior.

In this paper, we propose a secure information gathering agent system with a new scheme to protect IGAs. Combined with the traditional encryption techniques, a detection object is introduced to sense any little unauthorised modification made by any host. Meanwhile, nonrepudiation evidences are also reserved among every transit servers to help trace the malicious host should any illegal manipulations on the IGAs be detected. These measures effectively guarantee the security of IGA under the Internet trading scenario.

The rest of the paper is organised as follows: Section 2 describes the structure and information gathering procedure of the proposed system. Section 3 makes a detailed analysis on the security and performance of the system. Section 4 concludes the whole paper.

2 Description of the secure information gathering agent system

Similar to most of the secure distributed system, the proposed secure information gathering agent system utilizes a public key cryptosystem (e.g., RSA[3]) and a hash function (e.g., MD4[4], MD5[5]) to encipher and decipher data, provide certificates and generate digital signature.

Throughout the following discussion, each participant X in the system has a pair of keys associated with it, one of which being publicly known (X_p, X's public key), the other one only known to X (private or secret key X_s). X's public key is used to encrypt data meant to be read by X; X can decrypt the result using its private key: $D = X_s(X_p(D))$. X can use X_s create a digital signature, which can be verified by any party using X_p. The hash value of a message M with the hash function H is denoted as $H(M)$.

In addition, we need a hierarchical structure of certification authorities to provide certificates for all participants in the system. Their public keys of these certification authorities are known to every entity. In order to simplify description here, we assume that only a certification authority (CA) is in the system. In the case of a multitude of certification authorities, the description is almost the same as that of a certification authority except that some symbols are slight different.

X's certificate ($Cert_X$) issued by the CA is composed of the certificate content ($CertCont_X$), which mainly contains serial number, encryption algorithm identifier, hash function identifier, signature algorithm identifier, CA's name,

CA's public key, X's name, X's public key, validity period and so on, and the CA's signature on it.

$$Cert_X = CertCont_X \| CA_s(H(CertCont_X)) \tag{1}$$

The secure information gathering agent system mainly intends to solve security problems (prevent agent from malicious hosts) in the following case:

A user U wishes an Agent Service Center (ASC) to gather certain business information (such as the price of a commodity) on his behalf. According to user's requirements, the ASC will create an information gathering agent with the necessary domain knowledge. After some preliminary preparations (such as, through interactive training, let the IGA learn more about user's tastes), the ASC will furnish IGA with some initial routing information(some information servers' addresses) and send it out to the Internet.

The IGA will roam through the different Internet hosts, dynamically change its routing plan when new promising information servers are located, and use its domain knowledge to autonomously filter and collect the user interested information.

In order to ensure the security of the proposed information gathering agent system, the secure structure of the IGA needs to be considered firstly.

2.1 Structure of an IGA

In the proposed system, the basic structure of an IGA sent by the ASC can be divided into three distinct portions from the point of view of security.

1. Agent Certificate — ASC's certificate ($Cert_{ASC}$) issued by a certification authority (CA). On basis of (1), we know

   $$Cert_{ASC} = CertCont_{ASC} \| CA_s(H(CertCont_{ASC}))$$

2. Static Portion — Code, static data and $Sign_{ASC}$. While IGA jumps from host to host, it always executes the same codes and uses the uniform standard to filter the information. Therefore, IGA's codes are static during the information gathering procedure. To insure the integrity of this part, ASC signs on the IGA's codes and some static data before dispatching agent out

   $$Sign_{ASC} = ASC_s(H(Code \ and \ Static \ data)) \tag{2}$$

   After IGA returned, the ASC will verify $Sign_{ASC}$ to check IGA's integrity.

3. Dynamic Portion — Information base, routing table, time stamp and non-repudiation evidence. This portion will be changed during the information gathering procedure. Information base is used to store gathered business information. Routing table records the host list IGA plans to visit. Time stamp indicates the time when the IGA is sent out by a server. Nonrepudiation evidence includes $Cert_{send}$(the sender's certificate issued by the CA)

and $Sign_{send}$ (the signature of the sender on the part (M) from Agent Certificate to Time Stamp in the IGA).

$$Sign_{send} = Send_s(H(M)) \tag{3}$$

The information base is the part easy to incur host's attack. Under the Internet trading scenario, malicious actions on the information IGA gathered will cause big trouble. Consider the following example: an IGA is sent out to collect the information about the cheapest flight from Singapore to China. When it visits Fly-By-Night Airlines, the Fly-By-Night server erases all the information the agent has collected previously, so that the Fly-By-Night flight appears to be the cheapest. In addition, the leakage of the confidential information such as quotations will result in inequitable competition and give edge to the malicious breeder.

To secure information base, we introduce detection object(DO) technique. DO is a string of random bytes. Before sending IGA out to the Internet, the ASC generates a DO and put it into IGA's information base. During the information gathering procedure, any new information acquired by IGA will be encapsulated with DO using ASC_p as follows:

$$DO_n = ASC_p(I_n, ASC_p(I_{n-1}, \cdots, ASC_p(I_1, DO) \cdots)). \tag{4}$$

I_n stands for the information package provided by the nth server.

After IGA returns, the ASC will decapsulate the DO_n to obtain the information packages and check the DO to see whether the IGA has been tampered by malicious hosts.

The structure of an IGA can be illustrated in the following figure:

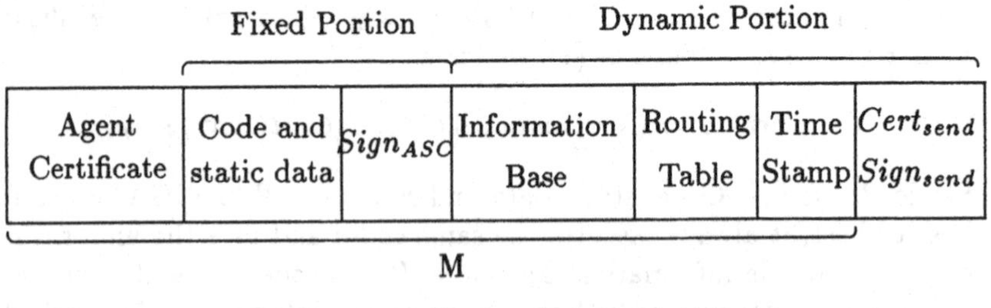

			Dynamic Portion			
Fixed Portion						
Agent Certificate	Code and static data	$Sign_{ASC}$	Information Base	Routing Table	Time Stamp	$Cert_{send}$ $Sign_{send}$

M

Fig.1: The structure of an information gathering agent

2.2 Structure of Login Data Bases (LDB) for servers

In the proposed system, each server involved in the information gathering needs a Login Data Base (LDB) saving some information from passing IGAs in order to provide the evidence that an IGA is authorized and not illegally modified by a server when any problem occurs.

Because there are probably a lot of IGAs entering a server to retrieve information every day, it is impossible for a server to keep whole passing IGA in its records. Otherwise, the LDB will occupy a great deal of storage space. In view of it, the structure of record of the LDB needs to be very optimal.

Our solution to this problem is setting up the LDB in the following record structure:

Agent Certificate	Time Stamp (0)	Previous Node	Time Stamp (1)	Signa- ture (1)	Informa- tion Package	Next Node	Time Stamp (2)	Signa- ture (2)

Fig.2: The structure of record of a Login Data Base (LDB)

In the above structure, the meaning of each field is illustrated as follows:

1. Time Stamp (0)—the time when the IGA is generated.
2. Previous Node—the certificate of the previous server from which the agent comes.
3. Time Stamp (1)—the time when the agent is out of the previous server.
4. Signature (1)—the signature of the previous server on the IGA.
5. Information Package —the business information the IGA collects from the server.
6. Next Node—the certificate of the next server to which the trade agent has gone.
7. Time Stamp (2)—the time when the agent goes to the next server from the server.
8. Signature (2)—the signature of the next server on the IGA.

All the information will be kept as non-repudiation evidence for every passing agent. The period to preserve a specified agent's record is highly depended on the agent's lifetime since ASC can make decision on whether to launch an investigation or not just a little later than the agent's life length is expired.

2.3 Information gathering procedure

The complete information gathering procedure can be illustrated with following figure:

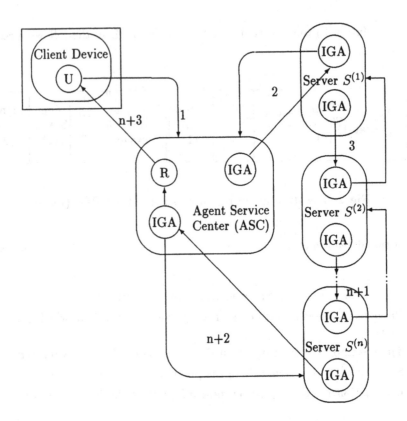

Fig.3: The proposed secure intelligent trade agent system

The detailed procedure is explained as follows:

Generation of an information gathering agent

Step 1: User $U \Rightarrow$ Agent Service Center (ASC)

1. User U, who wishes to obtain certain business information from web, get access to a client device connected to an Agent Service Center (ASC). From the client device, he transmits

$$Cert_U, ASC_p(R_U, t), U_s(H(R_U, t)) \tag{5}$$

to the ASC, where R_U states the user's detailed requirements and the current time t acts as time stamp of this communication.

2. After receiving (4) from U, the ASC checks the following items:
   (a) Is $Cert_U$ issued by the CA?
   (b) Has User U registered the ASC before?
   (c) Does the signature U on (R_U, t) correct?
   (d) Is the time stamp t valid?
   If all answers are certain, the ASC executes 3. Otherwise, the ASC refuses the requirement of User U.

3. On basis of R_U, the ASC creates an IGA according to the structure shown in Fig.2. A detection object denoted as DO_0 is generated by the ASC, one copy of it is reserved in the ASC's database, the other is put into IGA's information base.
4. The ASC provides some interactive interfaces to let user train the agent and a initial routing information which is put into IGA's routing table.
5. The IGA is sent out to roam the servers on the Internet.

An information the gathering agent roaming network

For simply description, the ASC is formally denoted as Server $S^{(0)}$ and $S^{(n+1)}$.

Step i+1: Server $S^{(i-1)} \Rightarrow$ Server $S^{(i)}, i = 1, 2, \cdots, n + 1$.

1. After IGA roams into Server $S^{(i)}$, $S^{(i)}$ checks the following items:
   (a) Is Agent Certification issued by the CA?
   (b) Is Time Stamp of IGA valid?
   (c) Is $Cert_{send}$ issued by the CA?
   (d) Does Equation $S_p^{(i-1)}(Sign_{send}) = H(M)$ hold?
   If all answers are certain, the $S^{(i)}$ executes 2. Otherwise, The IGA will be sent back to the ASC or simply discarded.
2. Server $S^{(i)}$ replies Server $S^{(i-1)}$ with

$$Cert_{S^{(i)}} \| S_s^{(i)}(H(M)) \tag{6}$$

It is saved into Server $S^{(i-1)}$'s LDB.
3. Server $S^{(i)}$ provides the IGA with an agent execution environment, in which IGA automatically retrieves business information from authorized resources supplied by $S^{(i)}$, analyses it and forms selected information package. $S^{(i)}$ signs on the package with his secret key and the result : $S_s^{(i)}(Information\ Package)$ combined with $Cert_i$ is denoted as I_i. The $S^{(i)}$ then encapsulates the I_i with DO_{i-1} using ASC_p.

$$DO_i = ASC_p(I_i, DO_{i-1}). \tag{7}$$

The DO_i will be put into IGA's information base.
4. IGA will also search the information about other potential information providers and update its routing table.
5. Time Stamp, $Cert_{send}$ and $Sign_{send}$ of the IGA are respectively replaced with the current time, $Cert_{S^{(i)}}$ and $Sign_{S^{(i)}}$.
6. $S^{(i)}$ sends IGA to Server $S^{(i+1)}$ and then gets back $Cert_{S^{(i+1)}} \| S_s^{(i+1)}(H(M))$ as confirmation. Server $S^{(i)}$ opens a new record of Login Data Base (LDB) and fills it with corresponding items according to the structure of record shown in Fig.3. If $S^{(i)}$ can not obtain $S^{(i+1)}$'s reply after several rounds of attempts, it will send IGA back to the ASC with an accident report.

Step n+3: Agent Service Center $\Rightarrow$ User U.

After the IGA sent out by the ASC returns, the ASC brings out the DO_n and keeps decapsulating it with ASC_s until DO_0 emerges. The DO_0 will be compared with its reserved copy. If these two match, the ASC can trust the information packages IGA collected. Otherwise, investigation process will be activated. Once ASC get the valid information packages, it can transmits

$$R = Cert_{ASC}, U_p(I_1, I_2 \cdots I_n; t), ASC_s(H(Packages, t)) \tag{8}$$

to User U, where $Packages = (I_1, I_2 \cdots I_n)$ and t is the current time. The user can obtain the interested materials by decrypting the information package with corresponding server's public key. So far, the information gathering procedure is successfully fulfilled.

3 Security and performance analysis on the information gathering agent system

3.1 Security of Agent Service Center against User U

In the proposed secure intelligent agent system, User U must provide his certificate $(Cent_U)$ and signature on (R_U, t) if he wishes to obtain information gathering agent services from Agent Service Center. An unauthorized user who intends to enter the ASC is certainly refused because he is not able to show an authorized certificate and signature at the same time. In addition, replaying attack is impossible and of no significance in view of the existence of the time stamp.

3.2 Protection of servers against malicious agents

An agent is unique in that its codes is executed by a server, thus an executing agent has automatic access to some of a server resources. With this level of access agents can mount attacks by altering other local agents, propagating viruses, worms and Trojan horses, impersonating other users and mounting denial of service attack. In proposed system, the certificate of the ASC can be used as the entrance passport. Based on it, the host can effectively reject untrusted IGAs. Some existed techniques as: the approaches of Telescript [6] and Safe-Tcl [7] also can be taken to reenforce the security management.

3.3 Protection of agents against malicious servers

In order for an agent to run, it must expose its codes and data to the host environment which supplies the means for that agent to run. The host can always scan the agent for information, alter the agent states and codes, even kill the agent. Thus, the agent is unprotected from the host.

Current consensus is that it is computationally impossible to protect mobile agents from malicious hosts. Instead of tackling the problem from a computational (difficult) point of view, most researches [2] are looking at sociological means of enforcing good host behavior.

The proposed system provides the protection of agents against malicious servers in the following aspects:

1. Attack Detection. During the information gathering procedure, any information IGA obtained will be encrypted with ASC_p, this precludes the unauthorized scan of the information base. Every information package server provided is combined with server's signature and certificate, which prevents the falsifier from supplying false materials. Although hosts can decompose IGA's codes, they can't modify it without being detected. The digital signature guarantees the integrity of the code and static data. The adoption of detection object makes malicious hosts hard to tamper the information IGA gathered. Consider the example we presented in the section 2. If Fly-By-Night Airline erases the information capsulated with DO, once IGA returns, the ASC will detect this tampering immediately. Because the lack of the preset DO means some information packages have already been deleted. In addition, ASC has set a time limitation to the IGA. IGA must return within its life time. Otherwise, it will be supposed to be killed by hosts.

   In a word, the proposed system can effectively detect most attacks from malicious hosts.

2. Attacker location. Once ASC detects any illegal actions on the IGA, an investigation procedure will be activated to locate the attacker. The investigation is based on the LDBs on the servers IGA passed by. Although IGA can dynamically changes it routing table during the information gathering procedure, its travel course will be recorded in the LDBs. LDB has fields to store the incoming and outgoing nodes of a special IGA. Therefore, IGA's course can be reconstructed by linking all the corresponding LDBs' records together and ASC can trace the course from the first server it sent IGA to. Furthermore, the LDB record can also act as a nonrepudiation evidence during the investigation. The investigation procedure is as follows:

   (a) From the first server IGA is dispatched to, the ASC traces every host IGA passed by and asks hosts to commit their records (denoted as $Rec^{(i)}$ ($i = 1, 2, \cdots, n$)) and $I_i(S_s^{(i)}(information\ package)\|Cert_{s^{(i)}})$about the IGA. The motivation to prove themselves to be innocent drives all servers except a malicious one to provide true records and I_i.

   (b) On basis of original IGA, $Rec^{(i)}$ and $I_i(i = 1, 2, \cdots, n)$ the ASC can reconstruct the IGA corresponding to every server step by step.

   (c) Suppose Servers $S^{(i)}$ ($i = 1, 2, \cdots, m - 1, m \leq n$) have no problem, the ASC checks whether $S_p^{(m+1)}(Signature\ (2))$ is equal to $H(M)$ (where M is the part of the IGA corresponding to $S^{(m)}$ from Agent Certificate to Time Stamp and $Signature(2)$ is from $Rec^{(m)}$). If so, Server $S^{(m)}$ has no problem. If not, Server $S^{(m)}$ will be identified as a malicious one because it can not provide the non-repudiation of receipt from Server

$S^{(m+1)}$ which states Server $S^{(m+1)}$ has successfully received the correct IGA. Server $S^{(m)}$ should repeatedly have transmitted IGA to Server $S^{(m+1)}$ until $S_p^{(m+1)}(Signature\ (2)) = H(M)$ or have delivered an error notification to the ASC.

3. If an IGA is killed by a malicious server, the above check procedure 2 can be also carried out to dig out the breeder. The first server which can not provide the correct record about the IGA will be identified as a malicious one.

3.4 Performance analysis

Although LDB based investigation mechanism can effectively capture most of attackers, the system performance seems degraded by the high expense it involved. The expense can be detailed into two parts: time and space. The investigation process is quite time consuming, therefore, it will be activated only if real attacks occur. There are many reasons to cause IGA damaged, such as network loss, server broken down etc. However, not all of them will activate expensive investigation process. For example, if network is error or receiving server is broken down, the sending server will not be able to obtain acceptor's confirmation. Then, it has to send IGA back to the ASC with an accident report. On the other hand, the restrict security measures will overawe some potential malicious breeders, they have to give up vicious intentions due to high risk and expense expected. This in turn reduces the chance to execute the investigation. So, the time expense of the scheme is still relevant in general. To keep nonrepudiation evidence, every server IGA passed by should reserve a record. This costs much storage space. However, it will not be kept for ever, because after IGA returned, ASC will exam it and decision on whether starts an investigation will be made soon after. Therefore, the record only needs to be preserved a little more than IGA's lifetime. The problem is how to set IGA's lifetime. If it is too long, LDB will consume too much server's space, if too short, IGA may be not in time to gather valuable information. This needs further investigation. We're developing a demo system based on Java and IBM Aglet. The further improvement of the scheme is undergoing.

4 Conclusion

A secure information gathering agent system is proposed above. The proposed system can effectively prevent the attack from malicious hosts because with proposed detection and investigation mechanism, any destructor can be easily dug out. In addition, some measures are also taken to inhibit untrusted IGA entering the host.

The secure information gathering agent system has two features: 1. The encryption technique and detection object are taken to sense any illegal manipulation to the agent body. 2. Investigation based on distributed login data base (LDB) can effectively capture misdeed breeders.

So far, most security weaknesses in the secure information gathering agent system has been overcome. However, the security of the proposed system needs further intensive investigation and some limitations need to be improved. We will continue to work on this field and some new advances are expected soon.

References

1. Jaco van der Merwe and S.H.von Solms, Electronic Commerce with Secure Intelligent Trade Agents, Proceedings of ICICS'97, LNCS 1334, November 1997, pp.452-462.
2. L.Rasmusson and S.Janson, Simulated Social Control for Secure Internet Commerce. In New Security Paradigms'96, ACM Press, September 1996.
3. R.Rivest, A.Shamir and L.M.Adleman, A Method for Obtaining Digital Signature and Public-Key Cryptosystem, Communications of ACM, v.21, n.2, February 1978, pp.120-126.
4. R.L.Rivest, The MD4 Message Digest Algorithm, RFC 1320, April 1992.
5. R.L.Rivest, The MD5 Message Digest Algorithm, RFC 1321, April 1992.
6. J.White, Telescript Technology: The Foundation of the Electronic Market Place, General Magic white paper 1995.
7. N.Borenstein, EMail with a Mind of its Own: The Safe-Tcl Language for Enabled Mail, IFIP WG 65 Conference, Barcelona, May, 1994, North Holland, Arnsterdam, 1994.

Author Index

Springer
and the
environment

At Springer we firmly believe that an
international science publisher has a
special obligation to the environment,
and our corporate policies consistently
reflect this conviction.
We also expect our business partners –
paper mills, printers, packaging
manufacturers, etc. – to commit
themselves to using materials and
production processes that do not harm
the environment. The paper in this
book is made from low- or no-chlorine
pulp and is acid free, in conformance
with international standards for paper
permanency.

Springer

Lecture Notes in Artificial Intelligence (LNAI)

Lecture Notes in Computer Science

Vol. 1506: R. Koch, L. van Gool (Eds.), 3D Structure from Multiple Images of Large-Scale Environments. Proceedings, 1998. VIII, 347 pages. 1998.

Vol. 1507: T.W. Ling, S. Ram, M.L. Lee (Eds.), Conceptual Modeling – ER '98. Proceedings, 1998. XVI, 482 pages. 1998.

Vol. 1508: S. Jajodia, M.T. Özsu, A. Dogac (Eds.), Advances in Multimedia Information Systems. Proceedings, 1998. VIII, 207 pages. 1998.

Vol. 1510: J.M. Zytkow, M. Quafafou (Eds.), Principles of Data Mining and Knowledge Discovery. Proceedings, 1998. XI, 482 pages. 1998. (Subseries LNAI).

Vol. 1511: D. O'Hallaron (Ed.), Languages, Compilers, and Run-Time Systems for Scalable Computers. Proceedings, 1998. IX, 412 pages. 1998.

Vol. 1512: E. Giménez, C. Paulin-Mohring (Eds.), Types for Proofs and Programs. Proceedings, 1996. VIII, 373 pages. 1998.

Vol. 1513: C. Nikolaou, C. Stephanidis (Eds.), Research and Advanced Technology for Digital Libraries. Proceedings, 1998. XV, 912 pages. 1998.

Vol. 1514: K. Ohta, D. Pei (Eds.), Advances in Cryptology – ASIACRYPT'98. Proceedings, 1998. XII, 436 pages. 1998.

Vol. 1515: F. Moreira de Oliveira (Ed.), Advances in Artificial Intelligence. Proceedings, 1998. X, 259 pages. 1998. (Subseries LNAI).

Vol. 1516: W. Ehrenberger (Ed.), Computer Safety, Reliability and Security. Proceedings, 1998. XVI, 392 pages. 1998.

Vol. 1517: J. Hromkovič, O. Sýkora (Eds.), Graph-Theoretic Concepts in Computer Science. Proceedings, 1998. X, 385 pages. 1998.

Vol. 1518: M. Luby, J. Rolim, M. Serna (Eds.), Randomization and Approximation Techniques in Computer Science. Proceedings, 1998. IX, 385 pages. 1998.

Vol. 1519: T. Ishida (Ed.), Community Computing and Support Systems. VIII, 393 pages. 1998. (Subseries LNAI).

Vol. 1520: M. Maher, J.-F. Puget (Eds.), Principles and Practice of Constraint Programming - CP98. Proceedings, 1998. XI, 482 pages. 1998.

Vol. 1521: B. Rovan (Ed.), SOFSEM'98: Theory and Practice of Informatics. Proceedings, 1998. XI, 453 pages. 1998.

Vol. 1522: G. Gopalakrishnan, P. Windley (Eds.), Formal Methods in Computer-Aided Design. Proceedings, 1998. IX, 529 pages. 1998.

Vol. 1524: K.-R. Müller, G. Orr (Eds.), How to Make Neural Networks Work. VI, 432 pages. 1998.

Vol. 1525: D. Aucsmith (Ed.), Information Hiding. Proceedings, 1998. IX, 369 pages. 1998.

Vol. 1526: M. Broy, B. Rumpe (Eds.), Requirements Targeting Software and Systems Engineering. Proceedings, 1997. VIII, 357 pages. 1998.

Vol. 1528: B. Preneel, V. Rijmen (Eds.), State of the Art in Applied Cryptography. Revised Lectures, 1997. VIII, 395 pages. 1998.

Vol. 1529: D. Farwell, L. Gerber, E. Hovy (Eds.), Machine Translation and the Information Soup. Proceedings, 1998. XIX, 532 pages. 1998. (Subseries LNAI).

Vol. 1530: V. Arvind, R. Ramanujam (Eds.), Foundations of Software Technology and Theoretical Computer Science. XII, 369 pages. 1998.

Vol. 1531: H.-Y. Lee, H. Motoda (Eds.), PRICAI'98: Topics in Artificial Intelligence. XIX, 646 pages. 1998. (Subseries LNAI).

Vol. 1096: T. Schael, Workflow Management Systems for Process Organisations. Second Edition. XII, 229 pages. 1998.

Vol. 1532: S. Arikawa, H. Motoda (Eds.), Discovery Science. Proceedings, 1998. XI, 456 pages. 1998. (Subseries LNAI).

Vol. 1533: K.-Y. Chwa, O.H. Ibarra (Eds.), Algorithms and Computation. Proceedings, 1998. XIII, 478 pages. 1998.

Vol. 1537: N. Magnenat-Thalmann, D. Thalmann (Eds.), Modelling and Motion Capture Techniques for Virtual Environments. Proceedings, 1998. IX, 273 pages. 1998. (Subseries LNAI).

Vol. 1538: J. Hsiang, A. Ohori (Eds.), Advances in Computing Science – ASIAN'98. Proceedings, 1998. X, 305 pages. 1998.

Vol. 1540: C. Beeri, P. Buneman (Eds.), Database Theory – ICDT'99. Proceedings, 1999. XI, 489 pages. 1999.

Vol. 1541: B. Kågström, J. Dongarra, E. Elmroth, J. Waśniewski (Eds.), Applied Parallel Computing. Proceedings, 1998. XIV, 586 pages. 1998.

Vol. 1542: H.I. Christensen (Ed.), Computer Vision Systems. Proceedings, 1999. XI, 554 pages. 1999.

Vol. 1543: S. Demeyer, J. Bosch (Eds.), Object-Oriented Technology ECOOP'98 Workshop Reader. 1998. XXI, 571 pages. 1998.

Vol. 1544: C. Zhang, D. Lukose (Eds.), Multi-Agent Systems. Proceedings, 1998. VII, 195 pages. 1998. (Subseries LNAI).

Vol. 1546: B. Möller, J.V. Tucker (Eds.), Prospects for Hardware Foundations. Survey Chapters, 1998. X, 468 pages. 1998.

Vol. 1548: A.M. Haeberer (Ed.), Algebraic Methodology and Software Technology. Proceedings, 1999. XI, 531 pages. 1999.